Alternative Theatre in South Africa

Alternative Theatre in South Africa

Talks with Prime Movers since the 1970s

Rolf Solberg

Hadeda Books
Pietermaritzburg
1999

© 1999   University of Natal
         Private Bag X01
         Scottsville 3209
         South Africa

All rights reserved. No part of this publication may be reproduced or transmitted, in any form or by any means, without permission of the publishers.

ISBN 0 86980 950 4

Cover Illustration by Basil Mills

Hadeda Books is an imprint of the University of Natal Press. These publications reach out beyond the academic community to the wider reading public. Like the bird for which they are named, they have a wide distribution and a loud voice.

Typeset by the University of Natal Press
Printed by Kohler Carton and Print
Box 955, Pinetown 3600, South Africa

Contents

Preface	vii
Author's Biography	ix
Introduction	1
Zakes Mda	31
Rob Amato	41
Skhala Leslie Xinwa	74
Gibson Kente	82
Rob McLaren	91
Fatima Dike	111
Julius Mtsaka	139
Ronnie Govender	149
Kessie Govender	160
Maishe Maponya	177
Matsemela Manaka	189
Thulani Sipheni	209
John Kani	223
Mannie Manim	242
Don Maclennon	259

Preface

I was fortunate enough to spend a year's sabbatical in South Africa in 1994–95, with the support of the Norwegian Research Council. My main objective was to get a picture of the country's cultural scene, hoping to catch glimpses of the moods and aspirations of writers and workers in various cultural fields during the dismantling of apartheid, and identify some of the themes and trends that were on the agenda in the wake of Nelson Mandela's declaration of his Reconstruction and Development Programme.

This year of studies in South Africa could be seen as one person's expression of Scandinavia's growing interest in South African developments, and the country's new departures within art and culture. Tangible results of the sabbatical are two collections of talks with writers and theatre practitioners. The first, which appeared in late 1996 in the NELM (National English Literacy Museum) series of interviews under the title of *Reflections: Perspectives on Writing in Post-Apartheid South Africa*, deals with black writers, with one exception, and their perceptions of their own and South Africa's new situation.

This volume deals with workers in drama, especially in 'alternative theatre', which is also called 'black theatre' or 'majority theatre'.

It has been my intention throughout the interviewing process to reflect as truthfully and objectively as possible the form as well as the content of these conversations. It should not, however, be regarded as a vain attempt to become, as one of the interviewees put it: '. . . one of those that say "I know black people", and then he's writing volumes and becomes "an authority" on them.'

In order to become an authority one must, at the very least, know the language of the people one is talking to. And it takes much more than a year's sojourn in a country to be able to get inside the skin of its inhabitants, the more so in view of the paucity of information and materials on South Africa in Europe during the last few decades, caused to a large extent by the cultural boycott. Hence one enters South Africa with a clean slate and is bound to start off fresh.

The language issue is the most obvious of the constraints implied in this situation. It is a complex situation. There are eleven official languages: nine indigenous ones and the two 'white' languages, English and Afrikaans, although some would claim that Afrikaans is an indigenous African language. Being restricted to written English and the use of English as a means of communication, one may easily be perceived as another neo-colonialist, hurrying down the much-used, ill-reputed road of cultural imperialism. A Zulu writer found it odd for a Norwegian like me to come to South Africa for a short period and then go home and write books in English about Zulus and Xhosas and Sothos, without knowing the first thing about their languages – a very valid point indeed. The question one must ask oneself is whether an examination through the medium of English of artistic manifestations would be at all likely to give a reasonably representative picture of cultural developments in South Africa. There is after all a good body of literary output both in Afrikaans and in the indigenous African languages.

However, I think one should not overlook at this point the fact that English is South Africa's first official language by the choice of its democratically elected organs of government, and hence the country's lingua franca. It seems fair, therefore, to assume that English-language literature and theatre may be seen as a reliable, if partial or incomplete, reflection of the South African cultural landscape, both during apartheid and now in the post-apartheid era. This is borne out by the fact that English was regarded by the great majority of the practitioners in alternative theatre as the dominant stage language.

The main objective of this collection of interviews, then, is to bring between two covers some of the personalities who have been central in South African theatre during the last twenty-five years. They are prominent writers, actors, directors, producers and organisers who have all contributed in their different ways to the development of an alternative South African theatre. The scope of this book of interviews clearly limits both the range and depth that can be achieved, and informed readers will miss important names. Some of the people that ought to have been included were not available. Maybe most obvious among those are Athol Fugard, Barney Simon and Mbongeni Ngema. Ngema could not find the time required for an interview. Fugard was unavailable because he was travelling overseas. With Barney Simon I had made an appointment for an interview in June 1995, but was cheated, sadly, by his death.

Author's Biography

Rolf Solberg is currently Assistant Professor at Stavanger College, in south-western Norway, where he has served most of his professional life as a teacher of English and Anglo-African literature. Over the past 30 years he has had the opportunity of spending time in different parts of Africa, working as a teacher and administrator. He has been based in Tanzania, Congo Brazzaville, Namibia and Zambia.

In Tanzania, where he was posted by the Norwegian Overseas Development Agency, Solberg taught English for three years around 1970 while Julius Nyerere was at the height of his power and popularity. Then in the mid-eighties he was part of a Norwegian team that planned and implemented the building of Loudima Secondary School for SWAPO refugee children in Congo Brazzaville, and served there as head of the foreign languages department for two years. Solberg also spent three summer vacations teaching Namibian adult education teachers of English inside Namibia during the late-eighties.

During 1994–95 Rolf Solberg spent a year's sabbatical in South Africa, where, among other things, he made this collection of interviews.

Introduction

Up until the middle of this century South African theatre would have been classified as a traditional 'western' type of established theatre. Drama in all its genres was used mainly 'as a means of strengthening affiliation with the colonial centre',[1] or as a way of countering discrimination against and exploitation of the black population by raising the level of art and culture among the (mainly) mission-educated black middle class.

Black Theatre had its modest beginnings in the late 1930s, especially, through the work of Herbert I. E. Dhlomo, but only became a force to be reckoned with in the second half of the century. As used today, the term 'Black Theatre' is wide enough to cover almost any type of South African theatrical activity run *by* and/or *for* blacks.[2]

Alternative Theatre is another term used to describe black South African theatre. Its present connotations probably date back to the 1960s, but experts claim that the concept was already lurking in the wings before the Second World War. As an umbrella term, it covers a wide range of theatrical activities, projects or groupings. There are general designations such as Majority Theatre, Committed Theatre, Contestatory Theatre, Community Theatre, Black Consciousness Theatre, etc., which denote theatrical modes and objectives. And there have been a great number of specific alternative theatre organisations, like the People's Experimental Theatre (PET), the Theatre Council of Natal (TECON), the Music, Dance, Art, Literature Institute (MDALI), as well as individual groups like the Phoenix Players, the Serpent Players, the Imitha Players and many, many more, all of which came into being to provide alternatives to white Established Theatre.

These alternatives represent a variety of different theatrical agendas – dramatic theories, political ideologies, social aspirations, etc. – and I will return to the most important of them after having drawn a thumb-nail sketch of the developments leading up to the period when South African Alternative Theatre came to prominence.

Towards an alternative South African theatre

The South African playwright Vusamazulu Credo Mutwa[3] and others have in recent years demonstrated that drama and theatrical activities in the broadest sense were not introduced to the African continent by the white colonisers. Long before western drama was enacted by and for whites at South African city venues there had been ceremonial ritual practices carried out by the local communities in southern Africa as well as in other parts of the continent. Mutwa claims, in an article titled 'Umlinganiso... The Living Imitation' in the 1974–75 summer issue of the radical theatre magazine *S'ketsh*, that African theatre is 'as old as Man himself', and he links scenes in southern African rock-paintings to theatrical practices. However, as Mutwa remarks, although Africans have always dramatised stories and songs, etc., entertainment *per se*, the formal processes of commercial and 'serious' metropolitan theatre, were not part of that tradition. He talks about prehistoric art and culture as being inseparable from religious rituals. He even calls them 'the slaves of religion'. When the native religion in many parts of Africa was destroyed by the advent of Christianity, 'traditional African theatre and other branches of African art and culture died with it', he contends. Whether that 'death' is final is another question.

According to Mutwa, 'Umlinganiso' was an ancient form of theatrical enactment of social and religious themes passed on in traditional stories. 'The stories were dramatised and acted out as plays by trained players under the keen supervision of *inyanga* (praise singers) and *isangoma* (diviners), with audience participation in the singing and dancing.'

One important purpose of this form of drama, Mutwa points out, was to keep society united, as well as controlled, through fear. The one thing in which the *inyanga* and *isangoma* of old were united, was their fight against change, against anything that threatened to disrupt the order of things. As chief mediators between the living and the ancestors and gods, they ruthlessly dominated the community, and were 'so powerful, so feared that they actually managed to freeze the development of the black man throughout Africa'. Mutwa maintains that the black man was just as imaginative and creative as his white brother in the west. And he claims that the black man would have been just as inventive, had it not been for the way in which these religious leaders, the *inyanga* and *isangoma*, selected and promoted

Introduction

only what they deemed to be good for the cohesion of the tribe, suppressing everything else.

When the whites arrived on the continent they failed to see the organic function of such dramatic activities, and were on the whole unable to appreciate their qualities and originality.

There are some interesting records of early European missionary encounters with ceremonial enactment in southern Africa, dating back to the middle of the nineteenth century. In a report written in 1859, from present-day Malawi, Dr John Kirk, a member of David Livingstone's exploration team, praised the dancers at a funeral ceremony for their elegance. Christopher Kamlongera cites the following episode from the report:

> The motions too were quite elegant and had the great advantage that people seemed happy, no confounded white chokers about them. They clapped their hands which might with great advantage be added to the European style . . .[4]

However, positive reactions like this one were not the order of the day. After the European empire-builders and missionaries had established a proper foothold in southern Africa, the well-known white paternalistic attitudes crept in. In a book called *Winning a Primitive People*, published in 1914, D. Fraser, writing about some kind of 'native' performance, was disgusted at what he saw as an 'obscene' spectacle:

> I turned aside to my tent ashamed for what I saw, and burning with a sense of the loathesomeness that had been let loose. Next morning I assembled the village, and spoke to them about the degradation of last night's performance. I blushed to speak of those things, while the old women and men looked up, unashamed and wondering at my denunciation.[5]

There are many testimonies from the 1920s and 1930s from colonial officers and missionaries concerning the state of drama among the Africans. Much of this material is uninformed, and most of it tends to be negatively biased. There are some reports, however, that do recognise the 'potential' of dramatic art in African dancing and 'primitive theatre',[6] one such being the following extract from a scholarly report by Mary Kelly, which suggests, in the usual condescending language, that

> We may look to the African to show us, as a thing still alive, the origin of all our art . . . The art of drama is so very young in the mind of the African that it can hardly be said to exist. And yet the seed of the idea is there, for the African is by nature as full of drama as he is of music . . .[7]

However, things were on the move in South African drama before the Second World War, although modern black South African theatre did not begin to make a substantial impact until the 1960s and 1970s. Prior to that the western tradition and white city venues had set both the pace and the agenda. The conservative South African theatre was, in the view of Hauptfleish and Steadman,

> seldom experimental and often focused on light entertainment, a purely bourgeoise undertaking for a very specific market – the well-to-do white South African . . . The popular productions were farces, musicals, the occasional thrillers and – of course – Shaw and Shakespeare. Ibsen, Strindberg, O'Neill, Tennessee Williams, and other more serious fare was also occasionally presented, but once more within the formal tradition of 'legitimate' theatre.[8]

Herbert Dhlomo

Black theatre, with roots in ancient African traditions as pointed out by Credo Mutwa, was already germinating in the 1930s, especially in the works of Herbert I. E. Dhlomo, who was the first modern black African dramatist of real stature. He was a prolific writer and journalist, and wrote more than twenty plays, most of which have unfortunately not been preserved.

His 'possession' was the development and promotion of the concept of the 'New African' – the urban black educated middle-class person. Having established the Bantu Dramatic Society at the Bantu Men's Social Centre in Johannesburg in the early 1930s, he insisted that although it was vital for the liberation of the black South African to study the tribal past, it should be done in the light of the situation of the day:

> The African dramatist cannot delve into the Past unless he has grasped the Present. African art can grow and thrive not only by going back and excavating the archaical art forms, but by grappling with the present-day realities . . . art must deal with the things that are vital and near the African today . . .[9]

Introduction

Yet, Dhlomo did not want to cut the links to western dramatic traditions. He was himself educated in a mission school. This is reflected in what he wrote in an article in 1936, which appears very much like a balancing act, in which balance is achieved:

> The development of African drama cannot be purely from African roots. It must be grafted in Western drama. It must be inspired by, shoot from European dramatic art forms, and be tainted by exotic influences. The African dramatist should not fear being mocked as an 'imitator' of European art. Only he should write and produce his plays as he feels. His work should be marked by his own soul and individuality, for in drama as in life it is not so much what is done but how it is done.

About this time, Dhlomo's Christian assimilationist attitude began to change, as did his ideology of 'progressive individualism'. He began to take a new interest in his African roots and in 'native culture'. Three years later he wrote:

> The African dramatist has an important part to play. In the story of the African Travail, Birth and Progress, lies an inexhaustible source of African dramatic creations. We want African playwrights who will dramatise and expound a philosophy of our modern history. We want dramatic representations of African Oppression, Emancipation and Evolution. To do this the African dramatist must be an artist before being a propagandist; a philosopher before a reformer; a psychologist before a patriot; he must be true to himself and not be a mere prey to popular artistic fashions which, like the gardens of Adonis, soon melt away.[10]

Although still preoccupied with interiority, Dhlomo's focus by 1939, was clearly on the social and political plight of the black man. His first play, *The Girl Who Killed to Save: Nonqause the Liberator*, was based on the historical incident of the young Xhosa woman U-Nonqause's fatal attempt to save her people from defeat through the killing of their cattle. This was the first play in English by a black African to be published (1935). Ian Steadman points out that this was also the first 'significant attempt to create a play which was substantially alternative to the established white theatre'.[11]

In this play, as well as in *Cetshwayo* (1936–37) and *Moshoeshoe* (1938) *inter alia*, Dhlomo delved into Xhosa myths and history for dramatic material. From the late 1930s onward, he turned his attention more towards his own times, and Martin Orkin, in his authoritative work on African theatre, reinforces Steadman's claim that Dhlomo's output was an early precursor of 'alternative theatre':

> The dramatic projects which Herbert Dhlomo undertook in the 1930s and 1940s in South Africa may be said to mark the first significant attempt in drama to challenge the dominance of the imperial and colonialist centre as well as to contest aspects of prevailing ruling class discourse emanating from the white-settler culture.[12]

The 1940s and 1950s was the period when drama also began to appear in the townships, aimed at black audiences. These attempts were mainly based on western theatre, and introduced and supported in the early phases by 'white liberals'. However, as David Coplan points out, the township audiences were not too interested in plays based on the western literary kind of theatre: '. . . most urban Africans held the traditional preference for verbal expression linked to music, dance and dramatic action.'[13]

In the early days, theatre also encountered strong opposition from the rapidly growing cinematic industry. Despite the fact that indigenous theatre productions were occasionally mounted, and enjoyed good reviews, it took a long time for theatre to establish a foothold in the townships.

Another negative factor was the general lack of support from established professional theatre practitioners, as well as the paucity of capital. So nothing momentous happened in the field of black theatre until the 1950s.

Then, in the late 1950s and early 1960s, one began to see a new pattern in South African theatrical activities, namely the incipient collaboration between black and white intellectuals.[14] This collaboration marked the effective beginnings of what has come to be known as

Alternative Theatre

One such development was the formation in 1952–53 of the Union of South African Artists, 'Union Artists' for short, which operated from Dorkey House in Johannesburg. This proved to be a largely positive venture as far as indigenous music and theatre were concerned, even though it was run mainly on white capital, and was gradually seen to be syphoning black artists into the white sector. But it also gave vent to anti-

Introduction

establishment feelings and attitudes through some of its theatrical activities.

Major dramatic events of this period were the production of the jazz opera *King Kong* (1959), written by the banned lawyer Harry Bloom, and the staging of the early works of Athol Fugard, notably *No Good Friday* (1958). The production of *King Kong* by Union Artists in 1959 is regarded as one of the watersheds in the history of South African theatre. It was the first play based on a situation in a black township, and with an all-black cast, to be staged with great success at a white theatre venue. Among *King Kong*'s musical antecedents was the group Mthethwa's Lucky Stars, which enjoyed great popularity, and led to a proliferation of jazz music and the South African folk singing tradition during the 1930s and 1940s.

Union Artists did not, however, invite blacks to take part in the writing and production of *King Kong*. Its goals were predominantly commercial, as it was first and foremost aimed at white audiences. The only black person directly involved in the production was the writer of the music, Todd Matshikiza. The rest of the group was white. Leon Gluckman, the liberal director of the project, wrote:

> This [*King Kong*] was a show by Black artists, with a white nucleus training, organizing and producing. As time goes on the African will learn to do more and more of this work for himself . . . I see the theatre as a civilizing force – one of the last channels open in a country that is violently political and ferociously materialistic. The theatre recognizes and accepts the basic spirituality of man. On those terms everyone can meet.

In a comment on the patronising attitude of Gluckman's article Rob McLaren wrote:

> The characteristic relations of the white liberals with black South Africans emerge quite clearly here . . . They [the liberals] did not realize that such 'collaboration' could not prove that blacks were capable of their own cultural achievements. It could only show that blacks could be taught to participate on a simple level in theirs.[15]

McLaren emphasised that, compared to what he calls the 'rabid racialists', *King Kong* was conceived in a spirit of commendable 'recognition of the potential of black people to create'. And yet,

> because they both romanticized the culture in which the play was situated and underestimated the performers who were to perform it, they simplified, trivialized, even distorted, its content and failed to exploit the real strengths of its form.[16]

McLaren sees the Black Consciousness Theatre of the 1970s as the necessary corrective to this attitude.

The Sharpeville massacres of 21 March 1960 marked a fundamental change in modern South African history. Lewis Nkosi wrote in an article in 1965:

> The fifties were important to us as a decade because finally they spelled out the end of one kind of South Africa and foreshadowed the beginning of another. Sharpeville was the culmination of a political turmoil during a decade in which it was still possible in South Africa to pretend to the viability of extra-parliamentary opposition.[17]

Among the restrictive apartheid measures of this period were the prohibition of blacks in cinemas in white areas, and the Group Areas Act of 1960, which prohibited 'the association of different races in clubs, cinemas and restaurants'.

Racially mixed casts, however, could still perform before segregated audiences at the time of *King Kong* and Fugard's early plays, before an amended Group Areas Act put an end to that as well in 1965.

Lewis Nkosi's play *The Rhythms of Violence* (1962) belongs to the category termed Protest Theatre, and should be mentioned as an important contribution to the development of political black theatre. The core of the action in Nkosi's play is a bomb attack on the City Hall, where the father of the white girl, Sarie, is attending a meeting. The bomb is planted by the black student Gama, whose brother, Tula, is Sarie's boyfriend. When Tula gets wind of the bomb attack, he tries unsuccessfully to ward off the blast, and is killed in the explosion together with Sarie's father.

A major theme is the demand for violent action against apartheid among the radical students after years and years of talking and inaction on the part of the ANC. And although the play is cast in the European dramatic mould, it can be seen as an early expression of incipient black consciousness, albeit a consciousness more related to black middle-class values than to the township proletariat. (The fact that the leaders within the Black Consciousness Movement have almost all been black middle-class intellectuals seems to have been somewhat problematic all along.)

The Rhythms of Violence was published and produced in exile. It could, consequently, not be performed in South Africa, and its direct impact on the struggle was limited.

Nkosi's main dramatic shortcoming was a weakness which he shared with most other South African dramatists of the 1950s and early 1960s, as Martin Orkin pointed out: '. . . these writers seem to have had their eyes fixed upon the printed page more clearly than upon theatrical performance.'[18] The play gained praise, though, for its insights into the political situation in post-Sharpeville South Africa, and also for some of the devices employed to underscore the theme of violence, especially the dramatic use of jazz music. But it has been strongly criticised for its 'literariness' and also for its somewhat heavy use of sentimental clichés.

Athol Fugard

It was partly because of the 'more fluid theatre-based and less literary dramatic practice' associated with Union Artists dramatists that the township theatre developed its new styles, in the wake of the successes of *King Kong* and of Fugard's early plays. *King Kong*, Athol Fugard's *No Good Friday* (1958) and *The Blood Knot* (1961) and Lewis Nkosi's *The Rhythms of Violence* all marked important advances in South African alternative theatre in their different ways. However, whereas Nkosi's play marks a sort of blind alley theatrically, due to its literary bent, *King Kong* subsequently came to be a sort of matrix for the township musical. As for Fugard he was still, generally, operating within the liberal South African dramatic tradition. As Martin Orkin put it,

> while [Fugard's early plays] begin to register the existence of townships and a black population within an urban space, none of these plays focuses upon family life and its problems within the confines of apartheid, to which Mandela's statement at his trial at times pointed.[19]

The emphasis is still on 'an interiority in the central characters, largely indifferent to the social order within which these characters are positioned'.[20]

> ... it is the absence of any recognition of resistance and contestation in the construction of the oppressed subject in both rural and urban space in all these plays that is most noteworthy.[21]

It was only with Fugard's collaboration with John Kani and Winston Ntshona in the early 1970s, resulting in the famous *Sizwe Bansi Is Dead* (1972) and *The Island* (1973) that he is seen to move into Protest Theatre, which gradually developed into the mode of Theatre of Resistance in later contemporary dramatists, or into Contestatory Theatre, to use Orkin's nomenclature.

Fugard's prominent place in the history of South African alternative theatre is due, for one thing, to the impetus he gave to collaborative dramatic ventures. He began in a small theatre in Port Elizabeth with his wife in the 1950s (Circle Players), carried on at Dorkay House in Johannesburg, and then enjoyed great successes in Europe in the late 1950s and 1960s. In 1962 he mentions in his *Notebooks* the literary slant in T. S. Eliot and Alan Paton's dramatic works. He refers to them as naïve dramatic craftsmen, adding: 'Again it has been proved: a play is an actor before an audience. We had nothing else.'[22]

The Serpent Players was formed in 1963, and in a comment after a successful performance, Fugard wrote:

> A completely bare stage except for one black applebox, and then the actors – on and off, running about etc. in a series of short pithy scenes. For the first time I feel I really sense the potential in truly improvised theatre.[23]

Orkin made the comment about *Sizwe Bansi Is Dead* that it made an enormous impact upon its audiences and was itself influential in encouraging the realisation that theatre space might be used to present oppressed-class subjects and experience. Kani and Ntshona also provided continual demonstration of oppressed-class empowerment within the theatre, something Gibson Kente had in other ways achieved in the late 1960s, and something which the adherents of black consciousness in their own particular way, were urging . . .

> The collaboration of Kani, Ntshona and Fugard, which itself transgressed apartheid laws insisting on segregation in theatre, was to provide a new impetus to South African theatre, showing the value of group improvisation and workshop for South African theatre practitioners coming from different spaces and classes and isolated from one another through apartheid legislation . . .[24]

However, a major criticism of *Sizwe Bansi* was that it did not incite active resistance. Hilary Seymore, looking at the play from a class angle, states that Styles, the play's main character, barely goes beyond reminding 'guilty liberal consciences, especially outside South Africa, that the Pass Law system is inhuman, unworkable, and absurd'.[25]

Seymore maintains that 'statements on racism which ignore its class basis are not in essence radical,'[26] and sees Styles' establishment of his own photographic business as an assertion of reprehensible middle-class individualism. The play does attack certain social themes – the pass-book issue for instance.[27]

It also exposes the question of economic exploitation and the hopeless work conditions in South Africa, but it does not transcend the perimeter of the protest play. The same applies to *The Island*, which basically deals with the prison conditions on Robben Island. (The play was staged again in 1994 at the Market Theatre, twenty-one years later, with the original cast, John Kani and Winston Ntshona, and with Nelson Mandela and other prominent ex-convicts as guests of honour.)

Township Theatre

White theatre venues were still operating, of course, while these alternative theatrical forms were developing, but failed to make much of an impact on the attitudes of the township population during this period. In contrast to 'establishment dramatists' like Guy Butler, whose productions were to a large extent state funded (e.g. through the Performing Arts Councils) but usually seen only by a small number of whites, black writers like Gibson Kente and Sam Mhangwane, though unsponsored, drew huge township crowds.

Gibson Kente began his artistic career as a musician and worked for a couple of years as a talent scout for Gallo Record Company. His theatrical ventures started in Johannesburg in the late 1950s, where later, as a director, he became involved in the running of Union Artists at Dorkay House. The first play he wrote and produced was *Manana*, *the Jazz Prophet* (1963). After a couple of early successes he broke with Union Artists in 1966, and went his own way, perfecting over the next decade what has come to be known as the South African township musical. In 1967 he established his own theatre company, producing his own musical plays.

During the 1960s and 1970s, some of the most repressive apartheid years, he was the person that almost single-handedly kept the township masses entertained. He is seen as the grand old man of the 'popular' entertainment line of South African alternative theatre.

In the post-Sharpville period he toured the length and breadth of the country with his band of actors in the famous green bus with the slogan 'Gibson Kente, Slick Musicals' painted on it. He wrote and produced a string of very popular musicals, with *Sikalo*, *Lifa* and *Zwi* among the most popular. By the 1970s he was a well-established black commercial theatrical entrepreneur.

S'ketsh Magazine ran a series of features on Kente in its summer 1972 issue. 'Mshengu', alias Rob McLaren, calls him 'a phenomenon', in an article where he seeks to evaluate the Kente theatre. He says about Kente that at this stage acting styles hardly vary. There is superficial story development and an absence of any conflict but physical fights and slanging matches. McLaren praises the musical side very highly, and adds, 'Perhaps this is the secret of Kente's success – a discipline and control over the cast which drives them to greater and greater effort.'

He blames Kente, though, for glorifying some of the negative sides of township life, for instance the *tsotsis* (street hooligans), and asks

> Should plays depict tsotsis so that the audience admires and likes them on the stage, whereas they don't in real life? Should plays present a flattering mirror to the tsotsis themselves, and young people who have tsotsi tendencies?[28]

McLaren also looks at Kente's dialogue and states that

> Most of it is inaudible – because of band, audience response, bad voice projection, unfamiliarity with the words. Lines do get laughs, but this is usually more to do with the clownish antics of the speaker than the words themselves.[29]

This looks even worse than killing with faint praise, but his evaluation ends in a very different tone of voice:

> But for the moment there is no one to match Kente the musician, the choreographer, the director and the man with his finger on the popular pulse, Kente, the magician.[30]

About this time a new dimension seems to be added to Gibson Kente's artistic stature. It seems hardly probable that the change was due to the kind of criticism quoted above. It is more likely that it was prompted by the Kani-Ntshona-Fugard success with *Sizwe Bansi Is Dead* in 1972, and he may have been influenced by the politically loaded play *Shanti* by Mthuli Shezi, produced by PET the following year. But the most important cause may have been the mounting pressure from politically conscientised black township youths. In any event, these were probably contributing factors in the process that made Gibson Kente switch into a more serious and politically motivating mode of writing. Between 1973 and 1975 came three plays that were very different from his earlier productions, namely *How Long*, *I Believe* and *Too Late*. They were felt by the authorities to be so radical and potentially dangerous that in 1976, when *Too Late* appeared, Kente was detained. And on his release he was sternly cautioned by the police and told to toe the line, or else – which, many people argue, he felt obliged to do.

After that he seems to have fallen back to where he started, commented Sipho Sepamla in *S'ketsh Magazine* in 1979, and added, 'I have not seen his latest offerings. I am scared to be disappointed by him.' Gibson Kente more or less disappeared from centre stage as a creative force, until he surfaced again after independence as a filmmaker for the big screen. He now regards himself as 'the luckiest man to be alive at this time', as he puts it in the present interview, feeling he can make a significant contribution in this transitional period of South African history. This he hopes to achieve through a string of new TV films with a strong emphasis on the message of peace and reconciliation, which he is making in support of Nelson Mandela's nation-building.

There are conflicting opinions among the interviewees concerning Kente's contribution towards the struggle during the apartheid era. But his position as a leading South African theatre practitioner is never questioned. Even those who regard him merely as a 'slick entertainer', show great respect for his professionalism as a theatre personality, for his versatility and artistic skills.

Furthermore, younger 'serious' black playwrights concede, however grudgingly, that he has set a pattern with his musicals that nobody can afford to ignore. Matsemela Manaka recounts in his interview, a humorous episode that shows how practitioners of 'committed theatre' were generally losing out to Kente when it came to drawing the big township audiences.

The musical element in Gibson Kente's productions seems to have been what contributed most to his great popularity in the townships. The effects of the music apparently account for the deep involvement and personal identification evinced by his black audiences. His plays are written in English, but Rob McLaren points out in his analysis of *Too Late*[31] that the many songs in Kente's plays are invariably in an indigenous African language, which, of course, enhances the identification process. The profound effect of all this on the township population was probably the main reason why the police gave him that strong warning when he was released from detention. Kente says in the interview that the police told him that they regarded his musical appeal to the township audiences to be a danger to the government: 'People carry it home, they sing about it because it is in musicals. It's very dangerous. We are watching you.'

'Black Drama' and 'Drama for Blacks'

The poet Pascal Gwala made the distinction between 'drama for blacks' and 'black drama', in an editorial in the radical magazine *Black Review*, in 1973. 'Drama for blacks', in Gwela's view, denotes the exploitative and largely white-sponsored theatre feeding off the township blacks, as well as Gibson Kente's genre of 'popular' theatre.

'Black drama', on the other hand, is, for Gwala, theatre that promotes dignity and self-reliance and affirms new, positive self-images for blacks, and not merely 'drama of protest and lament'.[32]

Among the most prominent 'black drama' groups and institutions that mushroomed in the wake of Dorkay House and the Phoenix Players in the early 1970s were PET (People's Experimental Theatre) in Lenasia; MDALI (The Music, Dance, Art, Literature Institute) in Soweto; TECON (The Theatre Council of Natal); MAD (Music and Drama); Shah Theatre Academy and the Stable Theatre in Durban.

Among hands-on theatre groups were, Workshop '71, the Ikhwezi Players, the Serpent Players, and the Imitha Players.

The serious, politically motivated black drama groups and fringe theatre companies that sprang up during the 1970s and 1980s have been variously called 'committed theatre', 'worker theatre', 'majority theatre', 'black consciousness (BC) theatre', etc., depending on their composition and their differing agendas.

Black Consciousness Theatre

The most effective among alternative theatre groups when it comes to political conscientisation in the townships, was without a doubt Black Consciousness Theatre. Like the Black Consciousness Movement (BCM), which sprang out of SASO (South African Students' Organisation), in the late 1960s, BC theatre was exclusively black. The journalist Mango Tshabangu stated:

> It is not the duty of black theatre to conscientise the white man . . . Right now black consciousness must take up all the room and refuse to be prostituted . . . We say that if the white man wants to see what is going on in our world let him do the impossible, get a permit and come into our township . . . To perform before whites in their own plush places serves to preserve the status quo.[33]

McLaren and other white practitioners have tended to avoid the term 'black theatre'. This is probably partly due to the exclusive stance adopted by BCM on racial issues. We shall come back to this point shortly, after a brief comment on BC theatre and the play *Shanti*, its first significant success.

Shanti by Mtuli Shhezi was the first 'declared' black consciousness play of importance. It was first staged in 1973, by PET, which regarded itself as BC's cultural wing.

Shezi started his career as a student politician, and was later elected the first Vice-President of BPC (Black People's Convention), which, together with SASO was the backbone of the BCM. Shezi wrote *Shanti* in 1972, during his short period as Vice-President of the BPC, but did not live to see it performed. He was pushed before a train at Germiston railway station in December 1972 by a white conductor and killed, after standing up to defend a black woman against white abuse.

PET saw theatre as a means of '. . . assisting Blacks to re-assert their pride, human dignity, group identity and solidarity . . .'[34] A person working with BC drama wrote in a PET newsletter in connection with the production of *Shanti*: 'We cannot waste time on comical dramas. We live in times of war where a black man cannot stop thinking of his liberation. We are determined to fight for our rights.'[35]

It is interesting to note that the townships that were visited by the PET *Shanti* performance in 1973–74, were the very townships where the spontaneous rioting broke out in 1976. This seems to confirm that the conscientisation work which was promoted through the BC cultural and political branches at the time was effective.

Shanti is made up of thirteen scenes, built around the love story of the Indian girl Shanti and her African lover Thabo. The third central character is a coloured man, Koos, and the basic message is the need for unity among all black groups in the fight against their common enemy.

Thabo, who refuses to accept violence as a means to promote the black fight for human dignity, is incarcerated on some trumped-up crime charge, but succeeds in breaking out of jail. He escapes to Mozambique and joins the freedom-fighters. As it is put in the play, 'verbal confrontation' has now been 'sent to the museum'. Thabo is later killed because of intrigues in the freedom-fighters' own ranks.

Shanti is different from earlier black dramas in that it breaks away from the traditional literary dialogue:

> The scenes are presented in too staccato a fashion to allow for any literary sophistication. Far more important than involved verbal dialogue are physical tableaux, of which there are a number in the play.[36]

However, the play failed to establish an immediate rapport with township audiences. This was partly because the dialogue was not in one of the local African languages, but mainly in English, the lingua franca of black resistance, and also the language of the educated black middle class.

This is where Gibson Kente and the township musical genre struck a new chord by using *tsotsitaal* (gangster talk) or South African 'pidgin', blended in with English. This had a much greater appeal to the township audiences, as Matsemela Manaka pointed out in his interview.

There is an ideological, as well as theatrical, reason that *Shanti* did not catch on, namely its blatant didacticism. *Shanti* was intended by both Shezi and PET 'to present information and argument through polemical means'. The play makes a clear move away from Protest Theatre into Theatre of Resistance, as did BC plays generally. They were 'agit-prop' productions created primarily for didactic purposes, and must be judged as such. Aesthetic considerations were secondary to that objective.

Trial against Black Consciousness activities

In 1975 the state mounted a trial to put an end to the Black Consciousness Movement and its 'subsidiaries' once and for all. PET and TECON, together with three political BC organisations: SASO, BPC and SRC (the Students' Representative Council of the University of the North), were put on trial, accused of activities that were regarded by the state as '. . . inflammatory, provocative, anti-white, racialistic, subversive and/or revolutionary'.[37] Most of their leaders were convicted and imprisoned, and although they were not formally convicted as representatives of the theatre, the result was that all these theatrical organisations were effectively put out of action.

One point worth considering, briefly, before moving away from BC theatre, is the contentious problem of race and class in BC plays. Most critics who have pronounced on the question seem to hold the opinion that race takes precedence over class in *Shanti* and BC plays in general. Marxist critics like Rob McLaren, on the other hand, see class rather than race as the basic issue behind apartheid, and consider *Shanti* in the light of class struggle. This is probably another major reason why McLaren prefers the term 'majority theatre' to 'black theatre'.

The experimental theatre group Workshop '71 was a nucleus of politically progressive practitioners. The four initiators, Rob McLaren, James Mthoba, Selaelo Maredi and Bess Finney, started out by workshopping and producing the play *Crossroads*, and continued with a number of important productions in the half-dozen years they were functioning, including a play about black prison life, *Survival* (1975), which was technically a very innovative production, mixing stage realism with dramatic narrative,[38] pointing forward, dramaturgically, to Mbongeni Ngema's productions of the 1980s.

Another interesting theatrical development came with the Workshop '71 production of Credo Mutwa's play *uNosilimela* in 1973, directed by McLaren.

Credo Mutwa: Rediscovering African Myth

This play marks a contrast to BC theatre in a number of ways, and stakes out a new course for alternative South African theatre.

It is a tale based on the myth of a girl who travels through time, and in the play she is carried along on a wave of dancing and singing. In a critique of *uNosilimela* in *S'ketsh Magazine*, summer 1974–75, Vincent Kunene underlined very strongly the important function in black African society of the musical element in the play and in black drama generally:

> Electrifying traditional dances are no doubt creditably what reveals to us what Blacks are. If you are black and you are in the audience, and you can see what the artists do and say as they dance, you cannot avoid feeling the energy within you developing and being transmitted through the ages of time to some era unknown and incomprehensible to you, a call of mother origin, a self-realisation that propels you to reveal yourself to yourself.[39]

The play can be seen as a romantic allegory of African history. It consists of a number of scenes tied together by a storyteller and a band of dancers/singers. The storyteller tells us that this is a story of self-understanding, neighbourly love and respect for the ancestors.

uNosilimela is born to the Princess of the Stars in the remote Amariri, the mythical land of the Children of the Star. On the basis of a prophesy she is declared to be a goddess and she is to be worshipped. She will, therefore, be denied love. However, she does not comply with this provision, and after an illicit love affair she is banned and has to go into exile. Uprooted from her traditional environment she gradually gets corrupted by life in the urban areas. First she gets married to and abandoned by a railway worker in Transkei. Then she is 'saved' by white nuns and educated as a teacher, and finally ends up as a prostitute in Johannesburg. Again she runs away into exile, ending up in the Northern Transvaal. It all ends with her being killed – and resurrected – and an ancient prophesy is fulfilled: Johannesburg, symbol of the present colonial dispensation, is consumed in a nuclear war and South Africa is purged. The play ends about the year 2500, with happy people celebrating rituals of peace, which have been observed during five hundred years of peaceful living.

The character of uNosilimela is clearly conceived by Mutwa as a symbol of African rural values, both past and future. The play was regarded by BC adherents as reactionary, which calls to mind H. Dhlomo's warning not to return to 'tribalism': Black South Africans should, according to his advice, move forward into modernity, and become the New Urban Africans.

One reason for Mutwa's negative response to the BC approach is the movement's exclusivist stance in racial matters. Mutwa spoke up for understanding between black and white, and had little time for BC's 'black man you are on your own' attitude.

However, Ian Steadman stated in his analysis of the play that through his research into African mythology, Mutwa had created a piece of uniquely indigenous African drama:

> In form and language Mutwa's plays generally straddle European and American elements and succeed in combining them into a work which is as rich as anything by Wole Soyinka or John Pepper Clark . . . [But *uNosilimela* could never] find favour with the proletarianised audiences looking for internationalism in their black culture.[40]

Steadman added the following appraisal of Mutwa's theatrical work: 'There is no doubt that Mutwa's play made an enormous contribution to the process of discovering an authentic African identity in the theatre.'[41]

And he continued:

> [Mutwa] achieves through drama an important cultural statement with political implications. Ideologically distanced from the radical politics of Black Consciousness, he created a play which exactly served that movement's intentions for black culture.[42]

N. C. Manganyi also lent support to Mutwa's critical stance regarding the exclusiveness of BC in an article published in 1981. He extended the points made by Steadman, and placed Africanisation in a broader, humanist tradition:

> I think blacks understand intuitively that black consciousness will have remained a dismal failure if it has failed to develop beyond its erstwhile preoccupation with race. The prospects as I see them are for a humanism that would come into being and thrive as a new cultural belief system which Dreyer Kruger and I have described as Africanisation.

Despite the banning of the organs of the black consciousness movement, I believe that a natural pattern of socio-cultural evolution has come into being and the emergence of Africanisation as a humanism for this country is assured. It certainly is not naive or idealistic to believe, as I do, that we blacks have a historical advantage that propels us towards this humanism, a challenge which the exponent of Afrikaaner *volk-nasionalisme* have failed to grasp.[43]

The role of white practitioners within alternative theatre

In the 1960s and 1970s, a number of the groups dominating South African alternative theatre were run by white dissident directors and managers who pursued a policy of non-racialism. They were all radical or liberal groups. People that made a mark in this way were – besides Athol Fugard – Barney Simon, Mannie Manim, Rob McLaren, Brian Astbury, Rob Amato, Don Maclennan, Ari Sitas and a number of others.

Simon and Manim were the driving forces behind the establishment of the Company and the Market Theatre in the mid 1970s. Marxist Rob McLaren headed the team that started Workshop '71 in Johannesburg. Amato began his theatrical work with the group Imitha Players in East London in the early 1970s, in collaboration with Leslie Schala Xinwa, a journalist on the East London *Daily Dispatch*. Amato was later involved in alternative theatre venues in Cape Town, firstly the Space Theatre, initiated by Brian Astbury, and when that was shut down in 1979 he carried on with the People's Space. Also in the seventies, the poet and university lecturer Don Maclennan did theatrical work in Grahamstown with a group called the Ikhwezi Players. Ari Sitas was involved in the establishment of the very radical Junction Avenue Theatre with Malcolm Purkey, as well as being one of the initiators of worker theatre in Durban in 1982.

Since there were hardly any official ways for black practitioners to develop their dramatic skills or competence at the time, they had to fall back on this sort of 'apprenticeship' situation under white 'tuition'. This must have been humiliating for those who had felt the scourge of apartheid impinging most keenly on their lives, and even on their bodies, as was the case with John Kani and his family.

Kani gives a very vivid and interesting description in his interview of the profound scepticism with which he, as a conscientised black youth, met Athol Fugard, a representative of the 'enemy' – a 'white honkey' doing drama with some of Kani's best friends.[44] However, after a long 'incubation period' a relationship of trust and friendship gradually grew between them, which resulted, among other things, in the well-known collaboration between Fugard, Ntshona and himself on *Sizwe Bansi Is Dead* and *The Island*.

Makwedini Julius Mtsaka is another prominent black theatre personality who is voicing mixed feelings concerning his experiences with whites in the early days of alternative theatre. In his interview he puts his finger on what he perceives as the failure of some of the white directors/producers to accord due recognition to black actors and other practitioners for their contribution to the development of black theatre. He was one of the leading actors in the Imitha Players in the early 1970s, and highly regarded as a talented actor. Rob Amato describes him in his interview as an interesting man – 'not a trained actor, but a wonderful emoter', who later went on to teach at Wits University.

Mtsaka feels that there have been many episodes over the years where the relationship between white and black practitioners went sour. In the interview he regrets that there is no Truth Commission set up to investigate problems in arts and culture, as he claims that he and some of his colleagues have on occasions in the past been insulted by liberal friends. He refers to a particular incident in Soweto in the early 1970s involving a white theatre director who made a humiliating and unacceptable offer of financial aid to his group.[45] From such criticism, and from similar comments from other sources, it seems to an outsider that there must have been cases where appropriate recognition was not given.

Whether this was because of racialist attitudes is a very different matter. It is hard to believe that any white South African persons with racial grudges would give of their time and money to support the struggle for racial equality. What assistance was given by people like Amato, Astbury, Maclennan, Manim, McLaren, Simon and the other white theatrical moguls of the time, must clearly have been a valuable contribution to the struggle for black empowerment and the fight against racial oppression. It probably boils down in some cases to bad chemistry, or lack of personal trust. But again – there is never smoke without fire – there are bound to have been cases of white arrogance like the one quoted by Mtsaka, and also examples of exploitation and failure to acknowledge valuable contributions from the black participants in the early labours in alternative theatre. The problem also has an obvious Black Consciousness side to it, namely the movement's almost total rejection of white liberal support, based on BC's ideological programme.

When it comes to the situation today, one would expect that considerable changes have taken place in the white-black relationship in theatre. Matsemela Manaka speaks at some length about this issue in his interview.

Alternative Theatre after 1976

Black or alternative theatre emerged after the Soweto riots of June 1976 as a force that the white South African cultural hegemony could no longer afford to ignore. Africanisation was now the major factor behind the growing influence of alternative theatre. The establishment of the Market Theatre in 1976, the Space Theatre in Cape Town and a host of fringe theatres around the country reflected and helped the growing social consciousness in South Africa.

The vice-like grip of government control and repression following the ruthless policy of mass removals of the late 1950s, and the Sharpville massacre in 1960, led to increased racial tension. With the new vigilance on the part of the government censors the latitude of critical writing was severely limited, bringing prose literature virtually to a standstill during the 1960s. This led to a steadily increasing exodus of black writers. Those who remained behind tended to switch more and more to poetry, where anti-apartheid criticism could more easily be camouflaged in emblematic language.

Drama was also a mode of expression that lent itself fairly readily to devious practices in this situation, despite obvious problems with the heightened government attention and sharpened race relations legislation. Most township plays of this period were never written down, and were therefore not open to detailed government control. And by operating through private drama clubs and special invitations to theatrical performances, one could circumvent some of the assembly restrictions, and it was possible to carry on with a modicum of dramatic activity and development. This was how the early mixed drama groups had to operate.

Committed Theatre

Among the many interesting 'committed' black dramatists and thea-

Introduction 23

tre practitioners appearing about this time were Fatima Dike, Ronnie and Kessie Govender, Matsemela Manaka, Maishe Maponya and Zakes Mda.

There was also Julius Mtsaka, whose first play, *Not His Pride* (1978), is a bitter attack on the cruelty and injustice suffered by the black population through the implementation of the bantustan policies of the South African government. The play was later published by Ravan Press. Among his other plays are *The Last Man*, produced 1979, *The Bargain*, *Bongi's Struggle* and *This or Nothing*, which was produced in 1990.

Fatima Dike wrote three plays in the 1970s, *The Sacrifice of Kreli* (1976), *The First South African* (1978) and *Glasshouse* (1979), which were all first performed at the Space Theatre in Cape Town. Her fourth play, *So What's New?*, was written and produced in 1990.

The action of *The Sacrifice of Kreli* takes place in 1885. It is another rendering of the Xhosa's defeat by the British a few years earlier, and harks back to the Xhosa cattle-killing catastrophe in the 1850s. But this time the historic events are partly used to make a very crass comment on the contemporary political situation in South Africa. The performance got very good reviews. Fatima Dike talks at some length about her work in her interview.

Ronnie and Kessie Govender both write their plays from the point of view of the Indian community, and their names are closely associated with the Shah Theatre Academy, which was founded by Ronnie Govender. They are, however, still in the tradition of Black Consciousness Theatre. Ronnie Govender's greatest success was *The Lahnee's Pleasure*, and one of the most prominent of Kessie Govender's satirical plays is the award-winning *Working Class Hero*. The title suggests its political leanings. It was regarded as a very provocative play, and caused quite a stir when it was first produced in 1974.

Matsemela Manaka was born and lives in Soweto. He is one of the most productive and versatile of the younger South African dramatists. He is a painter, composer, musician and teacher as well as a writer and philosopher. Among his plays are *Egoli* (1979), *Vuka* (1980), *Pula* (1982) and *Children of Asazi* (1984). The best known is probably *Egoli* (City of Gold), which is a metaphor for the black man's enslavement by South Africa's exploitative contract labour system. It is a harsh criticism of the social conditions in the worker hostels and the atrocious conditions in the mines underground. The main characters are two ex-convicts, who escape chained together. Ian Steadman sees that as a symbol of the men being 'chained in bondage to the economic system', and it is these men's, and all South African workers' goal to break the chains.

David Coplan points to the imagistic qualities of *Egoli*, which, like traditional African theatre, relies on improvisation and episode rather than on firm plotting, and Manaka makes extensive use of flashbacks and dream sequences in the play.

Both Manaka and Maponya are firmly anchored in the tradition of black consciousness, which comes out very clearly in the language used in *Egoli*. Manaka is evidently and openly a great admirer of Bertold Brecht's dramaturgical practices, and was subsequently invited to take his production of *Egoli* on a tour to Germany.[46] This happened in 1982, and Manaka stayed on in Germany as a student until 1986.

Maishe Maponya has until very recently worked as a drama teacher at Wits University. He is, like Manaka, one of the radical young writers who kept the BC beacons burning during the last decade of the struggle. Orkin pointed out in his analysis that the two playwrights are both driven in their work by the urge to conscientise. However, in recent years both of them have gone one step beyond the old BC tenets, showing 'an increased interest in the exploration of interiority in the attempt to assert a sense of identity and self in the erasures of apartheid discourse'.[47]

Maponya's first play, *The Cry*, came in 1976. Then followed, among others, *Peace and Forgive* (1978), *The Hungry Earth* (1978), *Umangikazi* (1983) and *Gangsters* (1984). The two best known are probably *The Hungry Earth* and *Gangsters*.

Gangsters is a critique of the prison system of South Africa. It focuses, among other things, on police violence and on blacks that are prepared to betray the black cause for personal gains. When the play was first produced it was restricted to 'small intimate four-wall theatres, of the experimental or avant-garde type', with reference to Section 30 of the Publications Act of 1974. It was thus prohibited from being shown in the townships. This meant in effect that its function was reduced to 'preaching to the converted', mainly liberal whites, and it would pose little threat to the system.

Gangsters is a mixture of interiority and black consciousness ideology, typical of a number of the later works of Maponya and Manaka. The poet Rasechaba, one of the three main characters of the play, is described as a man who '... if the spirit of the nation moves him, [he] will write about the nation. He will talk about man, he'll talk about pain and he'll talk about that which moves the people.'⁴⁸

Zanemvula Mda, more commonly known as Zakes Mda, is another very versatile artist. He grew up in Lesotho, and spent several years studying and teaching in the USA. He is today rated as one of the most influential of the 'new' South African dramatists. Apart from writing and producing a string of plays, he has written and published poetry, award-winning novels and other books, scripted and produced films, and he is an acknowledged painter. Among his plays are *We Shall Sing for the Fatherland* (written 1973) and *Dark Voices Ring* (1979), which were first produced in 1979, and *The Hill* (1980). As Michael Chapman pointed out in his new book on southern African literature, they 'owe as much to Beckett as to African storytelling'.⁴⁹

Coming from a highly politicised family, Zakes Mda joined the 'theatre of resistance' early in his career and has been one of the champions of community theatre in southern Africa. In his book *When People Play People* (1993) he puts theatre on top of the list of cultural institutions capable of liberating the minds of the masses. He contends, however, that this is not attainable through top-downward governmental prescription. It can only be achieved by way of active grassroots participation with the assistance of expert facilitators. He claims, with reference to Kamlongera and others, that when thus creating theatre for the people *with* the people, one is building on ancient African traditions. This kind of theatre could be turned into an effective method of adult education.⁵⁰ With this approach Mda seems to be in line with the thinking of worker-theatre practitioners and theorists such as Ari Sitas, Keyan Tomaselli and others.

One of the younger practitioners, who takes a clearly positive view of theatrical developments in South Africa, is Thulani Sifeni. Like Mda he sees grassroots activities as a condition for real progress within South African theatre. He wants theatre to look back to the past and try to develop some of the good aspects of the old family pattern, and thereby alleviate prevailing social ills such as the abuse of women. He blames the problems of divorce on Women's Liberation in the European feminist sense, and is about to take up the whole gender issue in a new play called *We Men*. In this piece he reflects upon the relationship between a couple, and explores what it is that causes problems. 'I know it is industrialisation and money that are the bottom line, but I'm trying to explore it to find out what is important and what is not.'⁵¹

Before turning our attention to worker theatre and to the latest brand of commercial theatre, mention should be made of a couple of very interesting plays that emerged in the early eighties. One was a Market Theatre collaborative production which occurred in 1981, namely *Woza Albert*. It is a biting political comedy workshopped by Percy Mtwa, Mbongeni Ngema and Barney Simon and produced by Mannie Manim. The play turns the tables on apartheid theologians, advocating a kind of Black Theology and toying with the idea of a Second Coming of Christ to South Africa. The play ends on the note of a new South Africa resurrected on the traditions of the old South African social order. This play had considerable impact both in South Africa and internationally.

In 1985 Mtwa and Ngema followed up the success of *Woza Albert*, each with a new play: Mtwa with *Bopha!*, and Ngema with *Asinamali!* ('we have no money'). In a sense these plays reflect the situation in the wake of the turbulent strikes and worker unrest around 1980, and were, in a way, a warning of what was to come in the following years: police and crowd violence, 'necklacing' and repeated states of emergency. Both plays take up the urgent social problems of the day – *Bopha!* against a family background and *Asinamali!* in a broader context. The latter especially embodies interesting theatrical developments by mixing stage realism, and dramatic narrative, the speakers addressing the audience and in the next moment breaking into song or dance.[52]

The plays could also be perceived as arguments for the oppressed – in real terms the black working class – which is an interesting point. In this way they would appear to be related to the movement started in Durban in the early eighties by Ari Sitas, namely

Worker theatre

Ari Sitas, one of the founders of the Johannesburg-based Junction Avenue Theatre in the late 1970s, moved to Durban in 1982 where he got involved, together with Astrid von Kotze, in the production of *Ilanga*, also known as *The Dunlop Play*. This project came up in connection with a court case against the workers at the Durban Dunlop factory, who were unjustly accused of staging an unlawful strike in 1980. The workers' trade union lawyer, Halton Cheadle, wanted to establish the truth of what happened by re-enacting the events leading up to the conflict. Through a series of role-play discussions among the workers they arrived at what was seen as the true sequence of events, and this

Introduction

dramatic enactment was subsequently used by the defence at the trial.

Sitas and Kotze joined the enactments together into the Zulu play called *Ilanga*, which was played by the workers themselves for their fellow workers at the Dunlop plant.

Through the efforts of Sitas, Kotze and local cultural workers like Nise Malange, Alfred Qabula and Mie Hlatshwayo the Dunlop Cultural Local was formed in collaboration with the local branch of the Congress of South African Trade Unions (COSATU), and in the course of a few years in the mid-eighties more than a dozen worker plays were produced in the region as part of a conscientisation drive aimed at the workers. Unfortunately most of these plays were not recorded, and are probably lost to posterity.[53]

'Neo-Commercial' theatre

In diametrical contrast to this kind of work in recent South African theatre comes a new wave of productions resembling in significant ways the mode of *Ipi Tombi* (1974), regarded by many as purely exploitative speculation. Others choose to see this development in a more positive light – as a legacy of Gibson Kente's 'popular' township musicals from the 1960s and 1970s. This wave has been epitomised by the career of Mbongemi Ngema in his post-apartheid commercial theatre ventures, especially *Sarafina II*. After the popular and artistic – and also commercial – successes of *Woza Albert* and *Asinamali!*, Ngema wrote and produced the musical *Sarafina* in the early nineties, based on the township riots by the school children in Soweto. This became a runaway success both technically and commercially. As he wanted to pursue this success with the sequel *Sarafina II*, purporting to be a countrywide information drive in the fight against AIDS, he came under fire from radical critics and others. From being one of Kente's protegés, and a playwright that Mannie Manim supported and regarded as one of the most promising young South African theatre personalities in the early stages of his career,[54] he has become the target of a lot of negative media attention. Unfortunately he was not available when I approached him for an interview in January 1996, so I was unable to ask him about his visions of the future of South African theatre, or about his personal career plans. However, his position as heir-apparent of 'popular' theatre along the Gibson Kente lines no longer seems to be assured.[55]

Where does South African alternative theatre actually stand today, when all is said and done?

The director of the Nimble Leap Theatre Company in Cape Town, one of the youngest fringe theatre companies in the country, has the following to say:

> Theatre's desperately struggling in South Africa and worldwide, but here it's suffering even more because of what happened in the past. I say promoters should bring all the West End and Broadway hits out here to get people interested in going to the theatre again. Bring all the big stuff, then we can establish a solid fringe that will grow. Right now, South African theatre is a fringe without a mainstream. We need to create a sense of theatre in Cape Town again . . .

A viewpoint which without a doubt will provoke many Young Turks in South African theatre. This is, however, where we must leave it.

Notes

1. Martin Orkin, *Drama and the South African State*, 1993 (p. 22).
2. For a fuller account I would refer to seminal works on modern South African culture and theatre such as David B. Coplan, *In Township Tonight*, 1985; Peter Larlham, *Black Theatre, Dance, and Ritual in South Africa*, 1985; Rob McLaren/Kavanagh, *Theatre and Cultural Struggle in South Africa*, 1985; Orkin, *Drama and the South African State*, 1993; Ian Steadman, 'Drama and Social Consciousness', (Ph.D. thesis, University of the Witwatersrand, 1985).
3. Credo Mutwa is wearing a number of different hats: in *The Sunday Times'*, *Sunday Life*, 9 December 1996, he is described as 'a keeper of traditional knowledge and a healer. He is also an author, poet, linguist, historian, prophet, conservationist, artist, blacksmith – and communicator . . .' (from Lynne Stafford's presentation of Mutwa's stone sculpture Mother Earth).
4. Christopher Kamlongera, *Theatre for Development in Africa with Case Studies from Malawi and Zambia*, 1988 (p. 1).
5. D. Fraser, *Winning a Primitive People,* London, 1914 (p. 76).
6. Kamlongera, *Theatre for Development in Africa* (p. 3).
7. Mary Kelly, 'African Drama', *Overseas Education*, Vol. II, No. 3, April 1931.
8. T. Hauptfleish and Ian Steadman (eds.), *South African Theatre: Four Plays and an Introduction*, 1984 (pp. 80–81).

Introduction

9. N.W. Visser (ed.), 'Literary Theory and Criticism of H. I. E. Dhlomo, 1939', *English in Africa*, 4, 2, 1977.
10. H. Dhlomo, 'Why Study Tribal Dramatic Forms? 1939', *English in Africa*, 4, 2, 1977 (pp. 37–42)
11. Ian Steadman, *Drama and Social Consciousness*, 1985 (p. 66).
12. Orkin, *Drama and the South African State*.
13. Coplan, *In Township Tonight* (p. 149).
14. See Robert Mshengu Kavanagh, *Theatre and Cultural Struggle in South Africa*, 1985 (pp. 60–61 ff).
15. Kavanagh, *Theatre and Cultural Struggle* (p. 94). Note: Rob McLaren operates under several aliases: Rob(ert) McLaren, Mshengu Kavanagh. In the following I shall refer to him as Rob McLaren.
16. Kavanagh, *Theatre and Cultural Struggle* (p. 97).
17. Lewis Nkosi, *Home and Exile*, Longmans, 1965 (p. 8).
18. Orkin, *Drama and the South African State* (p. 119).
19. Orkin, *Drama and the South African State* (p. 76).
20. Orkin, *Drama and the South African State* (p. 75).
21. Orkin, *Drama and the South African State* (p. 79).
22. Athol Fugard, *Notebooks 1960/1977* (ed. M. Benson), Faber & Faber, 1983 (p. 65).
23. Fugard, *Notebooks* (p. 94).
24. Orkin, *Drama and the South African State* (pp. 158–59).
25. Hilary Seymore, 'Sizwe Bansi Is Dead: A Study of Artistic Ambivalence', *Race and Class*, 21, 3, 1980 (p. 284).
26. Seymore, 'Sizwe Bansi Is Dead' (p. 275).
27. Statistical information for 1972/73 shows that an avergage of 1 413 trials for pass law offences took place every day, including Sundays, which was a decrease from previous years.
28. Kavanagh in *S'ketsh Magazine*, Summer 1972.
29. Kavanagh in *S'ketsh Magazine*, Summer 1972.
30. Kavanagh in *S'ketsh Magazine*, Summer 1972.
31. Kavanagh, *Theatre and Cultural Struggle*.
32. Coplan, *In Township Tonight* (pp.222–23).
33. Mango Tshabangu, *S'ketsh Magazine*, Summer 1974–1975 (p. 19).
34. PET Newsletter, cited in *Black Theatre in South Africa. Fact Paper on Southern Africa*, No. 2, June 1976 (p. 5).
35. PET Newsletter, cited in *Black Theatre in South Africa* (p. 5).
36. Steadman, *Drama and Social Consciousness* (p. 159).
37. Steadman, *Drama and Social Consciousness* (p. 152).
38. For further detail see Orkin, *Drama and the South African State* (pp. 173–74).
39. Vincent Kunene, *S'ketsh Magazine*, Summer 1974–75.
40. Steadman, 'Drama and Social Consciousness' (pp. 246–47).

41. Steadman, 'Drama and Social Consciousness' (p. 249).
42. Steadman, 'Drama and Social Consciousness' (p. 253).
43. From Linn I. Dalrympie, 'Explorations in Drama, Theatre and Education: A Critique of Theatre Studies in South Africa', (Ph.D. thesis, University of Zululand, 1987, p. 146), citing N. Chabani Manganyi, *Looking Through the Keyhole: Dissenting Essays on the Black Experience*, Johannesburg: Ravan Press, 1981.
44. See Kani interview.
45. See Mtsaka interview.
46. See Manaka interview.
47. Orkin, *Drama and the South African State* (p. 221).
48. Moishe Maponya, *Gangsters*, 1984 (p. 64).
49. Michael Chapman, *Southern African Literatures*, Longman, 1996 (p. 360).
50. Zakes Mda, *When People Play People*, Witwatersrand University Press, Zed Books, 1993 (pp. 9–10).
51. See Sifeni interview.
52. Orkin, *Drama and the South African State* (pp. 227–30).
53. See Ari Sitas interview in *Reflections: Perspectives on Writing in Post-Apartheid South Africa*, NELM, 1996 (pp. 44–45); Hlatshwayo, 'Culture and Organisation in the Labour Movement', *Staffrider*, VIII, 3/4, 1989 (pp. 40–42).
54. See Mannie Manim interview.
55. See interviews with Fatima Dike, Gibson Kente and especially Rob McLaren, who is very critical in his comments on Ngema.
56. Owen de Jager, director of The Nimble Leap Theatre, Cape Town, in an interview with the *Cape Argus*, 24.12.1996.

Zakes Mda

Zakes Mda, I wonder if we could we start with a bit of background information? You work mainly in drama, isn't that so?

Yes, I work in drama, mainly, but I'm also a painter. The paintings you see on the walls here are my paintings, except for two, which are made by my son. The ones that are predominantly brown and red are mine. And I also write other things than drama. Right now I am working on a novel. It's a novel that I want to finish in December, because I have this contract with the publisher, who wants to release it in March. So I am quite busy with that. As you can see I am doing a number of things. I began as a painter, but I think I gained more recognition as a theatre person, as a playwright, and most people know me as a playwright, more than as a painter. But I am involved in all kinds of art. I am involved in film making as well, and I am a musical composer.

At Wits you are involved with theatre?

Yes, at Wits I am a visiting professor, for one year. I was teaching at the University of Vermont, USA, but at the end of my year as visiting professor at Wits I will stay on in South Africa and do other things in theatre, and in film. The main thing I'll be staying for is the production of a movie.

What's the theme?

Well, it's a story based on real life about a black soccer star in the fifties, a South African football star who went to England and played there, as the first black to play for England. And from there he played for quite a few teams in Europe – he played for Barcelona, he played in Italy as well; he played in France. And from there he went to the

United States where he went to school and did a Ph.D. in psychology and became an assistant professor in psychology. And then he ended up in jail. He served twelve years for allegedly assaulting his wife and his wife's lawyer with acid.

Then recently he was released from jail, and he is teaching again, in New York, in one of the universities there. It is a human interest story, you know, the rise and fall of this soccer star, and also it's a sports story as well, and it features a lot of the court cases involved, because there was a lot of intrigue – the CIA was involved, South Africa was involved. He claimed that he was framed by the CIA and South Africa, because he used to campaign for the boycott of South Africa and so on.

It's that kind of a story. I scripted it when I was in America, so it's ready. I am just waiting to finish the work, and then I'll start on the production together with another producer in America, because more than half of the story takes place there, especially in the jail where this guy served twelve years of his sentence. He was actually sentenced for much more.

Let's return to South Africa for a while. Could you say something about drama during the Struggle?

OK. There were several phases in South African drama. We had a phase, for instance, when the Township Musical was the predominant genre, in the '60s.

And this genre was not political at all. It was mostly for entertainment. It was a most popular period of theatre in South Africa, because there were a lot of travelling theatrical companies that used to go even to the smallest towns. So the theatre was very close to the people, and the audiences cut across all classes those days, you know, from the labourers who worked digging the roads to the highest level that you can think of. It was not an élitist kind of activity.

And then there was at that same time another kind of theatre that happened at the city venues, which was political. It was Protest Theatre, which was practised mostly by white practitioners, like Athol Fugard, sometimes together with the black intermediate classes. It was mostly Protest Theatre.

Let me define what I mean when I talk of Protest Theatre. You see, after that Protest Theatre we had another phase which came as a result of the Black Consciousness movement, but which was taken over by other movements as well. It was a phase of the Theatre for Resistance, which was quite different from the Protest Theatre. Protest Theatre was a kind of theatre which addressed itself to the oppressor, like *King Kong*, with a view, perhaps, to appealing to his conscience; with a view, perhaps, to making him see how terrible his laws were.

In other words, it was mostly a theatre of self pity, and a theatre of mourning and of weeping and so on and so forth. It showed how people were oppressed – it showed also the effect of that oppression on the people, but only went as far as that.

But when we came to the phase of the Theatre for Resistance, which was now a different phase altogether, the black theatre people consciously moved away from Protest Theatre. They created a new kind of theatre which no longer aimed to address itself to the oppressor. It addressed itself to the oppressed, with a view to mobilising the oppressed to fight against oppression. One realised that it was futile to protest to the oppressor. One realised that he knew what he was doing. And in any case the oppressor never saw these plays, you know. These plays, like the Fugard ones, were played in the city venues where they were seen by white liberals, who were already converted. So they didn't serve any useful function in that sense, except reinforcing already existing convictions.

Now, Theatre for Resistance came into its own in the late '70s and '80s. It was a very effective kind of theatre in many instances, because in the beginning it was performed everywhere – it was performed at political rallies, it was performed at funerals, it was performed even at weddings. But it was also performed at city venues, for instance at the Market Theatre and other places.

And the oppressors allowed it to carry on?

Yes, but there was a reason for that. You see, in the beginning, as I told you, this theatre happened also in the townships, Theatre for Resistance. And during that period when it happened in the townships, the theatre practitioners were harassed. They would be arrested and harassed in many different ways. But when the Theatre for Resistance became the main genre in South Africa, the most popular, it replaced the Township Musical and the Protest Theatre of people like Fugard and others, as the main genre. This was also the time when the city venues were opened for black people as well. And then the theatre practitioners moved to the cities to do it there, you see. So we came to a stage in the mid-eighties whereby almost all Theatre for Resistance was no longer happening in the townships; most of it was happening in the city venues. And the audiences in the cities were not the same as those that were the consumers of theatre before, in the townships, and in the most marginalised parts of South Africa. The audiences at that time were the white liberals again, and a few black middle class people who could afford to drive from the townships to go to the city, or a few already living in the cities by now.

But only ten percent would be black. However, although this Theatre for Resistance was much more radical in content – it was much more revolutionary than the previous genres, the Protest Theatre and the Township Musical – its resistance was only in content, but not in function. Why? Because it was no longer with the people out there in the townships. Its consumers were the white liberals here in the cities. And of course at that stage, when the theatre was performed in the cities, the government would not bother with it. Because when it was performed here it was quite harmless. You preach to the white liberals, and when they go home they have seen the play, and it's terrible what has happened there. They go home to the comfort of their middle class homes, as do the black middle class people as well, and then forget about the whole thing.

Whereas it's the people out there who are capable of taking revolutionary action to change things. So these plays could go on, they were allowed to go on, because they would not do any harm to the government, they would not instigate anybody to do anything.

But weren't there any moves to take the plays out there, to the people, where they could have a real impact?

No. It's only now that people are becoming aware of that. When the city venues opened, it was the ambition of every playwright of note to have his plays performed in the city venues rather than in the townships, because that's where they got recognition. And then, of course, after that those plays would go abroad – they would go to England, or to America or to Europe. And that's where everybody wanted to be. So people who used to create theatre, even those who had their roots in the township, and who originally, in the seventies and early eighties, used to do that theatre in the townships, were now doing it in the city venues. We only had a few groups which continued to do some theatre there, but even those groups had no choice: they were doing their theatre there, but their ambition was to move into the city.

Would this be where the worker culture and the worker theatre groups took over?

Well, you see, that worker culture did not become as widespread as the theatre that I am talking about. That worker culture was mostly in Natal, and it didn't come to much in other places. And it was mostly confined to the workers themselves. It was the kind of theatre that discussed their own particular issues, the shop floor issues and so on. And most of the audiences would be the workers themselves, about their own particular problems.

Sometimes, of course, such plays would be performed for their brother audiences. But it was not the kind of theatre you could find wherever you went, as was the case with the township musicals. Those you would find everywhere you went in the sixties, even in the smaller places. And they would be much closer to the people, of course, than the new Theatre for Resistance, which was really confined to the Market Theatre and such places.

Someone working in drama suggested recently that the musical might be on the way in again because it is a popular genre among township people, and also because of its educational potential. Have you any views on that?

Right now I think people are trying various things to see what can be done. The musical was popular because it was using the most popular performance mode of the people. These are the modes that are used in the township every day. When people are happy, or even when they are sad or angry, they dance and sing. It is part and parcel of the popular culture. So the township musical was very popular.

But also the practitioners of theatre were very good at the township musical. Gibson Kente was a very good choreographer, but he was poor as a playwright. But the people didn't care about the story not being so good. He composed the songs himself, and was a very good composer as well.

Now, to take the theatre back to the people, the main thing that practitioners can do is to create the kind of theatre that uses the performance mode of the people themselves. Because the people don't live in a cultural vacuum. They have never lived in a cultural vacuum at all. Culture is always dynamic, you know. And at any point you will find that people have popular modes of culture that operate in their midst. And any theatre which exploits those modes to create a theatre where the people themselves are participants, and not mere consumers of a finished product which comes from outside, you know, people with superior knowledge, who'll come and bring it here and say, 'OK, this is what you people must do about your life': that's the kind of theatre which the people themselves are involved in the creation of, and it is created from their own perspective. Because they know their life better than I will ever know it.

Do you think the writers of today – when things begin to get stabilised – will be going back to these sources and exploiting them, and creating a new vibrant theatre, which may also have as a purpose to educate people for democracy and all that?

Well, as I said before, there are already people who are trying to do that. There are practitioners like Peter Gwenya, for instance, who are creating plays with the people about various issues. It is something which has not taken off – it is a very new concept in South Africa. But it is an old concept in Africa generally, you know. Yes, of course, I believe in it, because I have been involved in it myself, for many years. I worked in the mountains of Lesotho, for example, doing theatre with the peasants there about their own situation, about their own problems. And I mean doing theatre *with* them, not doing theatre *for* them. I being there as a catalyst, who facilitates.

I spent many years doing that. It resulted in my writing the book *When People Play People*, which discusses different methodologies, based on my experiences in those mountain areas where I was doing this theatre with the peasants. So this book is both a theoretical book about development of communication and of theatre itself, and a practical book about the actual case studies, the successes and failures of this theatre – its strengths and weaknesses. Because like most things it had both its strengths and its weaknesses.

South African literature is still, I believe, in the doldrums after the liberation struggle. Can you see any ways in which South African literature may move now, in its wake?

That's what I can't understand. Why should it be in the doldrums? Were writers writing because of apartheid? Were writers created by apartheid? You see, I've been to many countries of the world where there was no apartheid, but the writers there continued to write. How do the writers in America or Nigeria or Norway write without apartheid? It is not apartheid which makes writers. Writers wrote about apartheid merely because they were responding to what was happening at the time in this country. Now, after apartheid, they will continue to respond to what is happening at a particular time.

The writer who will have a problem, because there were such writers as well in South Africa, is the writer who depended on apartheid to create stories for him or for her. Our apartheid was so bizarre and so ridiculous that it created stories. So those writers were just taking the situations as they were, or within their imagination to create his or her own world, as it was out of that apartheid situation, and then just transfer them to the page in a generalistic manner. This is the writer that will be in the doldrums. Writers, you see, who are talented in the craft, in the art of writing, the Njabulo Ndebeles and so on, will continue to write.

Ndebele, in his collection of essays Rediscovery of the Ordinary, *seems to stake out a new direction for South African writing generally. He is critical of the externalising tendency in recent struggle literature, and suggests a turning away from the townships and urban scenes for relevant literary topics, and rather looking to the issues of ordinary people in the rural areas for themes and inspiration. Would you go along with that?*

Well, I don't believe in prescribing a new genre. But I believe a critic has the right to point these things out. And I actually agree with the things he has pointed out. I actually pointed them out myself in theatre. Our theatre was very much urban-based in its setting, in its characters and so on, and there was very little theatre that explored what was going on in the rural areas. And it was also a very male-based and sexist kind of theatre. So I do point these things out. And I am sure the more critics point out things like those – and they are *not* prescribing when they are doing that: they are criticising trends, they are criticising the times, they are criticising genres – those artists who are able to, will move, will expand their horizon.

I stress the artists who are able to do so, because you cannot write about the rural areas when you know nothing about it. Many of our writers here are born and bred in the cities. I myself am writing a novel which is set in the rural areas now. I can do that because I have interacted with the rural environment in my life in Africa and elsewhere and can recreate that. But I don't know if it is possible to recreate the rural environment solely from imagination, in otherwords from what you think the rural areas are like. I have set my works in all kinds of environments, including the rural areas, because I am quite familiar with the rural areas. But as new writers come up who have their roots in the rural environment, they'll be able to recreate that environment in their work. I am sure we are going to see more of that literature as well.

I talked to a writer the other day who categorically declared that he was not going to do anything in his writing with a view to educating people. He didn't feel it was his job. He would write about his personal longings, about things that mattered to him personally, from his heart. So that revealed a strand that is not really based in African reality, or is it?

But then, so what? It's a free country, it's supposed to be a free country, isn't it? Now, an artist must be free to express himself the way he wants, without anybody prescribing that. The public out there will determine whether that artist is valid or not, whether they are interested in his personal longings or not. It is the public who will decide, isn't it?

There should be nobody to prescribe what feelings that writer should have, or what that writer should be writing about. You see? All I can say is that for me, I think I can use my heart to transform society.

You mentioned that you are about to finish a novel shortly?

Yes, it is going to be finished this month.

What is it about?

It is called *She Plays with Darkness*. And what is it about, man? It is difficult to say what it is about. But it is set in Lesotho, partly influenced by my experiences there. I am writing in the mode of Magical Realism, which is a mode I've always used from the time I began to write, even in my plays, without knowing that there was something called Magical Realism; it was just that I felt like writing that way. It is only later that I realised that, ah, there are other people writing in that manner, and that the name it has been given is Magical Realism. That was only three or four years ago, you see.

But it is a mode that I am more comfortable with. So the novel I'm writing is in that mode. I explore reality, you know – not in an objective manner, not as objective reality, but reality governed by magic and the supernatural. The supernatural is taken for granted. In other words, my characters interact with the supernatural forces in their day-to-day living – it's a natural thing to do. They don't find the supernatural problematic.

This novel is set in the mountains of Lesotho, in the rural areas, but some characters do go to the town at times to do their work there. And it's the interaction of the mountain people: how they live their real lives, their loves and so on. It's also a love story of sorts, and I stress of sorts, because it's not a romance in the normal sense.

I suppose this must be something that is close to the African cultural roots, the way you apparently depart from the 'barren rationalism of the west', wouldn't you say?

Yes, I think so. That's why, you see – this is something that comes naturally to me. If you go the rural areas, to the mountains, there are still beliefs and practices which are based on the supernatural world. And people interact with those beliefs, as if indeed they were real. To them they are real. In my novels, of course, those beliefs are real, and things happen in the very magical way in which these people live. Actually, people there live lives which are full of magic. Yeah. . .

Have you read Ben Okri's novel The Famished Road *by any chance? He is into a similar way of writing.*

No, I have not. But I have read some reviews of that novel, and I'm sure that when I have finished writing my novel, I will read that one.

And indeed, I think that it is the same mode he uses. I think he was quite correct when he took offence when the critics thought that he was trying to mimic the Latin American magical realists, you see. *His Magical Realism is based on his own situation here, which is just as magical. Which is the same thing!* That's why I tell you that the earliest plays I wrote were not naturalistic. Things happen in that 'supernatural' manner. I wrote them when I was at high school, and I had not read any Latin American writers.

But for me it was natural for things to happen in that 'un-natural' manner. You see that? It was only later when I got to know that – Ah, there's a mode like that, and it's called Magical Realism! And people have been using it for years – even before I was born. But to me it just came on its own, you understand? But it would be just crazy for anybody to say that these works have been influenced by Latin Americans and so on. There is only one Latin American that I have have read so far, and that is Gabriel García Márquez in *One Hundred Years of Solitude*. And that one, I only read it two years ago when I was in Britain. Then I saw that – Ah, man, that guy is doing some of the things that I am doing. And I have been doing this without knowing that there is such a mode, in fact, in existence.

Rob Amato

Could we begin the interview by you reflecting a bit on your background – educational, theatrical, etc.?

Well, as the son of an industrialist and a very beautiful socialite I grew up in a mansion in Johannesburg: six acres of ground and a river running past the bottom of the garden. I was a very lonely child. My sister was eight years older than I was, and my mother travelled a lot.

But at six something happened to me. My mother took me and my sister on a wonderful journey from Durban through the Suez Canal up to Stockholm through the Mediterranean; from there to England, and to France. We went to London, and to Madame Tussaud's. And all the right things happened. I thought the policeman standing on the stair was real. And then we went past a door which said – my sister had taught me to read very young – so I saw this line saying 'Adults Only', and promptly parted the curtains to see this man hanging by his guts, literally, on a hook. Which nearly wiped me out. Feel these fear images!

Then we went to Paris. And my mother decided she wanted to have a couple of months without the kids, so she put me into a French boarding school with my elder sister, which was sort of an institution from *l'Histoire d'O* or something like that. It was a weird place, where nobody wanted to look after the kids. I don't know why there was that strange combination of young kids and sixteen-year-old girls. A very bad combination. Sixteen-year-old girls are not very good for little boys. They manipulate them in all sorts of untutored ways, sorts of false motherhood and, well, that was a very strange experience. I remember my mother visited me with an old Jewish uncle, who looked at me, and I remember him saying this: 'This child does not look happy.' He said this to her in French, in an undertone, but I was now able to understand it.

They then took me into town, and we went, month in month out, to the Tuilleries, and there was le Petit Guignol, the puppet show, in a big green tent, wonderful! It took about a hundred children. They rang the bell on the hour and you came and paid your ten *sous,* and they did three shows a day in several languages, because Paris was full of tourists, and it was the great time for Americans in Paris '49, '50. I loved the sets and the changings and the puppets.

A little side story about this is that I was writing for *South,* a Cape Town magazine, about two or three years ago, and I wrote an article about how I would love to see such a puppet theatre in the Gardens of Cape Town. And the editor of *South* said that this was a Eurocentric conception, and I lost my rag and gave her such a blast that I never wrote for the magazine again. This just as an interesting little sideline to show how things do reach from six to fifty. They do, they often do!

When I went back with Hildur, my wife, in '69, I was twenty-five; le Petit Guignol was still operating in its green tent in the park, and perhaps it's still there. And one of the marvels of it was its sets, it had full scale stage opera flies, I mean tiny scale copies of opera flies, so they could do the country, the forest, the palace, the dungeons, all in the matter of moments. There were short scenes; they were always changing. And it was in this magnificent garden, this strange garden, with gravel under the trees. That's another association with Cape Town's Gardens – there's similar gravel in a circle opposite the beautiful old Orthodox synagogue (built by a Christian late nineteenth century architects' firm!) that looks like the set for the *Merchant of Venice*.

Then, on returning to South Africa on the Union Castle mail-ship, the *Pretoria Castle*, I lost a red-haired monkey puppet over the side of the ship. My first death by water. My mother was to die in the sea, at seventy-two, at Sea Point, in 1978, twenty-nine years later.

On the *Pretoria Castle* children weren't allowed to sit with their parents at dinner, or to go through various doors: I was full of resentment, because it was as if I were an adult being forced into childhood again. It was the English class system, something which later at Oxford, I also loathed. I was very unhappy there. I am really a republican, that's a very real part of the whole fucking thing. A poor capitalist, a republican with pretensions to grandeur! And now I'm worried about 'Traditional Leaders'!

What took you to Oxford?

A Rhodes scholarship.

Studying what?

We are jumping to twenty-four now. I must tell you some other things before coming there. I went to a Catholic school, which was also very theatrical. Catholicism is one of the most theatrical religions. If you are going to be a Christian, you might as well be a Catholic, for at least the theatre is good. Better than the Jews who always cut out the visual images and actually make their services as undramatic as possible, especially the 'Reformed' Jews. When I was barmitzvahed they tried to tell me how to read the *English translation* from the Torah in my performance before the assembled congregation (isn't that what it's supposed to be?). I was prepared to parrot the Hebrew, but English was mine, and the Bible is a drama, to be acted. That was the end of them, I moved on. And what about the Protestants who also cut out all the visual images? Their God is too jealous, like that of the Jews. I mean, what the devil, the battering down of all the little statues and the stained glass in Ely Cathedral: that shattered Britain! It's understandable that people want to talk privately to God rather than through the church, but with a bit of imagery, for God's sake!

So that was a Catholic school for a Jew. And there were several other Jews. My mother sent me there, because she liked the idea of the 'celibataires', devoting themselves to education. It was actually a very good school, because the Catholics, even in the rich suburbs of Northern Johannesburg, had a policy of admitting all sorts of children, also from poor homes – but all white until 1962–63, after I'd left. I was there for twelve solid years, 1948–60. It was a good barbaric school: lots of corporal punishment, lots of dramas, lots of perversities. But also an extraordinary devotion, a Catholic sort of energy which was quite interesting. All the Jews in our class were very clever boys. There were four or five of us who were among the top boys, and it was a kind of embarrassment for us. When we finally came to matric they couldn't make a head prefect because there were too many clever Jewish boys in this Catholic school, so they decided not to appoint one that year. It was funny!

That was quite good, but I was rather reactionary, I think, as a child. I matriculated in 1960 in Sharpeville, you see. And I saw Sharpeville as the media wanted me to. I still see in my mind's eye the African Mirror 'news' movies, put out by African Consolidated Films. That was where the main propaganda of the state operated. An evening at the movie house was serious in the fifties. You stood at the end for 'God Save the Queen'. And when they told you that the South African Police were firing in self-defence and to stop chaos you believed them. You worried that everybody was shot in the back, but you understood why. God!

And I spoke of myself as a Nationalist at the age of eighteen or so. I was what one commonly regards as a racist. But I used to have to deal with the ideas of my father, which were quite different in some ways. He never talked to me about the war and the Holocaust, but he had been a very important figure in the Congo and in the southern continent altogether during the time of the war. Actually, in 1979, when he died, at his funeral there were four or five hundred people I had never seen before, and I discovered that they were people that he had taken from the island of Rhodes in 1937–38, and that he had been in a sort of small way a Schindler, but just as an industrialist, not a person who risked his life to save people. He brought a lot of people out. He ran many industries from the Congo down to here. One would need a whole book to talk about him. His characteristics were enormous strength and enormous respect for people. He was actually very much loved later on. But he was an emotional bully.

He was fighting for the introduction of sunflower and cottonseed into South Africa while my mother was in America having an ear operation (she had fallen off a horse at nineteen and always had trouble with her hearing and balance, so that this beautiful woman looked always slightly drunk), or in Europe. Later she would visit the chateaux and palazzos of all the Viscomptes and Barons that she knew. That's another dimension: she was an aristocrat-lover, and they loved her too, her entrée was never in question because of her beauty, her charm, and her bad enthusiastic French.

But my father was staying in Johannesburg in this mansion that she had already furnished with eighteenth-century stuff. And this, or the early 1950s, was the time when he was making money: the 1950s was when white South Africans were really making money in a big way. He used to say things like 'A man must take the world as he finds it. Good luck to those who can be intellectuals and artists, but we've got to make food for tummies and work for people. And it'll take *siècles* and *siècles* for Africa to become industrial. You do what you can in your humble way.' He also used to say that when apartheid ends the Xhosas and the Zulus would start fighting each other. I think in his life he made over 10 000 jobs. He never took anything out of the business, never mind out of the country. No reserves, always expanding the businesses, paint, oils, animal feeds, textiles, blankets, grain bags. This was very important, strategically important during the war. Smuts and Churchill exchanged telegrams on the shipping under convoy (again a convoy – I'm going to make a convoy movie!) of an entire textile plant and 400 Yorkshiremen from Leeds to Benoni, to make tyres and tarpaulins. Imagine the management: here were 400 immigrants coming in one group. And he worked with them very well all the way through the years, this short Levantine Jew with all these Yorkshiremen. He always spoke with a very thick sort of Ladino accent, but my mother was from Holland.

The names are interesting. The family name on his side was Amado at the time of the Inquisition, the sixteenth century. Her family also came from Spain then, and were called di Leone. Amado was Italianized to Amato in the family's long move across the Mediterranean to Turkey, where my grandfather was born. My mother's side went to Holland and became de Leeuw. They married and the common languages were French and English. Both were actually Sephardic Jews.

What happened as you finished your schooling?

We are talking of the early sixties now. When I was eighteen my father falls. Big fall. Main headlines. And he's actually charged with fraud. It was later withdrawn. But the Amato group went insolvent. It was a question of contested valuation of stocks. A major development resulting from a change of policy in Pakistan, which was now determined to export bags, not hemp. Huge jump in raw material costs on a product that directly affected agricultural prices. Valuation problems surrounding hemp and sisal, stocks of fibre and bags used as security against bank loans, and the huge government and bank support.

Whatever the reasons were, he used to believe that they were out to get him. They were getting him out so they could move in, which is in fact what happened historically. He lost the industries.

And until his fall I was this millionaire's son who was going to take over all this. And we started all over again when I was eighteen. As I came out of school he had nothing. He had to bring down an old plant from the Congo. And that was the second time he had got an old plant, because that was the way it started in the Congo in the

1930s. He had started with a little oil-crushing plant from America, so he had to do a reliving of his twenties in his fifties, but I was eighteen at the time. I was going to the university, but I couldn't until I was twenty-two or twenty-three. I went from school to East London and started a new business with him, from an old plant in a little town away from everyone. A difficult time, cut off from culture.

But there, educationally speaking, I met a German couple who saved my bones. Do you know how they did that? They saw that this was a kid that liked to follow what was going on in the world, who was interested in literature or whatever. And they bought me a subscription. They were strangers: I went to dinner one night with them. And two months after that, you know, I suddenly received the first copy of a year's subscription to *The Spectator*. I've always thought of those people as the most extraordinary benefactors. Because, while I was stuck in that little town, every week I knew what was happening in London – two months late, but I *knew* it. And I knew how it was being reviewed, so by the time I got to university I could write.

And how was your life at university? Where did you enter the world of the theatre?

I was the typical South African rugby young fifties-youth at university: no involvement with black theatre or any contact with blacks of any kind. Completely segregated. Well, that isn't quite true, actually. I mustn't forget my black nanny, Annah Gumede. I think she was very important. She was an apple-cheeked Zulu woman who looked after me in my youth in that great big mansion. And her sons were important companions to me. KaiKai was one. I called him KaiKai, but his name was Msilikazi. I called him KaiKai because he cried a lot when we were little, and I couldn't say *cry*, so it became KaiKai. We lived together till I was about ten. He in a little room at the back of the house, and me upstairs in my huge bedroom.

Seems to be the ever-recurring black-white story, doesn't it?

Yes. Later on I went to visit her, in the eighties, in Inanda, and in the middle of KwaZulu. She was always worried that I might get hurt when I was visiting her. It was the beginning of the terrors in that area. I don't know actually what has happened to her. I have lost contact now.

Which shames me, but I have. She might have died in the last few years.

Would you see her as a very formative influence in your early days?

Yes, a strict, uncompromising, gifted, loud person. A very good cook. Mistress of the household. There were several servants, you know, about six or seven, and she was the mistress of the whole scene. She called me *Robbert Louuuis*. When I hear my full name pronounced I always think it's her speaking. I think that the physical proximity of that woman, as for many whites in South Africa, the sense, the smell, the black face, the intimate knowledge of the smell of the breath, the heavy smell of the hair, the proximity that we felt to those who were looking after us as if they were our own mothers, is a very important counter to apartheid. As I told you, my politics at school was like that of any white racist, in many respects, but there is always this undercurrent, which I think is also common to many people, and the nature of our revolution has to do with those links. The horror that many, perhaps most, whites feel at the idea of forced separation, and the horror they feel at the sad fact that so much black blood is shed, is in many ways a function of the intimate knowledge they had of black people as servants and nannies.

One of the reasons why I am cautious in my book on the new South African Constitution in making the judgements of Inkatha, is the fact that if you go to an Inkatha rally now, you'll see fifty thousand nannies of the kind that brought me up. Some of them will say that they are forced to be there; some of them will say they don't like Buthelezi; some of them will say this, that and the other; but the fact is that those women are like ships of state. They are very powerful personalities; they're very conservative, they're very decent, they wear the quasi military uniform of Inkatha with great pride. They're very Christian. They are a force to be reckoned with. They're a constituency which must be respected.

But back to East London in 1962–63. I was having great battles with my father, because I wanted to get away. I wanted to do other things than industry. I wanted to go into the theatre. I had at school enjoyed doing little bits of *Julius Caesar*, played Mark Anthony, Scrooge in the *Christmas Carol* and that sort of thing, you know. I am not a good actor, but I did a bit of acting. I knew I was going to be a director. I wanted to be a film director, actually, and in East London it was difficult at the time. Later (1970–76) I was to spend seven years directing theatre in East London again: those were the happiest days. I'll come back to those – very productive. But in 1960–63 it was difficult, and I finally said to my father, 'I'm going now, I'm going to Jo'burg to make my own way. I am leaving, this is my life.'

He said, 'Well, we'll make a deal. You go to Durban, you do Law, and you sell the products of the factory in Durban, the oil.' I said all right. So I went to Durban, right in the middle of the year, and I went to every lecture available on the campus, one of each subject for six months. It is a little campus, but nobody seemed to kick me out. And besides I was going to English and Politics and Philosophy and French and Economics. Most important were English, Philosophy and Politics. I was duly working, and got into the second year. I was on the SRC, and I never told my father I wasn't doing Law all this time.

A little incident there: the first black man that really had an influence on me was a fairly famous black man. I was selling cooking oil in Stanger, and this very nice Indian man, Muslim – he knew I was a student, said to me, 'Would you like to meet the Chief?' I had come to sell him oil: it was in a wholesaler's shop. And I came to the back of the shop, and there sat Luthuli, Albert Luthuli, who'd been restricted to that area. And we sat down and had tea, and Luthuli asked me what I was doing. Now, I couldn't lie to Albert Luthuli. I told him what I had done, that I was pretending to be doing Law, but that I was actually doing the subjects that I loved, and that I was doing this business. He looked at me and he said: 'We need lawyers who love literature. You should do what you father wants, just keep both going.'

It's funny that I never took Law, because the first book I published was on the new South African Constitution last year. Funny sort of cross pattern. I was on the NUSAS (National Union of South African Students) Academic Freedom thing, which has always been one of my big numbers – academic freedom, freedom of the mind. I'm quite worried about it now. And I think there is quite a glutinous use of it now, abuse. It's very sweet. There is lots of velvet over the glove, but I'm having quite a lot of my work censored in *Constitutional Talk* at the moment. I am very conscious of a serious censorship of journalism in the parastatal world. Not in the state itself, but in the parastatal world, in the world of the Constitutional Assembly. I personally have just had three articles severely censored, because they were arguing for Winnie and for her constitutional freedoms. So, you know, there's always a continuity. Anyway, in those days I was academic freedom secretary for NUSAS on the campus, and I went to a NUSAS conference, and they were talking of bringing out Harold Macmillan. He had done his 'Winds of Change' speech and they wanted to bring him out again.

I had by that stage shifted my politics, as one often does at university. University was free enough for that to happen. Most of us went through some sort of transition of that kind. Most of us came from conservative homes and ended up radicals, as we called them. And I said, 'Macmillan is nothing, bring out Robert Kennedy.' Which they did. I never met him. But he was enormously successful. It was part of a huge mind-shift in South Africa. His visit meant we were on the same planet as the Americans who were going through the Civil Rights thing, and the Kennedy Magic growth, the liberalisation campaign, etc. was up. There were six thousand people to hear him on the campus.

In Durban?

In Durban. The crowd was outside, and they were kept waiting for three hours, Kennedy having been kept with other people in town. Amazing. The managers! Those politicians from America are crazy, keeping six thousand people waiting for three hours.

So when did you go to Oxford?

In 1966. Before going to Oxford I did *Twelfth Night*, which was my first production, in Mitchell Park in Durban. Hildur, my wife-to-be, played Viola, that's how we met. I was a complete amateur. I hadn't done anything before, but it was very lovely, physically, done in that park. And it was great fun to create a theatre. Oh, I was called by the Professor of Drama at the time, Professor Sneddon. I received a summons: 'I will be at home at 11 o'clock on Friday morning.' And I pitched up at this Grand Dame of Durban Theatre; she is still the Grand Dame of Durban theatre thirty years later, the Thousand-Year Reich.

She rises and sits me down. She says, 'Now, you've done three years here at Durban; you've done English and Philosophy and . . .' – she knew my whole curriculum – 'you've just done a production of *Twelfth Night* and you've never come to the Drama department. Why?'

Now, I'd just got the Rhodes scholarship, and thought the sun shone out of my backside. You know it was a terrible arrogance. I don't remember this with pleasure, but I said, 'Because I attended one of your lectures.' She said, 'Do you take honey or sugar in your tea?' I said, 'I take sugar.' And she said, 'You must learn to take honey,' and she put two large spoons of honey in my cup, stirred it very hard and changed the topic of conversation.

I go to Oxford, and before I go I meet my fellow Rhodes Scholar. He was from Cape Town. His name was Rob McLaren. We meet, and we meet like two young bulls. We're both big deals, you know, in our respective universities; big egos! And we fight but we become friends, at Oxford, very close friends, and we decide we're going to come back and work in the theatre here. And we do that, actually. Three years later, we come back, and I start the Imitha Players in East London, and he starts all sorts of wonderful things. I mean, he's the most extraordinary influence on South African culture, that one individual; a tall Scot with long hair and a big nose and a wicked smile, a bit of a Jacobean. He also played Jacobean parts wonderfully.

It was interesting with the two groups, because my group, the Imitha Players, (the Rays of the Sun), was a very classical group. It was made not by me, really, but by a man called Skhala Xinwa, who was a diminutive journalist I met through Donald Woods.

Was this a white group?

No-no-no. A Xhosa group. Skhala Xinwa was a journalist on the East London *Daily Dispatch*. Rob McLaren was starting Workshop '71, really revolutionary theatre. Now, the Imitha Players was following my bent and was quite a classical group. What we did was we started with *Oedipus Rex*. You see I chose *Oedipus Rex* because I didn't want to come with Shakespeare. My father, funnily enough, said, 'You are doing Shakespeare with the blacks?' 'No,' I said, 'I'm not doing Shakespeare with the blacks.' It was an absolute condition of my coming back to East London to work with him that I would carry on with the theatre in the evenings. There was no discussion. Actually I cut him out of whole sections of my life, to keep them free of his power. I never even invited him to my shows. Very cruel in some ways, when I think back on it now, I was a very cruel young man. And I see traces of cruelties in my sons and daughter. They are cruelties that tend to be nice, but they are quite complex cruelties. They come from all sorts of processes. One of my cruelties was that I never let my father come to the theatre, because he was slighting about that side of my life.

We did *Oedipus Rex*. The reason I chose that text was because it was written two thousand four hundred years ago by somebody whose language I didn't know any more than did the people I was directing. It was a distant culture we were picking up. That was my logic. The fact that it was aboriginal to western culture didn't really occur to me. Perhaps it's not; perhaps it is so great that it's from everywhere. You know it is the best written detective story for the theatre ever done. It was the revelations that kicked me with the construction of that play. It is as good as any movie could ever be today, in terms of revelatory techniques and shocks and the skill of the dialogue and the containment and the respecting of the unities. The whole structure is a work of absolute transcendent genius. And it is about things the Xhosas understand very well; it is about the problems of taboos and incest, about power. It's about illusions of grandeur; it's about corruption in high places, causing corruption through the society. It was extraordinary in its resonances. And the person who played Oedipus – a marvellous man. He was Julius Mtsaka who subsequently taught at Wits University. He was very interesting; not a trained actor, but a wonderful emoter, and I just remember one incident, a story which somehow determines how I feel about the theatre in some ways.

You see we had done the production with very respectful audiences, mixed audiences. It was of course illegal to have mixed audiences where we sold tickets at the door. But with typical South African compromise, what we did was we had an invitation club, and we invited people to come to see a show and afterwards they gave a donation. So we organised it all through one of the secretaries at the factory. I had some cards printed, and she had a list, and mailed tickets to Mr and Mrs Mtheba, Mr and Mrs January – all the black teachers, all the white, all the coloured, all the three communities in that town, and with the help of Schala Xinwa, this journalist whom I met through Donald Woods, we put the whole thing together. What he did, he went to a man called Cyril Mjo, who was in fact the leader of the group in some ways, who was running a Handel choir. Now this group that did the performance of Oedipus was about twelve people who were also an expert Handel choir.

Hildur, my wife, did the costumes in classical Greek; she cut them wonderfully from the interlock cotton fabric that we were making in the factory, in beautiful dark burgundies, the colours of the bloomers of the women of the Transkei; burgundies and dark greens and of course unbleached natural cotton. And it was very, very beautiful. The reviewers said that they were so surprised at how all these black men and women looked like Greeks in Greek costumes.

They were all very beautiful people, and they sang like gods. You see we have this great thing – 'Nkosi Sikileli' is an example of it – we have a very remarkable marriage of minds in music, which I think is deeply significant in this country; the marriage of the black late nineteenth-century Christian musical mind, with that of eighteenth-century Europe, Handel in particular. So we did an *Oedipus Rex*: black Xhosas speaking English, wearing Greek costumes and singing Handel without words. We just dropped all the words from the chorus. You know the choruses of the play are the weakest part of it. They are the most obscure to us; the religious references are incomprehensible and the metaphors are a bit syrupy, and so one drops that and replaces it with just emotion for the moment, pure sound, with these wonderful voices in harmony singing this Africanised Handel. It was extraordinarily beautiful.

And the story I am coming to is that we'd done this production in town in the church halls that we had hired, and the audiences had come and they were professional people, educated people, and they loved it, and it was very moving. And then we went to Durban, to the university there. We went to Pretoria, we went to Butterworth, we went to places in the countryside. They were able to translate into Xhosa as we went, they were so close to the text; they'd played for two years.

Then finally after a year or so we're back in East London – we had long runs, you see, and we played every month or so, rehearsed for a year or nine months. Second language work, you know, it takes a long time. They were deeply close to this ancient play. Now, back in East London, we decide we must go to Ndantsani, which is the black township from which they all come. We start the play. It's done in the round. What we used to do there would be halls – big dreadful barren halls with no carpets or curtains, dusty and falling apart. That was all that there was in those days in the black townships. Terrible halls, built by people who were totally distanced from the township population and who were never going to use them for themselves: a sort of nightmare, officialese buildings. To make the place a bit more human, what we did was we put chairs on the stage. There were lots of chairs, so we put chairs on top of chairs and made a kind of amphitheatre. And on the other side we did the same thing, so it was a kind of parliamentary size. The stage was long and narrow, with audience on both sides. It was very much theatre in the round, very close contact between the audience and the stage. But the problem was, in that performance, that nobody was going to accept the conventions of this piece. Because there was the Headmaster of the school, barefooted and pretending to be an old man. They had only seen him in a suit and being dignified. And there he was as Tyresius, bent double and cursing. And there was the beer salesman as Kreon, and there was a well-known beauty as Jocasta, and they just laughed every time an entrance happened, because they recognised everybody and shouted and laughed. And the actors couldn't get the play going at all, you see.

They finally got to the point where Oedipus in the shape of Julius Mtsaka, comes in with his eyes gouged out with the brooches of his wife who's hanged herself: he's taken the brooches from her body, his wife-mother. And he's stabbing his own eyes, and he comes in with tomato sauce all over his eyes, feeling his way. And a big, fat mamma in the front row, says, 'Agh, come on Julie, we know you're not blind'. The whole place packs up! What does an actor do with this? What he did was, he went and stood over her, and cried, as if saying 'Mama, I am talking about pain, I am talking about man, I am talking about ancient things.' And she fell silent, and the people around her fell silent and contrite, and the whole house became contrite and quiet. And he went on to the most wonderful climax to end the play. So it worked, but only by a rescue which was of extraordinary proportions.

Then we went on to do some Soyinka; we did some Sartre. In the meantime Athol Fugard was running the Serpent Players in Port Elizabeth, and Don Maclennan was running the Ikwezi Players in Grahamstown. So there were three troupes of serious artists in the Eastern Province from 1970 to 1975.

There were actually travelling theatre groups as late as the mid-'70s?

Mm. We exchanged productions, so that every two months or so somebody was given an invitation to see a new play, and often very good plays. Don did *Job Mawa*, which was a marvellous production about man's suffering, pure and not simple. Then there was *In Camera*, from Athol and Kani, and then a Camus play, I've dropped the name, and he did *Mandragola*, hilariously funny. It's a marvellous play, *Mandragola*, I don't know if you know it? Machiavelli's only play. It appeared in the 1540s, I believe, and is a great anticipation of Renaissance comedy. Machiavelli was ahead in so many ways. Francis Bacon said that he was the first man to write about what *is* rather than what *ought to be*.

In the meantime Rob is doing this radical stuff up in Johannesburg, you see – Rob McLaren – at the time when I am doing this deeply, deeply ancient stuff. It's a very interesting contrast. He brings shows down, I take shows up. He brings down his version of the English *Everyman*, which he calls *Crossroads*. He makes it as a voyage through Soweto, and one sees the life of Soweto, and farm life. One wonderful mock operatic song with the Boer watching his farm labourers: *'Kyk hoe my volkies werk!'* ('Look how my little people work!') sung to the tune of *La donna è mobile*. So we exchanged productions.

Rob also did a wonderful version of a Ben Jonson play called *Zzzip!*, which was so outrageous we nearly got kicked out of the church hall forever.

And I must speak of Don Maclennan (lots of Scots I love in my life). Don is an English lecturer at Rhodes University, just retiring this year. For me, one of the most magic of men. Coming back from Oxford and having to live in East London, he was the great source of intellectual advance for me, and spiritual joy and the great outdoors.

Something happened that profoundly influenced my family. We lost a child in this period. Our second child was a girl called Justine, who died of leukemia. After the trauma of death, which occurred over a long time, over two months or so, Don came to the funeral, and after the funeral he said to Hildur and me, 'Come with me. I'm taking you somewhere. I want to show you something. It's a long journey, it'll take seven hours, but I'm taking you.'

So we got into the car and drove for seven hours from East London to a little village called Rhodes, which is in the southern Drakensberg, inland from Umtata. And that night he sang to us. I remember, he sang 'The lark in the morning'. 'The lark in the morning, she rises from her nest, And goes up in the air with dew on her breast, Like the jolly ploughboy she whistles and she sings And comes home in the evening with the dew on her wings . . .' A song which, of course, goes to my heart now, completely; it's a wonderful song which he sang to us in this dark little hotel in this funny little ghost town in the middle of nowhere right up in the mountains. We bought for seventeen hundred rand a house there, which is of extraordinary beauty and which my children have been to every year forever since. So it was a way of making one deal with a loss and look to the future. It was an extraordinary thing for Don to do. It was typical of what Don is like. He looks like a thinner and more anguished Sean Connery, Don does. Shirley, his wife, an American, was equally important as a redemptive force which is what that family meant to us.

Don was also doing his plays in Grahamstown, and so we often went up and down. There is a dream river between Grahamstown and East London, like there is a real river between Oxford and London. There was the sense that there I was in a little industrial town, but inland there was this university town, and there was this river between them.

And at that time, 1970–73, Rob McLaren, Mango Tshabangu and I were also publishing a magazine called *S'ketsh*, which you will have difficulty in finding in the records. In fact I don't think the first edition exists anywhere. But every three months or so we got out this magazine on the performance arts of South Africa, on 'majority' arts, as Rob used to call it. And it was the first radical magazine, I think, of its kind: an arts magazine.

Just after the death of Justine we went to the United States to try and recover and get Hildur away from East London for a while. My mother looked after our son, Ben, and we went to New York. And there I interviewed people for *S'ketsh*. It's a whole other story, Douglas Turner Ward, and the American Negro, African Black connection. He was the Director of the *Negro Ensemble*, and I use the word *Negro* advisedly, because they still call themselves the *Negro Ensemble*. It was founded in 1902. It was a great historical Black company. They were doing *The River Niger*. It was the time of *Roots*.

And we also published materials on most of the black artists in this country. A lot of black reviewers, too. Indians in Durban, and the radical theatre all the way round. It was also the time when the theatre was strongly Grotowski-influenced. Fugard had also introduced Grotowski to us all. And the 'poor theatre ideology' was going to take form in the Space and the People's Space Theatre in the '70s, and this was the beginning of that. It was through the idea that all one needs is a body and a voice, and the fact that the body is something like a stage set itself: you can work through your belly or you can work through your knees, etc. The extraordinary philosophy of Grotowski. Very powerful.

Fugard's *Orestes*, a very famous production which was seen by very few people, and which is almost impossible to put down on a page, was a Grotowski piece. So we had that, combined with Rob's Marxism and my sort of interest in The Great Theatre. So I was trying to bring all the great traditions of European comedy or tragedy to bear – we were doing Molliére as well, we had a lot of fun with Molliére – and Rob was doing the same thing, but much more suffused with revolutionary politics than my work, which was actually in that dimension completely tame. I wanted analysis, not argument, generally speaking, from what I was doing.

In fact, it's interesting that all the years I worked in the black theatre, so tame was my work, or so decent or so something, that I was never ever troubled by the police during the whole period that I worked, even when I was doing quite tough stuff like *Egoli* later on. But I think that the Afrikaners, the police included, had a great respect for culture, actually, which I think has been proved. And one of the things that I'd like to say is that I am very proud of my country's treatment of political prisoners. Of course I abhor the *idea* of political prisoners, but look at the way they've emerged, those who were not killed or tortured. I think South Africa contrasts remarkably with many other countries I have heard about in its treatment of political prisoners. They've all come out with degrees and they're all in fat-suits in Parliament, and they didn't have to bleed to do that. They might have been abused, but they were patronisingly helped.

What precisely are you talking about now?

I'm talking about Robben Island. You can see the recent movie called 'Robben Island, The Story', and there are all these gentlemen, of a certain age, who at the expense of the state, studied a great deal for many, many years. Can you name another country where that has happened? Where all the political opposition was imprisoned, but made studious? And all came out as lawyers or doctors of philosophy or whatever it happens to be? I think it's remarkable. My point is that the 'miracle' as it has been called, is not only a function exclusively of this specifically black South African genius for taking up the modern world, which I think is very important. So they are not reactionary, which is why the current traditionalism is a very deep problem: feudalism which is coming back in the form of Patakile Holomisa. All of them. Mandela himself is a prince, so is Buthelezi. There is a subterranean feudalism running through, which is in danger of causing great difficulties. But that is another aside!

Maybe we could take it back to the seventies again?

Yes. By seventy-six I had sold the industry in East London. We had done seven or eight productions with the Imitha Players, and I became involved with the production of a play of my own called *The Mind Mirror*, which was a one-hander, a study of 'computer morality programming' in the 1990s, written in 1973, which postulated East London as a walled city in the 1990s. It was a mixture of Woody Allen and Kafka. It was this sex-obsessed man talking to his own computer which replied in his own voice. I used a tape-recorder as the computer and just recorded what it said, and so there are two versions of the same voice arguing with one another. It's quite a fun piece. And there was no television in this country and I used this video thing, and had some beautiful nudes doing the positions of the sun, to Vivaldi, and the idea was that there was some permanent porn channel on this television, soft, very soft porn.

That was a nice play, directed by Don Maclennan, which ran for about six weeks at the Space.

Directed by Maclennan and written by you?

Yes, written and acted by me. That was the only really long stint of acting that I had, and at the end, by the end of the fifth week I was suicidal. Absolutely hated it, having to go in every night, and enact emotions, which seemed to me the most exquisite torture in hell: I am no actor. I know long runs are difficult for all actors, but for non-actors they become a torture.

You couldn't switch off?

No, couldn't give another line.

Then I got involved with Fatima Dike, who was working at the Space. And I brought to her an idea which I had got when I was doing a series of articles for the *Daily Dispatch* called 'Marking Time'. You know these articles that newspapers sometimes run: 'A Hundred Years Ago what was this newspaper like?' To be frank, the *Daily Dispatch*, which was Donald Woods' big radical paper, was mortifyingly racist a hundred years before. It was one of the first independent newspapers in this country, and I had done a piece on Kreli, who was a small king, one of the many that occupied the 'Kafraria' in those days, because it wasn't unified, like the Zulu nation has been. (If indeed the Zulu nation was that unified — there's a lot of argument about that amongst historians now.) Now, there was this king who had been defeated by the British, and was living in what he called a hole, in Bomvanaland in the present Transkei. He had been banished there, rather Lear-like, with three hundred soldiers, and no women and children. And the women and children had been placed with other tribes. The British had very strange ways of dealing with people they defeated. And the play takes place in this valley.

And Fats took up the idea wonderfully. She took her own sense of Africa, for most Africans have their own sense, which is not informed by scholarship, but by instinct: by the scholarship of the word, but not by an historical study. I had done a piece of close historical study by getting the journals of people who visited this king, and giving the basic facts as they were recorded by Victorian Englishmen. Southey, the name given to the anonymous journalist in the play, had written a very large article in this 1870s newspaper about this king and appealing against the torture that the British were imposing upon this man. And in it we built up this idea of sacrifice: *Yakhal 'nKomo*, the cry of the bull at the sacrifice. You know that in the traditions of most of the peoples in this subcontinent, Nguni people as opposed to the Khoisan, the tradition was that you slaughtered a beast, and if the beast cried out at its moment of death, the sacrifice would be successful. If it did not, it would not be successful. It's the similarity to the Greeks that we're talking about, the essential nature of the purity of the beast. And the Romans also picked this up, you know, the purity of the beast at the moment of sacrifice is a great augur for the future.

And this play, which we did at the Space, was beautifully designed. You can see the colonialism, though, operating. Hildur and I design the set; Hildur does the costumes, I conceive the play, and I collaborate with a black woman and we get fourteen black actors, and we make a mythical portrait of nineteenth century black life, deeply informed by Greek tragedy. I'm not ashamed of the colonialism of it. I'm proud of that. But I see it as what it *is* now, more than I did then. For me it was just humankind, the great myths of humankind. How you make emotion reflect human truth, is via story and music and sound and sacrifice and drama.

The King, again played by Julius Mtsaka, stands up and wants to sacrifice the beast in order to determine whether they should fight the British again, or whether they should go and collect their women and children and bring them to this place; what they should do as a defeated people.

The sacrifice of the bull itself was done on the stage in the most wonderful way, if I may say so myself. What happened was that there was a bank of the audience behind which there was a corridor in the old Space building, where the people are making this cattle kraal, and there is this long speech where the king and the sangoma choose the bull, the big white bull which had gone mad at the time of the defeat. And they choose that bull for the sacrifice. And then the songs of the sacrifice begin, and at the end of the first act there are fourteen people bringing this imaginary beast in, which always got ovations. There are fourteen people in a co-ordinated mime, which was rehearsed with me being the bull, and they would bring me down while I put up all the resistance I could muster, just to get right the muscular tensions of the act. Five men at each of my arms, and, of course, I would go down. It was simply a way of rehearsing. A bit of symbolism there as well, I suppose.

Anyway, they pull it to the ground, and it falls with a great thump as it lands, and this is done by an actor, you know. You've got so many actors that you don't know who's doing the sound effects. Then the King passes the spear between the bull's legs and up and down the body, and then stabs it. And one of the actors cries out – you can't tell which, they're all bending down holding this thing, kneeling and holding it, and there's a lot of noise. And then comes this great *Yakhal 'nKomo*, the cry of the bull of sacrifice, which is the basis of Mankunku's jazz, you know, Winston Mankunku, the great jazz saxophonist. And there's also a poem by Serote called *Yakhal 'nKomo*. There is a whole nexus of symbolism surrounding the sacrifice of the bull.

And in the second act Fatima imported a myth from Nyasaland, I think, about the way in which a sangoma is tested for his truth. He's wrapped in a skin, a cattle skin, the skin of the beast that's just been slaughtered, tied up and put in the sun. And the skin shrinks about him. If he survives that, he is a soothsayer. And the second act unfolds that process.

It is rather hard to read all that out of the text, wouldn't you say?

Impossible to read that play in the form in which it was published. I mean, it's infuriating! Stephen Gray messed it up. I am angry about it twenty years later! He didn't consult me on the publication of a play I had conceived and directed. The main problems were that he left the Xhosa untranslated, and that the stage directions were inadequate and wrong. It's a source of resentment, because it was a very beautiful play, and I should sit down and redo it with her. It's lost to posterity in the form it is now.

Maybe it's time now to have it rewritten?

I think there might be a time, it might be now. I think you might be right. The play wants to be remade. Because the play ends after the sangoma comes out of the skin and is lying there in a sort of *pieta* at the knees of the King. He whispers 'It will change', or some phrase to that effect, and the King picks it up and says 'What you were seeing now will take a hundred years for it to come to fruition. We will free only our children's children's children.' It was written in 1976, but set in 1875. So the point was that the new revolution was a hundred years ahead.

Now it has happened. So there is a case for reviving the play. It's a wonderful piece of theatre! I think we should do it again. Fatima is a wonderful poetic writer, and we worked well together. What we did was parallel texts: she'd write in Xhosa, and then she would write with me in English, with me looking after the clarity in English, the grammar, the poetic power, etc. It was a real collaboration. And it was a very big hit in the Space. And then it went to the Market Theatre, where it was a relatively big hit. It was the second production at the Market Theatre, a very big production. Barney Simon took over the direction because I was in industry down here and couldn't go up an do it. And I think he did a fairly good job, although he kept my *pieta* rather low; couldn't handle the sentiment of the last moments of the play. Perhaps he was right, perhaps he was wrong. But I thought the sentiment, not sentimentality, was central. But he'd got rid of the Messianic tones at the end. He found the *pieta* just too much. But I thought it was just fine, and so did the audiences. But there we are. Barney Simon is a very great director.

After that I wrote a play of my own which was a hearty flop, called *Not for the Deserving*, which was a sort of Beckettesque account of my own tensions in industry, and between industry and art. It was three men in a park in a revolution: a blind old man called Clunch, and a sort of clown figure called Tron (an anagram of *torn*), and a priest called Hallow. It was directed by Mavis Taylor, who put us into clown costume, whereas in fact it was *not* conceived in clown costume.

I shall not dwell more on this play. What it led on to, however, was my involvement with the Space. The founder of the Space Theatre was a very remarkable man, called Brian Astbury, who'd been working since 1972 and had been very influential in the major Fugard productions with Yvonne Bryceland (Brian's wife) and that whole wonderful nexus of work, which is not sufficiently documented at all. Somebody should bring out a proper book on the Space and perhaps the People's Space which followed. But what happened was that Brian had had enough after some fifty productions and seven years at the Space, which was initially at the top end of Long Street, and then at 44 Long Street, in the old YMCA building. And as he moved there he decided, in fact, to move out and I was instrumental with others in forming the People's Space Theatre, where a board of trustees was established and where we did the plays that are perhaps of most interest to this discussion. The first production there was Matsemela Manaka's *Egoli*, which involved two actors, Hamilton Sylwane and John Ledwaba. John Ledwaba went on to write his own musicals and a whole lot of other stuff and was very influential. He wrote something called *Township Boy* later.

But this is now 1978–79 or so, and having done the *Sacrifice of Kreli*, I went to Johannesburg to the Market Theatre, and was looking around for new work. I asked Mannie Manim, who ran the Market Theatre, what was going in black writing in Johannesburg, and he said 'Well, there is this play called *Egoli*, which is about miners, and it was playing at the University Theatre, a play for three hours. And it was a strange play about just two men, sitting with blankets in a room and talking about their lives. They were in a miners' hostel. It was impossibly long, but it was very magical. I decided this would be the opening production for the new People's Space Theatre, and I brought the actors to

Cape Town. Although Matsemela was a strong, imaginative playwright, he, interestingly, was quite happy to let us work here, and the actors and I shortened the play to one hour and thirty minutes or something. It was a very interesting piece, because it was very much a play based on light, light as the way of creating space.

And these two very beautiful bodies involved in a whole series of powerful mimes. It was in the tradition of two-male black South African plays of which, as you know, there were many. It started with Fugard's *The Island* and *Sizwe Bansi Is Dead* 'dualogues', often of two prisoners or two men locked together in one way or another. And its climactic pieces were also very visual, the creation of a certain mind-space which was also poetic landscape. It depended very much on the magic of the two actors. It was their play, and it actually ran for about fifty performances here, and then many in Johannesburg. It ran for about three or four years, the actors making a living out of taking it around the country. And its beauty was again its combination of an elevated tone with a great realism. It was strange. It's an interesting piece. Matsemela is a very fine playwright. He became much more schooled later in doing his own editing. When he came down to see the production he was quite pleased to see how we had reduced it. It is quite rare for a writer to enjoy the way it was produced.

How do find that play reads?

I think it reads well. I did the stage directions, and they are very carefully written. I think I conveyed on the page how the play works physically. It's a very short play as a text. It played much longer than it reads, because there was a tremendous amount of mime. It is ingenuous and beautiful. About simple people with very deep passions. It's again about myths of the wisdom of the heart, the wisdom of the nation, mythological treatment of the imaginary African past. Which I think is a great virtue and a great problem for us. Because evidence is so slack and because black knowledge is largely based on white interpretation of the past, because it was an illiterate culture.

This clashes with Marxism, doesn't it, in a sense?

Well, everything clashes with Marxism. I mean, Marxist materialism clashing with the African spiritual worldview, the *idea of mythification, etc.*

Now that was a big difference between Rob McLaren and I, because he was a wild Marxist, also working in the great myths and actually a marvellous playwright. I always used to think that his Marxism was like a dam to his virtues. He's probably very good at channelling them, but there was a huge kind of tension between his passionate love of Renaissance drama and all matters Renaissance, his love of Italian and French, which he spoke very well – Rob McLaren speaks eight languages – and his doctrinaire modern Marxism. He teaches now at the University of Zimbabwe. Anybody writing the history of South African theatre will have to look at him. He wrote a book called *Theatre and Revolution* or something like that. It was a tendentious book which I rather resisted. A marvellous artist! In fact his best pieces were the ones he liked least, because they were the least Marxist. It was a very strange phenomenon. He did a wonderful thing called *Smallboy*, which was about homosexuality in the jails, which he virtually redesigned because it wasn't sufficiently revolutionary. It was initially merely a study of what actually happens. And he did it with the actors, and it was wonderful, it was a beautiful piece. He brought that down to the Space Theatre, not to the People's Space.

Well, that was *Egoli*. After that we did *Dark Voices Ring*, which was our first production of Zakes Mda. It's a very strange story in which Sam Philips, who's just done a movie with Marius Weyers, played a sort of vegetable who'd been damaged by some white atrocity, and this man sits in his little hut, immobile and being attended by a woman who looks after him, who was played by Nomhle Nkonyeni, now I believe very powerful in PACT, the official Performing Arts Council of the Transvaal, who'd worked with Athol Fugard and is a very fine actress. And she plays the strong African woman, and the play ends with the old man smiling for the first time with the knowledge that his son is going north to join the soldiers, to fight the liberation war.

Zakes is a strange playwright, because his imagination is in a sense symbolist, which is unusual in this country. And he is a master of the imagined stage. By which I mean that the person working as a director on his material is not invited to clarify or interpret for the audience what's going on. He's done that. Although his plays are obscure and the jumps of logic are often difficult to follow, the emotional jumps are not. And the theatrical jumps are not. Of the four black playwrights whose work I have directed, I would say he was the greatest craftsman and the one who makes the least demands on the director to clarify or improve the text. In fact I've never altered a line of his, I don't think, which was certainly not true with my work with Matsemela's play, which we reworked and reworked and reworked until the authorship question was very doubtful. But with Zakes Mda the authorship has never been doubtful, nor, later, with Fatima Dike and Matsemela.

The play *The Hill*, which is set in Maseru, is something that I should tell you about. The first production was at the People's Space. It was a considerable hit. But let me first tell you about the play itself. Very basically, first of all, it is about two men on a hill in Maseru. The Hill is the place where migrant workers wait for jobs on the mine. They wait, sitting there with their Lesotho blankets, for jobs to be given to them by an agency which is at the bottom of the Hill, and the Hill is actually next to the site of the present Hilton in Maseru, and near the Holiday Inn. And Maseru in those days, and perhaps still now, was the place of porn movies and gambling casinos. A rather sad city, really – a very depressing place, I thought. But there were some elations, involved. I'll be coming to them shortly.

But the two men are sitting there comparing actually the size of their shit. They are arguing that my shit was bigger than your shit. I ate better than you this last week. One of them is an old man, and the other is a youngster. And the youngster is a dreamer, hoping he will find everything he wants – his car, his radio and his girls, at the Reef. And the Old Man is one who's been there for a long time, and they are suddenly intruded upon by a man who has nothing but a shirt on, and a big suitcase. And it turns out that he has been robbed by the whores of Maseru, who took everything he'd got and earned while he was in the mines, you see. And there is a lot of song and comedy and irony about all this, and the whores appear in all their Foschini glory. And the piece continues with all the disillusionment of the young man.

But the women in the piece are remarkably strong and remarkably abusive, which was quite good theatre. And very accurate, as it turned out, because after a very successful run here in Cape Town, we went to take it to its home town, to Maseru. And while we were setting up at Roma University I went out to the car to get some lights. But my car had been occupied by four Maseru whores, who wouldn't get out, who offered me their services, very aggressively, and when I refused, refused to get out of my car. I had to go into the hall and do the play while the reality was occurring outside. There was a marvellous moment when I came down in the lift, I remember, in the Holiday Inn

Hotel. And there was this woman and the farmer, a black whore and a farmer from the Free State with his navel showing through the safari suit. You know how one knows when there is real tension between two people. In the lift I didn't say a word, but I knew it was all fury going on between them. And we stepped out of the lift, and the farmer went out into the car park towards his Mercedes. And she whistled, and from the bushes came two or three of them, and I've never seen a wallet open quicker, and money come out quicker, and he obviously hadn't paid her what she wanted upstairs, but he did down in the car park and then ran back to the Free State, fast!

Effective trade unionism that!

Absolutely, very tough. But the play ran for an hour longer in Maseru than it ran in Cape Town. Why? Because the audience packed up so much. It was an enormous success there. It was a great pity we had to go on to Jo'burg. There we didn't do as well. And Zakes Mda was there in Roma, and he was very kind about the production, he liked what we did. I put a whole lot of songs in, that was the only change I made. I remember the whores standing around. We did it in bright coloured light, it was a sort of fantasy, symbolist fantasy. It starts with a nun, it's got a religious overtone which is quite important. It starts with a nun in a graveyard with shadows saying 'mea maxima culpa, mea maxima culpa', sort of strange. The chorus of the play is religious, whereas the play itself is not at all. It's a very weird piece in which Mda's political irony, of which he is a master, becomes very present. He is an ironist, a symbolist ironist. I think the most intelligent writer in the South African stage.

He looks upon himself as a magical realist, doesn't he?

Well, I think that is a very good adjective for him, but he seems to me to have anticipated that field. He shouldn't use the South American term, because he was actually ahead of it. This was before that became parlance at all.

Actually I had an interesting thing with him. He came to Cape Town in the late eighties and wanted to do a play out of his experiences in San Salvador and I couldn't relate to the play. And I asked him to do something a bit more 'box-officy', and he became very angry with me, and I haven't really spoken to him since. He said 'Box-officy?' to me, as if I had asked him to sleep with the Devil or become friends with H. F. Verwoerd, you know. It was as if the Enemy was the box office, funnily enough. But I don't think he is like that. It could have been a little pious period of his.

Another anecdote about the production in Maseru was that the actors were all non-Sothos, you know. They were all from other nations. And there was a surreal quality about that. It was being done in English, in its home town, by blacks who were not from that area, and it was a portrait of that area, and I think there were all sorts of frissons which arose from that. And a comedy of your own town portrayed satirically is greater for those from that town when it is done by outsiders.

The other production which I didn't direct, but which was done at the People's Space, was *We Shall Sing for the Fatherland*. That is Zakes Mda's portrait of a post-liberation or post-revolutionary African country, which is duly cynical about African rule as well, and which is actually quite interesting now that we have so many Umkhonto we Sizwe (MK) people still in prison, the ones that Clarence Makwetu is still complaining about. I don't understand why they are still in prison now. There are several MK, PAC (Pan African Congress) people who were involved in illegal acts or atrocities against apartheid, and they are still in prison a number of them, and it is a mystery. I don't know *what* Mandela is doing about this and why Makwetu is correctly able to claim that they are not released because they are PAC. I mean, the ANC (African National Congress) people have been released, and there is no perceptible difference in my mind between what the two of them were doing. And if we're going to have amnesty, as we said in our constitution we're going to have, then we must have it, and I don't know what is going on. It's worrying. You know, the second wave revolution theory is forwarded by this kind of problem. It's the kind of thing that gives Winnie Mandela and Mokaba and others, the populists, gives them a tool, because it is actually true. I don't know why. I can offer no explanation. This is relevant, because Zakes Mda was a visionary writer, of course not a South African, but a Lesothan, so his mind-set is different from those who are South African citizens and subject to apartheid because he came from a country which *was* being black ruled, and not very well black ruled. And so, unlike many others, he didn't have a kind of millenarian approach, believing we would have the millennium and it would all be fine. In fact we have had the millennium, and it was not so bad, but, you know, it's not all fine. But in Mda's unnamed African country the old war veterans are sitting in the park, broke, as many of the MK people are now, the ones that were not such good soldiers. The unruly, the tramp-like elements that the army has, were abandoned by the new businessmen. The play is full of new-black-suited businessmen.

Must be an ideal play to produce these days?

I would say the same. It should be very good to do now, very good. Somebody should do it again. But Zakes has done another one now, in Johannesburg in the last few months, which I believe is equally fascinating. His plays should be read sequentially. They are all adventures of a very serious kind. They are unambiguously black plays. They are not the products of the kind of marriage that I have been talking about. Which I value! Please don't think that I think of cultural marriage in a negative sense. You can gather from what I have been saying that cultural marriage for me is the essence of progress. But his approach is in no way qualified by white ghost writing or patronage: he is his own man. As indeed is Matsemela Manaka now, and Fatima Dike, now, too. But in those days there was more catalysing being done by white participants like myself, or Rob McLaren or Barney Simon and others.

I regard my own role ambiguously. My world was the liberal world, as it were, and I have tended not to use that word perjoratively down the years. Others might use it more critically than I do about my work. I stopped working in that field about 1982, because I became tired of the role of catalyst for other people's art. I wanted to do more of my own. Not that I did a great deal after that. There's still time, some anyway.

I think also I had found the exhaustions of doing black theatre very taxing. And, of course, there was money involved. When I was a rich man it was easier. I could always solve problems with the cheque book. Logistical problems, people running out of money, you know. I could keep the group going through my own sponsorship, effectively. Quite a lot of money in the seventies, three or four hundred thousand rands, I would imagine. And I didn't have money in the eighties, so it was much more difficult. It was that factor. Liberals need bucks!

They are supposed to make them, aren't they?

They are supposed to make them, but I wasn't as good at that as I was at spending them.

Now, I have talked a bit about Matsemela Manaka and Zakes Mda. I want to talk a little about Fatima Dike. I would say about her that her humour and her irony and her poetic sense are very great. And her feminism, if that's the right word for it, is very subtle. She is full of shit in the most wonderful way. And she has a tragic perception, which I thought was unique. Not the tragedy of race, not the conventional tragedies of South Africa. Actually she did one play which was specifically South African called *The First South African*, which was about a man born white to a black woman, and living in Langa, based on a true story. A white child growing up in Langa, who went insane and ended up in an asylum.

Sounds like the inverse story of Bessie Head.

Yes, yes! There is quite a bit on the story in a magazine which we published, called *Speak*, which one can get in The South African Library. It went from about 1978 to '82. The first edition has a very extensive review of Fats' play *The First South African* in it, by me.

Her women characters, again played by Nomhle Nkonyeni in that particular case, are always loud, abrasive, big, and she wrote a couple of plays. She went to New York for a while, and wrote a play there called *The Glass House*. And now, I believe, she's done something more recently as well. So there is continuity there, but I'm not very much in contact with all that.

I moved from directing to teaching at universities from then on, and really in a way shifted largely back into the white world. And indeed today I would say that I am not nearly as involved in the black world as I used to be.

Would you like to be?

Yes, I would. I think I have to go through, as all South Africans whites do, a profound adjustment now. It is not difficult, it doesn't feel painful, it feels joyous most of the time, but we are following rather than leading.

Doesn't your present work on the RDP (the Reconstruction and Development Programme) and your recent book on the constitution put you in touch with the present reality of South Africa?

Interestingly enough I'm not concerning myself with the RDP. I'm concerning myself much more with the checks and balances of power and the issues of freedom and the issues of intellectual freedom and the issues of oppositional powers and Parliament and procedures.

And the RDP?

My present book is not about the RDP at all. I'm leaving that to others. I am not worrying about that at all. I am worried about the degree to which this is a just and liberal state.

And what is the title of the book?

The Way We Are Playing It. And the subtitle is *Constitutional Performance in South Africa*. You see, I am allowing myself to be a kind of theatre critic of Parliament. I am empowering myself to use these two ways of looking, the political analyst's and the theatrical director's. And I am observing now. I'm not catalysing. I don't want to take on the responsibility of shows again. I don't really know if I want to be in the theatre again. That's not the only thing that's important. What's more important for me now is checks and balances.

I was thinking, perhaps, that if you were to go into the theatre again, you would see that sort of work as a way of empowering black people today like you appear to have done in the 1970s? Or is that a phase passé, as you seem to suggest in what you have just said?

I think it's passé. The theatre as empowerment is less important than theatre as analysis, or as adventure or psychic adventure or as ironic investigation. Empowerment is a different activity.

What you're talking about here is for the élite, isn't it?

Yes, I am very concerned about the élite. Actually I like intelligent people more than unintelligent people. And refined people more than unrefined.

But intelligence needn't necessarily mean the same as élitism?

Oh, yes, I don't care the fuck where they come from. I just want to know whether they're bright or not. And I don't want to lower everything to the standard of the boors, of whatever nation or whatever origin. I think it is very important that the universities, for instance, don't lose their standards. I should imagine that most black educators' opinion would go along with that too.

That depends as well on whether the 'disempowered' masses will go along with it, doesn't it?

I will look after the élite and the masses will look after themselves, reactionary as that may sound. I actually don't think we need to patronise people too much now. I think there's a hell of a lot going for a hell of a lot of people. And if you've got talent now you've got all sorts of channels. And you will have more as the state begins to put its money behind the new arts.

That's another question which, I understand, is being raised: Is the Government actually actively interested in putting its money on culture? Winnie Mandela's position has been queried in that context.

What's her position in that context?

Well, I've heard people claim that as Assistant Minister she has been used in the horse-trading with the Inkatha Freedom Party (IFP), who got that ministry. A serious question that has been asked is 'What does Winnie Mandela know about art, culture, science and technology?'

Interesting things going on there, but I'm afraid I'm ignorant about that now. I am not attending to cultural matters now. I am sure there are interesting tensions. I don't know if Winnie, or Ben Ngubane, are at all tuned to the refined kinds of theatre that interest me now. I think Ben Ngubane is a marvellous intellect, but he has nothing to do with arts. I find that's a strange appointment. He's fine for technology and business, and he's the kind of person that wants to make a Taiwan of Natal. That's what his bid is. I respect him greatly, but I don't know if he's got anything to do with art. I also respect Winnie greatly, but I don't think she has anything to do with art either. I would like people like Matsemela Manaka or Zakes Mda to have an influence, to be ministers. They would be more fun because they would look for bright minds, as opposed to being politicos or self-seekers or . . .

So you wouldn't really support the idea that was launched by one of the people I interviewed, viz. that taking proper theatre into the townships seems a futile pursuit, since people won't go and see the plays. But by reverting to musicals again, exploiting the entertainment side of the theatrical process, one might smuggle in ideas and contribute to the education of the thousands of needy township dwellers. Wouldn't that be something worth considering?

Yes, the great one for doing that was Gibson Kente, who was active during the '60s and '70s especially. His plays were seen by more than anybody else's. And they are wonderful theatre. They are crazy new gospel musicals, moralistic, bombastic, enormously entertaining.

Couldn't that link up again with the theatrical writer, the playwright, as teacher? Does that conflict with your view?

No, I think they should do that. The more the merrier. Kente was wonderful. He used to travel the country in a big green bus. *He* didn't travel in that bus, he used to travel in his big BMW, but his actors travelled in a big green bus, with a sign on it saying 'Gibson Kente, Slick Musicals'. And they *were* slick and enormously powerful. We actually lost a church hall in East London because of one of them which was called *Lifa*. It starts with a gangster leaping on to the stage – everybody leaps on to the stage in his plays – and stripping his woman down to her panties at knife-point. And the church ladies nearly passed out and we lost the use of the hall because of this. And there's always lots of funerals, and the music is wonderful, Victorian melodrama updated, you see. I must say this, that the African sensibility is often very Victorian and melodramatic.

You see, the person who suggested this thing about musicals to the townships had himself produced The Marabi Dance *by Dicobe, in Natal last spring.*

Yes, the youngster there. He tried to stage a kind of Gibson Kente play without having seen one. We sat down and I said to him, 'We'll need to sit down and I'll have to tell you how to stage if you can't get to see one.' He didn't sit down and listen. He'll do his own thing.

There are also terrible breaks in continuity. One of the weaknesses in black cultures is that they are very bad on continuity. The youngsters don't know what the hell the older ones did, and there are not enough ways of conveying how you do it. Apart from the kind of scholarship you are engaged in there is little that's ever done to ensure continuity. It will be different now, I suppose, because the youngsters can get hold of the tapes of things like *Sizwe Bansi*, *Woza Albert* and all the great pieces which were in fact video-taped. So there will be material available for them. And there are great artists about.

I would like to know about the mysterious chaps. Not the political ones. I am not interested in empowerment. I think empowerment is a bore. I think politics and economics are not what the theatre should be engaged in, so much as spiritual crises: ironic comedy, not platitudes.

So what do see as the way forward in literature, in theatre?

Perversity is the way forward. I want the individuals who are capable of creating fascinating madness, a gay new perspective, the good story, the extraordinary personality, the unusual, not the usual. We have been trampled by the usual in this country. We have a very unusual man at the head, and the Parliament is full of characters, but the theatre has become terribly stereotyped, and it is in danger of dying from its stereotypical quality.

But we don't like personalities in the country. It's a high-coloured country. But we don't like personality in the pious world of progressive or radical or sensible or Marxist or all the other epithets that make people so boring when they stop being themselves and start being theorists and ideologues. Ideology has been the death of South African theatre in the last five to ten years. The 'pure of heart' carrying us to the Revolution are more boring than any other human beings on earth.

Who or what, would you say, got it into that state?

I won't accuse anybody in particular. But there was a certain piety, you know, a sort of revolutionary piety.

Was it because of the ANC 'edict', as it were, to use culture as weapon?

When they were talking of culture as a weapon, I think it had already done its job. So they were passé when they were saying it. I mean, theatre did its job in the '70s, a very powerful job. Rob McLaren was accused by Credo Mutwa, the author of *Indaba My Children*, of causing the 1976 uprising with his township theatre. The theatre was very powerful. The work of people like Kani and Ntshona and Fugard, and the work of people like Rob McLaren and Matsemela Manaka, Zakes and Fats and others had enormous effect on the people, the crowds that came to the shows, and the power of the emotions there.

Was this also the case in the townships, or was it mainly in the city venues?

We made a great point of taking the stuff to the townships, and sometimes it was very successful. The young people found great solace there, and great energy. But you can't always be in *soixante-huit*, you know. You can't always be on the streets of Paris proclaiming the Revolution. Time goes on, and art follows genius, it doesn't follow politics, it follows genius.

Skhala Leslie Xinwa

Mr Xinwa, you collaborated with Rob Amato and a number of other people involved in Black Theatre in the Eastern Cape in the early 1970s. Would you tell me about that, please?

Rob and I met socially in East London – I can't remember what occasion it was, and we started chatting. And in the course of the chat he mentioned that he wanted to start a theatre group. He had met Athol Fugard before that, who was running another group in Port Elizabeth called the Serpent Players.

Now I remember what actually happened then: this was late 1970, and the Serpent Players had come to perform in East London. He was very much impressed with their performances, and this was the group that had players like John Kani, Winston Ntshona, Welcome Duhu, Nomhle Nkonyeni, Manga Hlisa and others.

And when we met socially he asked me, 'Look, can't we get some people together so that we can start a theatre group?' I also had interest in theatre from my student days, but that was nine years ago, and I had gone into other things and left theatre. But when the Serpent Players started in Port Elizabeth in 1963 I was there. And I took an interest. I remember I saw *Woitsek*, one of their first productions, and liked it very much.

But then I was arrested. I drifted out, surfaced in East London a few years later, where Rob and I met. At the time he was running a family business in East London, and I was working for a British company which sold air compressors.

I got a few friends together. I think one of the first people I got was Julius Mtsaka, who I knew had a very keen interest in drama. There was Mtunsi Noganta, who was a former colleague at university, who I knew liked drama, but who had never been exposed to acting before. There was Jiki Givena; there was Maggie Mjo, her brother Cyril Mjo, Tex Mandi; there was Zips Sehawu and a few others. We were a group of about ten. We got these people together and then we started. We started with improvisations. Our first real production was of *Oedipus Rex*, which was quite strange, because at the time the general tendency in black theatre was to look around ourselves and at the way we lived – and make a statement about some of the things that were happening in our lives, in our daily lives. This is the trend that the Serpent Players had taken. There was another group in Durban which was called MAD; another group surfaced in Johannesburg, Workshop '71; and there were other groups in Cape Town and throughout the country.

But essentially these groups were a new kind of theatre, that were moving away from accepted practices, that would pick up a Shakespearean play, people that would do improvised, open sessions theatre. This was the intention. *Oedipus Rex* was a bit on the formal side, and it was pretty successful. I remember in East London we got a very good write-up from Shirley Smith, who was then the arts critic of the *Daily Despatch*. And we performed in Port Elizabeth, at Rhodes University, Durban, Pretoria, Wits, and even in the rural areas, in Umtata and various other places.

Then we got into other productions – Wole Soyinka, the *Swamp Dwellers* and others. And Rob actually made his own production, which was *Baas Botha Is Coming*, which was more on the racial situation. It is a farm situation where there are problems: a woman among the farmhands giving birth and all that. The guy who was expected to help was this Botha, who was another farmer.

It got a lot of criticism from other areas because they said that even the use of the word 'Baas', was capitulating to apartheid. But it made a statement about the relationships of people, a bland statement that would say that in the situation down there, even if people looked down upon others, they also have concern about their well-being. And I think this was the message that came through in *Baas Botha*.

There were other productions, but because of my other commitments, my work as a journalist and all that, I sort of drifted away from the Players. But most of the administration was done by me. And that was a very good association.

So much for Imitha Players, which was the group that was formed in East London. But we built up a wide net of associations with Workshop '71, with the Serpent Players, with MAD in Durban. And we were sharing productions – them coming to us in East London, and we going to perform in other areas. It was a very good time for the development of Black Theatre: people like Athol Fugard, Rob Amato, Benji Francis, Barney Simon, Rob McLaren and several others who really put in a lot in developing theatre, specially in the black community of that time. It is those efforts that brought about the professionalism that has been seen in people like John Kani and Winston Ntshona.

And I remember John Kani and Winston Ntshona in late 1971 had gone to perform in East London. And we were sitting there one Sunday morning chatting about many things. And they told us that they were going professional. This gave me a fright, and I wondered if those guys were mad. And professional they did turn, and they made it! And the rest is history – you know, winning awards and what have you.

But they grew from those small beginnings that were started then.

Are you acquainted with their early association with Fugard? I know John Kani was very suspicious of Fugard before he got to know him better: you know, one of those 'palefaces'.

You know, John Kani is a bit of a maverick. I knew him when he was still at high school in Port Elizabeth. And I remember Winston Ntshona when he played football – we were in the same rugby club. He was a wing forward and they used to call him Iron Man. Obviously, at the time there was a lot of political speculation, a lot of people were being arrested, and all that. And here were these white liberals moving into the black communities. And there were hardly any black people who were trained and understood drama well in the black communities. And there was a sense in which there was something to be gained in associating with these people, because they had the know-how. And they were prepared to give it.

But the suspicions were always there. I know when we were with Rob, some people were suspicious, but me – we met, we sat down, and I've accepted him as a friend since then. And I've never had reason to doubt him. Obviously we came from different backgrounds, and there were certain things he would take for granted that I didn't understand, and there were also certain things that I would take for granted that he didn't understand. He came from a very rich background: I came from a very poor background. And those things were to be expected. I don't know of any serious fall-outs in spite of that, but I know there were suspicions.

When one came into the early or mid-1970s and Black Consciousness really was on the agenda, did that in any way influence or impinge on your collaboration?

I don't think so, I don't think Black Consciousness impinged on our work. As a result of the work that was done by those groups at that time there was a phenomenal rise of consciousness about the importance of drama in the lives of people. That was one thing.

Even Black Consciousness benefited from this. Obviously Black Consciousness started questioning the involvement of whites in these productions. But on the other hand there was an awareness at levels which understood the realities of our life, that the expertise was on the other side. And we needed the expertise.

But it also led to a certain rise of interest in drama in the townships. Another person that made a great contribution to drama at the time was Gibson Kente. Gibson Kente is actually a phenomenon in South African Black Theatre, and because of the productions that he took around the country a lot of people tried their hand at it. And I think of guys like Ben Numoy, who's now one of the better directors and producers in television in South Africa – who started then with small plays, like Zenzile, developed them and later moved into films. Those were the early paces of the thrust that started at that time aiming to entertain people with meaningful productions.

On the other hand, one of the things that I learnt at the time was that the average township community was more interested in musicals, and we were not giving them musicals. We were giving them hard theatre! It took time to get them on board and to make them accept that theatre could be theatre without music.

The other thing is that they were more interested in comedies, and we were not giving them comedies. Right, there is Wole Soyinka's *Swamp Dwellers* and other comedies that were put up, but most of the work was serious theatre, not just straight comedies.

And I suppose another reason is that if you look at our lives at the time, we either had to find a way of laughing at ourselves, or presenting it in a hard, but theatrical manner.

You mentioned Gibson Kente. One seems always to come up against his name when one talks to people about South African theatre. How do you regard Kente's contribution to South African theatre?

His contribution has been very great, there's no running away from that. Art is art, and any art transcends even societies, even cultures, even ideologies. And a statement made centuries ago by, say, Sophocles, has some relevance even today.

I suppose you are alluding to The Island*?*

Yes, precisely. In *The Island* you see so much of it. It is so immediate, so real, and yet so ancient.

You say the public was presented with stark serious theatre – no music, no dancing, no comedy. Did this conscientise the population around Port Elizabeth at the time, or did it benefit mostly the well-educated blacks?

I think it cut across levels of sophistication. But I do not think it was deep enough into the grassroots. The other thing is there were no proper theatres. There were no halls in the black areas big enough where you could show these things. And another thing that sort of distracted the actors sometimes was to find that the people were not happy, they wanted music, they wanted comedy. This thing was too serious for them. There was that element.

Can you see theatre today as one way of redressing some of the balance and giving back something that the dispossessed can grasp and benefit from, something on which to move forward?

There is a sense in which it can. But there are other inbuilt problems. One is caught up in two problems here. The first one is: what can you provide? Because if you go and take theatre to any community, there has got to be something that appeals to them. You cannot get them to go and watch if it does not appeal. That's the first thing.

The second is, because there are no facilities for being able to draw these people to this, something has to be done in education initially to make people understand the importance of this and to appreciate the plays. No productions can have sufficient reach to conscientise people to the extent that they should do in order to have a lasting effect. You reach some, but you miss many.

A drama student at Durban last year dramatised Dikobe's Marabi Dance, *and claimed that the way to reach the disadvantaged people of the country was by means of taking musicals with a message to the townships, using the appeal of the musical as a vehicle. This is, of course, no novel idea, but how does it strike you?*

Yes, if you went into the townships with musicals, you could draw them. But one of the problems I have always found, is that they get carried away by the music, but miss the message. This is the other problem. You give them entertainment, which is what they are looking for, but you don't, in fact, give them any message. Even if you've got the message, they don't pick it up. They get lost in the lyrics.

Where do you see Mbongeni Ngema in all this?

Mbongeni Ngema is another phenomenon.

In what sense?

In the sense that he is able to come up with things that can draw the erudite and the rustic. He can provide something that I can relate to very well, but which can still draw from grassroots. That's the first thing about him. And in a sense I think he has demystified theatre. He has done that by putting up productions that appeal all along the spectrum. And I think this is what we need if we want to make theatre grow in this country.

On the other hand I have come across criticisms of the way he is doing his theatre, as creating a sort of myth that the country could do without.

I don't know if he is creating a myth. I would rather think that the criticism against Ngema is for oversimplifying the theatre. But then – we have rustic people who need theatre in its simplest form. And we can only make them understand it better if we start at their level, which is, I think, what he does. And that is why I said I think the man is a phenomenon.

Are you still keeping in touch with theatre?

No, not really. I enjoy going to the theatre and, watch, but without participating actively.

If you had a hand in mapping out the course for theatre in this country, what sort of directions would you recommend?

I would say, let's have more Mbongeni Ngemas. Let's have more Gibson Kentes, but linking up with those who are providing very sophisticated theatre in this country. Let there be links between the two areas, because we are building audiences, we are conscientising people of a very important part of their lives. And theatre can only grow if there is a link-up between entertainment and serious theatre.

You know Rob McLaren, of course – or Mshengu Kavanagh – he has used a number of different aliases. He appears to have had a very radical class-oriented approach in his theatrical work. How do you see his approach to Black Theatre compared to that of Rob Amato?

I must say that Rob Amato operated at a higher level than McLaren. McLaren wanted grassroots. He went to Soweto often, slept there, stayed with people there, understood their banalities, their levels of development. Rob was never really exposed to that. He met people like us: he never met the real grassroot people, except through the factory, his family factory that he managed in East London. Basically I think that there was a difference there.

On the other hand I think McLaren was perhaps too much off into grassroots for an intellectual (laughing). I think his politics pushed him too much into grassroots.

Did you meet and have any dealings with Fatima Dike?

Fatima I met once, when they came up to East London with the *Sacrifice of Kreli*. She was working with Julius Mtsaka, who was a former Imitha Players person. He is one of the most fascinating people in theatre in this country. He went overseas, studied drama, and is working in some education-related capacity. He has tried to revive drama in the township since he came back. He had his own productions before he met Rob Amato, and then joined us and acted the leading part in *Oedipus Rex* in our production.

Did you meet Athol Fugard?

Yes, I met him once or twice, but I knew Rob McLaren better than I knew Fugard.

And now you are into broadcasting?

Yes, I have been in broadcasting for quite some time. At the time when we were involved in theatre I was working as a journalist in East London, for the East London *Daily Dispatch*. I moved to Port Elizabeth. I edited a magazine in East London, which was more of an off-the-mainstream publication, and then we had to close it down, as it lacked advertising support – because of what we were saying. You know, we had the readers but we couldn't get the advertisers.

I moved to the University of Transkei and did publications for the university. And then from 1989 I moved to broadcasting in Umtata – I was running the broadcasting service there for the Transkei Broadcasting Corporation. And I was there till June of this year, when I came here.

What is your position here?

My position is Group Functions Co-ordinator, which essentially is overseeing all the services within Zwelakhe's (Sisulu) area of operation. In a sense I am his special assistant.

Gibson Kente

You started out as a musician, Mr Kente, isn't that so? I wonder if you would talk to me a bit about your background, and about how you came into South African theatre?

You know you are asking me one of the most difficult questions I have to answer, because I keep this thing inside me. It is not as with academics who go away and pick up a degree. It is a talent embedded in you by the Creator. At some stage you just feel you want to start writing.

    I started writing music at school, about the neighbours and the people around me. I just enjoyed writing about people. And this I also translated into my scripts – the kind of creative work writing about my environment, writing mainly about people around me. My terrain has not been the suburbs. Basically it's my interest in the lives of other people, especially ordinary people. I don't write about rich people, because I have never been rich, so I don't know that level of life. So basically that's it. I can't say there has been any outside influence when it comes to writing music, because I have been indigenous in many ways. And the same goes for theatre.

When you started doing music, was it plain jazz or what was it?

It was the whole spectrum, you know. I wrote traditional music, township jazz and some ballads, too – gospels, hymns, rituals and all that kind of stuff.

Later, when you started writing for the theatre, what were your aspirations? Did you write for entertainment, or was it a letting-out of creative impulses from within yourself?

I would say it was both, Rolf, I would say both. My first attempt will illustrate my point. It was called *Manana, the Jazz Prophet*. Here I believed that entertaining the kids in church and giving them bouncing entertaining music would get the elements off the street and make them look forward to coming to church on a Sunday.

Now that was *Manana, the Jazz Prophet*. Here was this guy, you know, bringing the kids together, and it was all American kind of bouncing gospel and so on. So this illustrates to you that I had entertainment in mind as well as satisfying social needs and aspirations.

From conversations I have had with various people I have found that everybody knows about Gibson Kente. Some see you as the as the heart and soul of South African theatre. Others see you as more of the popular entertainer. How do you yourself rate the different sides of your activities?

Look, let's face it, I have done so much here in focusing on issues that involve people, both politically, socially and sociologically, whatever the case may be. I have been a critic of the political scenery for a long time. I think one of my most popular shows, that even Mandela, Buthelezi and such people know very well, is *How Long?* This was the most popular play in terms of reflecting the life in the townships under the old regime. This was written in the mid-seventies. And here I was reflecting again the pain of the reference book, the influx control and so on. And it was extremely popular.

That was not the only one, because I had plays like *I Believe*, where I was saying, 'I believe that if the government can take note of the attitude of the youth, of the simmering impatience of the youth, the anger of the youth – if they can act now, we might save ourselves a lot of hardships in the future.' And for that play I was called the Prophet. Because what happened later on – there were these strikes and the kids, and June 16th and all that, you know, and they said: 'Gibson Kente said this would happen!'

This was extremely entertaining, because here were those kids in Casa Blanca, in a dance, stripping the stage as they entered, furious, but expressing it rhythmically and musically. And what I am trying to say to you is that I have been the custodian of standards in terms of politics here, in pointing an accusing finger and saying 'Be careful'. Later on, when I saw the white regime crumbling and succumbing, then I said, 'What is going to be the character of our politics?' Because

I could see us taking over. And again I highlighted trends that I feared would destroy us, like black on black violence, and sanctions, which I saw as digging our own graves, because tomorrow we're going to need these jobs. We were actually fighting to take over the economy, not politics, because politics is worthless without having control of the sources of wealth. So then I wrote that play, which was very popular with the moderates. But at that stage I was attacked by the radical politicians, who could not see what I was getting at. But today I have emerged again.

You know, I fought against interference in education; I fought against things like sanctions, because I felt we were destroying the very things we were fighting for. So basically I am saying to you – I still see myself as somebody who has fought on the side of what you could call sanity in this country.

Matsemela Manaka told a rather funny story about an occasion when he had had one of his experimental plays advertised during the performance of one of your plays, and, in consequence, had a packed house. But when he got on with his show, mayhem descended on the house, because the audience expected the Gibson Kente stuff. Where was the music? Where was the dancing? People felt they had been ripped off and demanded their money back. He mentioned this as an example of how hard it has been for his generation to break through the mode created by yourself. Would you care to comment on that?

I believe theatre is an instrument that has got to be used very subtly. Messages of every type and fashion must be delivered – yes. But they must sink in like soft waves. Theatre can't come begging on its knees. It has to be presented and shaped, like parts of the tapestry of the arts.

I was cautioned by the regime at the time. This was the time when they picked me up, you know, under the emergency, in 1976. They said, Mr Kente, you are the most dangerous person in this country, because your message, whatever it is – you make it stick. People carry it home, they sing about it because it is in musicals. It's very dangerous. We are watching you.

That's why they picked me up. I hadn't done anything. Just written my plays. And I am saying to you: Matsemela was wrong trying to ram the message down people's throats.

Right now I have written three scripts for the big screen, but the most important facet of this production is attitude. I am writing about education, for parent, child and everybody. This is from the perspective of a child who is frustrated through failure. If I gave the script to you now, and you had the money, I bet you would put all the money on the table right now and say, 'Let's go for it.' Because in it you would see money spinning in. And at the same time the message is going to reach so many people, because people are going to come for entertainment. They are going to come for the music, and for the quality of the action. These are the things I aspire to.

This is one of the aspects in this TV series, that is extremely pointed. Actually it's first-class writing. And I have told the actors that, Look, if you don't respect the nuances of this game you are no good for me. – You may have the looks, and you may have the voice. But you don't come rough. You come with those finer, suave qualities.

So what I am trying to say is that I aspire to uplift the people culturally, because they should not see second-grade actors, they should not see second-grade productions. I need role models as well, so again I go back to my original statement that I am a custodian of the values of my people, and I want them to be uplifted by what I do. I think I have actually been an instrument of influence in my society more than a mere entertainer.

Does that mean that you see popular but high quality theatre as a weapon in the struggle to empower the disadvantaged people in the townships?

Yes, Oh, yes. We must lead the way, we must show people the way. For instance, there was another production called *Generation*. I was initially supposed to have been heavily involved in that, but I said, 'It's a beautiful idea, but we are taking it at a level where township people won't identify with it.' Because we already see those big guys talking millions, staying in flush places. We're not showing people how we started down there. We're not showing them that it is possible for them to climb the ladder, so that they can say, 'Oh, it is possible for us to be like the lowly person we saw in that play.'

I saw in yesterday's paper that you are inviting people to come for auditions. Do you have any kind of philosophy or methodology behind your stage training programme? What's your key to excellence?

Well, through my experience I have refined some techniques in the various disciplines. I have not been to school myself. But then I have familiarised myself with the writings of people like the Russian Stanislavsky, and of Americans who have written about the actor. There is not much of that kind of literature here, but I have tried to follow their teachings, displays and other kinds of stuff.

I am a perfectionist, and I like something that is beautiful, and I believe an actress can only inspire the child out there if she can be aware of her deportment, and the mode in which she conducts her dialogue and so on, instead of just throwing things out without any awareness of the mode of presentation. So we do get them into extensive training after we have finished auditions. This is just to detect talent, and say, that's OK, that kid can be trained.

For instance at auditions I'll ask a person to deliver maybe a line, focusing on one spot without blinking and so on, in order to bring out the sort of self-discipline in the person's character. But there are those that simply rattle on.

I understand that some people tend to see a fusion of your entertainment productions with music, with song, with dance and sensuous appeal, and the so-called 'Committed Theatre' of Manaka and all these other young bloods. How would you respond to such an idea?

Yes, there's bound to be, because in the past people relied on Protest Theatre. We were exploiting the political situation and turmoil for our own coffers. But I think the day demands a more creative, artistic approach. The old mode cannot pass any more, because people want to be entertained, and they aspire to higher standards, especially because of the exposure to the American forms of entertainment. And people do not settle for less. So I see that as being the track, and I see that as being a very, very demanding period for many of us. There is no ready cut-and-dried material, like you had apartheid that could be 'hyped'. Subtlety and nuances are the stuff that has to be the order of the day if the writers are going to survive.

Mbongeni Ngema has been mentioned as somebody who is pursuing what might be perceived as your line of business. Would you see it that way?

No, I think the diametrically opposite is the case, much as he is my protegé. Mbongeni aspired to find his own identity along the way. But I think unfortunately he tackled that in a rather shabby way, because he was against anything that I taught. Instead of adding on top of the good things that I taught him, and developing like I did, with Stanislavsky and so on – he talks about sincerity, enthusiasm and all those things.

I must improvise: how can I translate this in terms of my own environment, my own culture, my own background? There is a standard determinant in our field, because it deals with human beings. So human beings have got to present themselves in order to impart their culture. But as everybody has his own special background, so the mode in which to present those things has got to vary. But otherwise it is basically the same thing.

So he decided not to stock anything from me, he wanted his own style. For instance, at one stage he tried to make people speak English like they were speaking Zulu. Stick to Zulu, then, if you want the bloody thing to be Zulu. Don't try to present a story in English and force the phonetics to be Zulu. You don't do that. But I think this was a drive to give up on Gibson Kente in order to have his own identity. I think he has actually gone off the way.

In fact, an acquaintance was watching his production in Durban recently, and was quite disturbed by the fact that Mbongeni is not bothered about how people carry themselves, how they throw their voice for instance. They are screaming in the theatre! There are no feelings, no awareness of space, no artistry.

So there he's my opposite. Mbongeni knows I am very sensitive to breathing, because that's how you bring the sound out of yourself, whatever language you speak. To bring the sound out of yourself there must be that internal thing, which has got to be built out of proper breathing.

You mentioned three productions that are under way. Are they television productions?

No, they are for the big screen, for the cinema.

Would you mind telling me about them?

Well, going back to your question about the direction I am pursuing –

whether I regard myself as an entertainer or whatever. These films are about certain aspects that I think might make things easier in South Africa, and bring some awareness to the people of the townships. Education is one of them, one of the films. Another one is about Community Policing. And I think these are well presented and will be able to arouse in the people a sense of responsibility, a sense of awareness of the role they can play in bettering the quality of their own lives, in their own areas. But at the same time they are spear-headed or propelled by entertainment.

Education and policing. And the third one, does it have a specific purpose as well?

The third one is about Reconciliation. Here I set myself up to exploit the good in everybody. I am having ANC, Inkatha, the National Party . . .

How does Buthelezi feature in all that?

He features quite well. He is a buddy of mine, and Mandela is my uncle: both of them are my friends, so I have no problems. But actually Buthelezi plays a central and quite important role in this film. But I see quite a lot of bad blood that has been caused during that period, and there were distortions, unfair distortions. So I think we've got to correct those wrongs if we are to achieve harmony. If the Zulus are going to accept the Xhosas, if Gatsha is to accept the ANC, those wrongs, those distortions, those stigmatisations have got to be straightened out, and we start over on a new leaf. But I think, Rolf, if you were to see that film, you'd respect what I've done. Really, I've decided not to say anything bad about anybody. I've tried to look for good. For instance, I don't know if you have read this article in today's newspaper – there was already a reaction from a writer concerning one particular issue. I was quoted as saying in the film that apartheid has been a blessing in disguise.

Yes, I remember reading that one.

Rolf, what I *actually* say in that film is that much as apartheid was fundamentally evil, we would not be having a Mandela of that stature today was it not for apartheid. And South Africa would not be in such a positive, favourable position to receive investments and the sympathy of the world were it not for apartheid. And were it not for apartheid maybe the communist forces would still be here and would be killing South Africans till this day . . . I say in the film, Yes, they were not aware of things – this they did unwittingly. They were the mere hand of history, just like Bishop Tutu, who resolved to use sanctions, which is quite evil! A man of God using evil to fight another evil! He called sanctions the lesser of two evils, but he admitted they were evil.

Now *there* is a holy man of God, using evil to fight evil. So this is what I am trying to say, some bad things are done at times, not because they were right, but for expedience.

Is that film in the process of being shot, or what?

We are auditioning for it now. We've got parts of it financed, and we are looking for more finance. But in my old tradition, I am auditioning now, so that I get those prospective kids into the machine, to groom them. I believe in good 'pre pre-production'.

Turning to a different issue. You said about language, in connection with Ngema, why pretend to use English when you want to twist something else out of the actors? You conduct your work mainly in English, as the lingua franca, don't you? Do you break into any kind of patois when you take your plays to the different townships, in the various areas?

No, no. In the films I'm going to do that. I use the odd word here and the odd phrase there which does not tamper with the flow of the story. It can do no harm if it makes the characters feel more at home with what they are doing, by establishing the environment in which the film is made – exclamations and set phrases and so on in my lingua, but not to interfere with the general message and the dialogue of the film.

What you have been saying, Mr Kente, suggests that you are actually back into the arena again at full speed, after some years of relative inactivity?

I am running on the rails again, strongly on the rails! I'll tell you something here, Rolf. I regard myself as the luckiest person to be alive at this time, because I feel there is so much I can contribute towards this transitional period. I know I have the capacity of saying many things better than Mandela, because my medium is such that it is open to anybody and I can send it in a flash to the whole country. The music tells the things rather sweetly, and it makes people ready to listen.

So you will not accept one of the main criticisms against you, namely that you have been trading in melodrama?

I don't know how you're going to define 'melodrama' to me. I understand it in one way, and I don't think I have at any stage been melodramatic. Anyway, that's a matter for the critics to decide . . .

Rob McLaren

Rob McLaren, could we start this interview with a few comments on your South African background?

Well, I think there's a little bit of it in the introduction to 'Theatre and Cultural Struggle' (Rob Mshengu Kavanagh, *Theatre and Cultural Struggle in South Africa*). Both sets of parents, almost all my ancestors, are from Scotland. But it was my grandparents on the one side, and the great-grandparents on the other that went to South Africa.

I was born in Durban in Natal. That's where I grew up and went to school. I went to Cape Town University, and then to Oxford. I met Rob Amato at Oxford, and it was when I came back from Oxford that I became involved in what I have always called Majority Theatre. I use that term, because obviously anything involving myself could not be called Black Theatre. And I doubt whether I would have been interested in anything called Black Theatre.

What I was interested in was theatre that expressed a sense of South Africa, you know, a theatre that expressed the aspirations and the culture of its majority. It was when I got back from Oxford in 1960 that I got involved in that kind of theatre.

I left South Africa in '76, and the reasons for leaving were complex. They related to certain philosophical questions which were raised by the intense sense of racial confrontation which took place in '76 as a result of the June 16 uprising. It ranged from that through to the fact that I was married, and the person I was married to was a black South African, and to other things related to the interest that the South African police were taking in me. And so I went out. I don't think it was clear to me at that stage that I was not going to come back, although if I had made an analysis, I would have realised that I was not coming back.

And from there I went and did a Ph.D. at Leeds. Then I wanted to return to Africa, but during that whole period I had become a socialist, and I wanted to go to a part of the world where I could really partake of an experience which I felt would be useful to a free South Africa. And that I felt was the experience of an independent African country that was trying to construct a socialist or, shall we say, economically independent society.

And so I went to Ethiopia. And I was in Ethiopia for four years. That was an extremely rich experience. It was really so rich and our own identification with it was so complete that I'm sure that people in Ethiopia were absolutely staggered to hear that we were leaving. I mean, from outward appearances one would have thought that we were really going to stay there for the rest of our lives. But we left largely because my wife's mother and my own mother and father were in South Africa. So we took an opportunity to come to Zimbabwe to be closer to them. And that brought me here in 1984. And I've been here since then. In 1990, with the unbanning and the release of Mandela I went back for the first time. And, of course, it was on the cards that this was the time when the exiles were going back.

I have not gone back, and once again the reasons for not going back were about as complicated as the reasons for leaving in the first place. But perhaps the overriding reason was simply that the children are doing their schooling, and really the Zimbabwean schooling system for them, anyway, is positive and so well balanced and sociable that I just didn't feel I could uproot them from that. Of course there have been other reasons as well. I'm also a kind of person that is interested in exile. But I feel you get two kinds of exiles. You get one, who, wherever he is, is always 'living his home', never putting down any roots, who just lives for all that he came from. Then there is the other kind of exile who, wherever he is, begins to develop an engagement. And I am the second type. So that when I came here I got very much involved in all sorts of things, and right now I am extremely involved in a lot of things which it would be very very difficult to extricate myself from. And there is also a feeling that I'm not really sure of a mission in the new South Africa, of a contribution, you know, an overriding one. I think that people down there are better at doing whatever they're doing than I would be.

If we could return to the early years, was there anything in your social background that pointed towards a socialist commitment?

I think there was. My father – I always called him an untutored communist – never read Communism, he never read Marx and Engels. But I think he came from a strong egalitarian Scottish tradition, a Protestant tradition, perhaps best expressed by Robbie Burns in poems like 'A Man's a Man for A' That'. He died last year, and that's, in fact, what we have written on his tombstone: 'A man's a man for a' that'. And I think for me I must have got my socialism from him through that kind of tradition. It is also in the other side of my family. I have a very strong feeling that I don't care about people's rank. I don't want anybody to pull rank over anybody. Every human being is a dignified person, is given that sense of dignity. And in that sense we have to be all equal. I think that a very strong egalitarian tradition lays the foundation for a kind of socialist ideology.

Were you involved with the Black Consciousness movement at all?

No, by definition the nature of Black Consciousness was, you know, that 'Black man, you are on your own'. And possibly part of the motivation of Black Consciousness was precisely to move away from what was conceived as the hegemony of whites, even within theatre groups where the members were black. I mean, one aspect was that invariably you very seldom got a white South African who was prepared just to be a member of the group. Invariably the white South African involved was some kind of director. It would vary from one group to another, but that was the pattern, and I think that was one of the aspects which Black Consciousness groups felt quite irritated by.

So you were not actually supporting them in any way through your theatrical work?

It wasn't really from our side. I think that, speaking for Workshop '71, we were open to supporting other groups, and that included Black Consciousness groups, and in fact if you look at the pages of *S'ketsh Magazine*, and if you get hold of some of our earlier pronouncements in Workshop '71 – Workshop '71 was a sort of anomalous company in so far as it to a large extent favoured Black Consciousness. It favoured and supported the positions of Black Consciousness – the presence of myself notwithstanding. And not just me – Sarah Weinberg, Shirley Weinberg as she was called then, Shirley Pendlebury – there were a number of whites involved. And also a number of black members who were not African in the sense of racial classification. It really was, I think, a rather premature effort to create a non-racial collaboration. But premature perhaps in the sense that Black Consciousness had not reared its head and run its course. I think one had to go through the Black Consciousness experience before the non-racial experience could really take root.

As a theatre director you were hassled and intimidated by censorship and the police, weren't you?

We worked in a virtually independent sphere.

As whites?

No, no, I mean in terms of our situation. I didn't work in any grouping that would link me with any other whites in terms of our work within Workshop '71, where we performed, and with the associations that we made. We really did what we wanted and we had no examples of censorship. We were aware of censorship and therefore we devised our strategies in the light of it. Our first play, *Crossroads*, was an overtly political play. We then went on to a play called *Zzzip!*, which was a musical farce. What we were trying to do, consciously, was to achieve a mass audience without too prematurely attracting the attention of the authorities, hoping that we could use that mass theatre audience in order then to achieve more of our political objectives.

Why do you use different names when publishing your work – you are Mshengu Kavanagh, you are McLaren etc.? You are McLaren, really, aren't you?

Yes, I am McLaren. You take for instance a person who is South African High Commissioner right now in Zimbabwe. During the time before South African freedom he was Kingsley Xuma. Now he is Mamabolo. And you have the same thing in the Zimbabwean situation where, during periods of political activism, they would use other names to be able to say what they wanted, do what they wanted, without being identified. But the reason why I combined Mshengu and Kavanagh was, you see, that if I'd used Mshengu, which was what I was widely known by in theatre circles in South Africa, then and now, I would have done what other people who were working for the South African communists did, when they used names like ANC Khumalo, and that gives the impression that the person actually is a black South African. And I don't think that was right. So I took the name Kavanagh, which is a Celtic name which I got from a James Joyce novel. And then I used Mshengu so that people who knew me could identify who that Kavanagh was.

Nationalism is a concept that is topical in this part of the world today. Is that an acceptable concept in the South African situation?

Nationalism . . . Well, I think certain nationalist sentiments have some use, but I think the dangers of nationalism far outweigh the positive factors. And I feel that nationalisms like all chauvinisms are largely manipulated by a minority, often of ambitious people who use them to achieve the support of a mass base in a cause which will provide them the mass support, but ultimately enables them really to achieve their private agendas. And I think that whether people use gender chauvinism, racial chauvinism, nationalist chauvinism – whichever chauvinism – I always feel that there are tremendous dangers of that kind of manipulation process.

But wouldn't you agree that the way in which the 'Rainbow' concept has been presented seems not to include so much of the chauvinist aspect?

A non-racial South African nationalism? Yes, it's like all these words, you have to consider what you are differentiating the term from. Here we're talking about a nationalism where we are perceiving ourselves as One Nation. And I think that is a very positive patriotism, if you like. It's like Samora Machel, for instance. One of the big slogans in his work in Mozambique was *Povo Mozambicano da Rovuma ao Maputo.* (The Mozambican nation from Rovuma to Maputo.) He knew that in a society that stretches right down the eastern coast like that – as you move you go from one language group to the other, and somehow all those people had to see themselves as Mozambicans. So we were talking about *Povo Mozambicano.* I thought you were referring more to the kind of narrow nationalism, the Yugoslavian type.

Could you see the theatre as a weapon or tool in such a conscientising process here in South Africa?

Right. You see, you are putting things to me which right now I am not thinking about, because you are now asking contemporary questions. So that you are forcing me really to think on my feet. But once again I definitely think the theatre can play a part and there can be no doubt about that. But, looking at the 'Rainbowism', it reminds me of reconciliation in this country. They are relatively equivalent phrases. And I think that 'Rainbowism' and reconciliation cannot be used as romantic escapes from the reality on the ground. With the concept of 'Rainbowism' we can't look with shiny eyes at an ideal situation where we actually forget inequalities, forget lack of opportunities, forget historical injustices and just wave a wand in the spirit of the Rainbow, as it were, and pretend that we are all one people. The Rainbow concept I believe has got to be worked hard for and on the basis of frank realisations and acceptances of the need for change. We can't just say: 'We are one people, colour doesn't mean anything', and just wish it were all like that. But to come back to your question, I believe extremely strongly that theatre is in all these areas, in all these ideological areas, an extremely powerful way of getting people to conceptualise, concretise, discuss, debate, have dialogue.

I came across a young student who has dramatised Dikobe's The Marabi Dance *as part of his drama course at the University of Natal – he made it into a musical. He says that in his view the best way of bringing theatre to the people is through township musicals. Now, against the long career of Gibson Kente, would you think that is a viable idea at all? Can that co-exist with committed theatre and have a function in the townships – amongst the dispossessed?*

Well, I don't know to what extent the whole concept of musicals has currency in South Africa. It is difficult to look at the South African situation in the parameters of South African thought, but for us here in Zimbabwe we identify those kinds of categories as basically – I'll try to find a word for them – as not really in touch with the realities of African theatre, because it implies that there are dialogue plays that are all words. Then there is another kind of play where you use a lot of songs and dance like in Broadway, etc.

For us, I think, for the performing arts in Africa, both in the modern and in the traditional context, we don't see that kind of articulation between music, dance, dialogue, poetry, mime, storytelling. So that in our theatre, in order to get through to the people and come across in a medium that people are going to relate to, I really think we have to use them all together. So I would say, don't let us call it *musical*, let's just use theatre in the way that the people themselves relate to it, and the way they themselves create theatre in their lives, which is through songs and through dances, through mime, through stories, and dialogue of course, and poetry.

What do you think of the way in which a writer like Mbongeni Ngema presents the struggle through his musical version Sarafina*?*

To be honest, I also saw *Magic at 4 a.m.* and I saw the later version of *Sarafina* at the Market. And let me just be blunt: I would like to write an article about South African theatre entitled 'Screwing the Struggle'. And I think that Mbongeni Ngema is one of the screwers. I think he is just a plain commercial opportunist. And he'll make anything that is going to sell in the United States.

There was very recently a biting article about him in the Cape Argus *to the same effect.*

Yes, and then he will bring in gobbets of apparently political-sounding rhetoric, but only for its commercial value.

OK. Could we return to the early days of majority theatre again: How did Workshop '71 come about?

I've just written an article in the *Contemporary Theatre Review*, but I don't know when it's going to come out. There is an issue that is going to concentrate on South African theatre. I tried to write a story to get an idea of the genesis of Workshop '71.

You'd have to look also at the lives and the hopes of the people who came together to make it. You'd have to look at James Mthoba, working at Federated Union of Black Artists (FUBA) – he'd be a good person to speak to – Selaelo Maredi, who's now back from the States, who is also still in theatre in Johannesburg, working largely at the Windybrow.

Then Bess Finney, who is an actress and drama teacher in Johannesburg, and myself.

It was really a coming together of those four people and then all the other people that were involved. But it originally began in the Institute of Race Relations in Johannesburg where the idea was that we would set up a drama workshop. I remember when we all got together at the first meeting, somebody said, 'What is the aim of all this?' And one of the Race Relations people immediately said, 'Contact.' So from the perspective of race relations it was to try and get something going to involve South Africans from different segregated groups. But the point was that all of us came into it with our own hopes and it was transformed from what was originally envisaged by Race Relations, and it became what the people in it wanted it to be.

There remained an element of race relations, of contact, you know, but we all had different aims for it. Maredi, for instance, I think Maredi to a large extent was aiming to create a theatre which was going to make some money. James Mthoba was very, very much interested in theatre itself, especially in the experimental theatre aspect. What he liked so much in the work we were doing was that it wasn't the usual jazz opera, or dialogue theatre. There was a lot of experimental type of theatre, you know – mime, different kinds of workshop techniques, so he was fascinated by that. I had a relatively political agenda, and so Workshop '71 is really a kind of fusion of different perspectives.

This was an established theatre, wasn't it? But you did go to the townships with your productions?

Yes, yes. In fact, funnily enough, when we did *Crossroads*, that play was in a way the Race Relations ideal. The cast was South African from all sorts of different backgrounds. The message was a relatively liberal one. It had a lot of satire in it, but all from that perspective. It was played originally at the Institute of Race Relations and was extremely popular with white liberal audiences. We performed that in black townships. The experimental theatre aspect of the production was something which intrigued white town audiences, for up to that point in South Africa there had been very little of this kind of experimental theatre that came up in the late '60s and '70s in the States and Europe etc., you know, bare-foot, using the actor's body, not a lot of props and costumes – all that sort of thing – mime, etc.

But when we got to the townships, people just thought we were poor, and they felt sorry for us. We didn't have proper costumes because we couldn't afford it! We did a fantastic band scene with no instruments at all. I think this was the first time this was used in South African theatre. I know it is very dangerous, especially, I have noticed, in a South African theatre context, to say this was the first time something was done, because it could just show one's ignorance of what has been done before. But I just don't know of this kind of theatre having been done before. This is the first time that a jazz band was created just using vocal sounds and things, and Dan Maredi played a fantastic trumpet. There was one time, for instance, when we decided to bring in real instruments because of this problem we were having in the townships, – and he did a kind of a duet with his 'lip trumpet' and the real trumpet, and really, he held his own.

And so we took it to the townships; people got the message, people understood what was going on. But this kind of experimental theatre was alien to the townships, so that is why we decided that our next play was going to be *Zzzip!* We didn't feel that we were making theatre like Race Relations, we didn't feel that we were making theatre simply for inter-racial contact, and we were suspicious of the fact that *Crossroads* was a darling in town, and it was not speaking the people's language in the townships. So that's why went for *Zzzip!* and we made that a musical in the sense that you were talking about before. We used Soweto soul music of the time, and made it a comedy; lots of music with a band, with proper costumes and everything, and we felt that that way we would get the audiences that we were looking for in the townships.

Zzzip! was designed in such a way that it could not be performed for whites. It was in all the township lingo, you know, Zulu, Xhosa, Tsotsitaal, etc. There was hardly any English. And the only time we ever played it to a white audience was actually with Rob Amato's group, Imitha Players. They organised a performance in East London, which was a disaster. And we skipped Grahamstown, where there was another white audience waiting for us, and we only did the black audiences. Because white audiences could make nothing of that play. So that play, *Zzzip!*, was designed specifically for performances in black townships. And that's where it performed all over the country and in the Johannesburg-Witwatersrand-Gauteng area.

Then, the next production, Credo Mutwa's *u'Nosilimela* was a production which had a lot in it for South Africans of all backgrounds. That is one of the African masterpieces, considered in a continental perspective. It was a pity, but it was performed by non-professional actors, by really young people, by unemployed youths from the ghetto, from Soweto, which meant that a lot of its spectacle was under-achieved. Had that been done professionally it would have been just amazing. And that was performed in town, but also in townships, and for one thing it was done in runs, which was absolutely unheard of in those days – to do a run in Soweto! To set up we created like a tennis court with a scaffolding and with seats on either side, because it had a unique form of staging. It took us a day's hard labour to set it up, which meant we could not play it and take it down the next day, which is what normally happens. So we ran it for four or five days at township venues, which was something new as well.

Then the next play was *uHlanga*, which was a one-man play by James Mthoba. That was mainly performed at town venues. It was an extremely dense poetical, literary work based very much in African history, close to Negritude, African poetical tradition – in the tradition of black American writers, the writings of people like for instance Eldridge Cleaver. So that was performed to a large extent in town. I think it had one performance in Soweto, but generally speaking it was performed in town. Then there was *Survival*, which was the last rather political piece. That was extremely popular at town venues. Town venues of course were where blacks and whites could meet – forerunners, if you like, of the Market, and places like the Space, the Box Theatre at the University of the Witwatersrand, the Window Theatre in East London. And it also performed in the townships in the Cape Town area. But that was an interesting play in that when we performed it for a black audience, we had to actually re-stage it, because there were passages of challenge, which, if the audience was black, you didn't want confrontation with the audience. You had to turn it around and carry the audience with you. So we had to actually re-stage certain sequences, whereas with the audience that was predominantly white there was more of the 'offending-the-audience' type of element, you know.

There is something that has baffled me: how come that there was such a cluster of gifted, dedicated whites at the time working for black or majority theatre in the early '70s?

Well, I've no idea. I have no ability to extrapolate from our own involvement.

Did you support each other? Did you influence one another? Or were you a number of independent theatrical personalities that happened to be operating at the same time?

I don't think there was a consciousness of there being a group. The fact that there was something of a network emerged to some extent in the pages of *S'ketsh Magazine*, where you would see a group in Grahamstown, a group in East London, a group in Johannesburg, etc., but I think we rather saw it as a general quickening of the theatrical pace in the townships and in non-apartheid spheres in the country overall, because it happened at the same time, for instance, as the Black Consciousness groups were also becoming quite active. So there was a general countrywide increase in interest and activity in the field of the performing arts.

You mentioned your Marxist leaning initially. Your friend Rob Amato takes the view that maybe your political involvement to some extent has blocked your development as an artist – that the politicised theatre practitioner stands in the way of your achievement as an artist. Have your views changed noticeably since your turbulent youth?

No, I think if you were to speak to Malcolm Purkey and other friends of mine in the theatre who are not Marxist, they would say the same thing. Let's take *Simuka Zimbabwe* (Zimbabwe Arise) as an example to clarify my position. In that play we are dealing with the IMF (the International Monetary Fund). We are using a play to try and explain the IMF, to explain the Structural Adjustment Programme, where it came from, etc., and we look for artistic and theatrical ways of communicating that. We are not starting by looking for theatre, just making theatre. We are trying to get across heavy, difficult stuff and we are using theatre because we feel that through theatre we can clarify it and we can bring it to life and we can communicate it effectively. And ultimately we're trying to do that as artistically and as entertainingly as we can. If ultimately it means that the theatrical product is not as great, perhaps, as if we were doing some other theme, or, perhaps, compromising and simplifying, etc., I would rather have it that we get that thing across, that we set up the debate, that people get the ideas, and that the political message gets across even at the expense of the theatre stuff.

Right. I am into theatre. But to me what is really important is what I see around me. And what I see around me is a situation where a lot of things are really unfair, where a lot of people are not getting what they should get. And this reality that I see is to me the overriding reality. And I can't make theatre or paint pictures or do anything and feel justified or happy just doing that, when the rest of it is not being addressed. For me the important thing is not to be the consummate artist, but to use my theatrical talents and my gifts in order to engage and in some way make a contribution to changing or preparing for some change in all these things that I see about me. Because I know that a lot of people can live with the things they see about them, and do live with these things. But they really get to me. They frustrate me. They make me very angry. And they make me very sad, just like living in apartheid. For me what I saw in South Africa and what was happening in South Africa had such an impact on me, that it didn't matter to me whether my plays were suffering in theatrical terms by the fact that I was trying to conscientise people, trying to bring people's attention to what was going on. That to me was a more important mission. And it remains that. The fact that South Africa is free, you know, the fact that Zimbabwe is independent, has not brought all this injustice to an end. It is there. And I feel that those are the important things, and if it means that the plays that we do are not as artistically pure, perhaps, I don't mind.

But then, on the other hand, I think that is the perspective that a person, perhaps like Rob Amato, and like Malcolm Purkey, would expect. But our audiences don't feel that. It's like Brecht said, that the working class audiences are not interested in whether you use realism or non-realism, symbolism or whatever. Their concern is that what you are portraying is real to them, that they recognise it to be what they live. How you do it is not the important thing. They will recognise it whichever way you do it if it's real. And I don't think that our audiences are saying that the plays are suffering from the fact that they deal with those issues.

I don't think that's what Rob Amato meant. I don't think that he is at all critical of what you are doing per se. By suggesting that your politics acts as a sort of dam, I believe what he was really saying was that in his view you might have got even further as a theatrical artist had you not been so politicised. His clearly not being a Marxist, of course, colours his view, but his comment was not meant to be denigrating.

No, but it's a very fresh question, because when we did *Simuka Zimbabwe* in Johannesburg, it was really interesting to hear, say, Malcolm – you know the man who did *Sophiatown* in Junction Avenue, and the *Marabi Dance* recently at Rhodes. He was associated with Workshop '71 in the beginning. And when we all left and there weren't many actors left behind, many of them went into the theatre company that he was in, people like Ramolao Makhene and Sipho Khumalo. And this was a question that Malcolm Purkey was raising. He was wondering whether theatre or art should be dealing with such economic issues. He went on to say that there is not enough subtlety, and this is a common thing which he and a number of people in his circle were saying – and this is obviously an ideological circle as well, and an aesthetic as well as a social circle. Also William Kentridge, the famous painter and film-maker, also in theatre in South Africa, would say the same thing.

One realises the extent to which subtlety is not only culture based, but class based as well, so that what is completely unsubtle to somebody who does not identify with its paradigm, if you like, is very subtle to somebody else to whom the nuances are available. So that Julie Frederikse for instance – the author of the recent very important book *None but Ourselves*, which was basically about the information and versions of history which lay behind the *Chimurenga*, the armed struggle here in Zimbabwe – you know the myths of the white government and then the realities and the myths and the different perceptions of the opposing side. She also did something in South Africa, *A Different Kind of War*, and she's also got a book out on the tradition of non-racialism in South Africa.

Anyway, she was here in Zimbabwe. So when she went to see the play, she came back afterwards and said: 'I was constantly flabbergasted, stunned, all the time at the layers – layer upon layer of meaning.' So you get that kind of perception of an extremely dense work, which, to somebody else, who doesn't identify with what you're doing, appears to be straightforward and predictable, not subtle.

From what you are saying it does not seem to be true what I hear people in South Africa saying, viz. that South African theatre is in a limbo. Your theatrical work seems to be full of the present-day problems, the present-day struggle.

Well, this is a thing that really interests me. When going back to South Africa, hearing people sort of say that now that democratic elections have been held, people don't know what to do with theatre, one realises that all this time, you know, everything was given focus by the anti-apartheid struggle. That is something that I really don't understand at all, because I suppose I've never seen the end of formal apartheid as the end simply of social issues, things to engage with. And I would have thought, 'Right! Thank goodness, now we've got rid of that stuff. Now we can get on to the real thing.'

And when we did *Simuka Zimbabwe* this is what quite a lot of black theatre personalities and some of the reviewers were saying about the play: 'We see from the play that we're not talking about the death of political theatre. With the end of apartheid as such political theatre renews its mission and continues.' In fact David Kerr, who is at the University of Botswana, who saw our production when we went down there, wrote an article where he's pursuing precisely that: the relationship between the agenda of political theatre as expressed in *Simuka Zimbabwe* and the feeling that with the end of apartheid in the region, politics is dead.

This is a question I have also asked some of the other writers I have interviewed – what they envisage by way of new themes after the end of the Struggle, and what they see as being on the agenda in the years ahead. Some are inclined to sit back and look at the Struggle and ponder the many untold stories, while others, like yourself, are more preoccupied with present problems. When it comes to the untold stories in literature and in theatre, what language are these stories going to be told in? You mentioned the kind of Creole that is emerging in the townships.

They have actually emerged a long time ago.

Yes, and are used in umpteen different constellations. In your view, is English going to remain the main theatrical language in Southern Africa, or will this mixed lingua take over? Or will they co-exist?

No, I really think that in a multilingual society like South Africa, where theatre is going to have all sorts of different missions, it will be impossible to generalise. There's always going to be that kind of theatre which people are going to do in English, or predominantly English, and then there will be scope and need for theatre in predominantly Zulu, predominantly Xhosa, predominantly Sotho, etc. And then there will be those plays which will reflect that mixture.

I think it will all depend on what the individual company is trying to achieve. It happens here as it happened when we took *Zzzip!* round the countryside in South Africa. Mostly it was done in Zulu and Sotho. But when we came to the Cape, people there don't speak Zulu, they speak Xhosa. As the actors live mostly in Johannesburg they've got a good idea of Xhosa, so what they did, on stage, was they just changed their register. They changed the words and made the Zulu more accessible to Xhosa speakers. In *Simuka Zimbabwe*, we've got a predominantly Shona version, but we prepared a predominantly English version for Botswana and South Africa.

We've taken our plays to a community like the Mhangura Copper Mine. In the afternoon when we performed in the amphitheatre to the ordinary workers, the play had to be in Shona. In the evening we performed in English in the left-over of the colonial theatre which the white community once had there, for the 'higher' people in the mine, you know. All on the same day.

And the actors switch from one language to the other, just like that?

Well, it's not just God-given. You have to work at it. But at least there is a basic language ability that you can build on. People, especially in Johannesburg, are very good at moving from Sotho to Zulu, and they will know some Xhosa and they will know some Tswana, etc. etc.

The collaboration between black and white theatre practitioners is something that will expand, isn't it? How do you view that – will there be a merger between the so-called dedicated or serious city venue theatre and the typical township theatre? Will there be an approximation between those two modes, or will they develop separately?

Well, if you are asking me to predict and extrapolate from the present South African situation, I don't think I can do that, because I don't really think I know enough about what is going on right now in South Africa to be able to tell what is going to happen. But in terms of blacks and whites working together, looking at Zimbabwe, it's interesting to note that there is very little inter-racial co-operation here. Generally speaking whites are very uncomfortable when participating in anything in which they are not numerically superior or predominant, and culturally dominant. So they don't mind doing a play which is *their* play, based in *their* culture, and bringing in a few black actors, etc. But ask them to actually participate in something which is rooted perhaps in a black view of history or in black life! Very difficult. They won't! Even ask them to participate in a situation where there are three whites and fifteen blacks! – That's this country!

Now, one thing that we have noticed, amazingly enough, is that in South Africa, despite its far more rigid apartheid and polarisation of the races, there's a much greater willingness on the part of whites and blacks to work together as opposed to here. I can give you one experience, because one can only talk of what one knows. At the University of Witwatersrand, I and another member of our theatre group were invited down to do a play that we had done here, about Mozambique, with the students of the School of Dramatic Art there. You have to know that this play is set in Mozambique; the culture is just completely Mozambican/black Zimbabwean. Its Frelimo songs, languages of Mozambique etc. Whites appear only when they are satirised as part of the colonial process.

We go down there; we discover that we have a cast of fifty percent white students, fifty percent black students. The guy I went with, Walter Kawisi, a black Zimbabwean, took one look at them and covered his face in his hands. He just didn't believe that it was possible. Then, as we were late because of work permit problems, they started showing us what they had been working on. They had been working on South African freedom songs about Mozambique, or changed to fit in with Mozambique, and this opened his eyes. There were these young white students, dancing, singing in harmony, fully participating in black South African culture. And that changed his mind.

We did that play – there were some problems, of course, that was to be expected, but those dozen or so white students went into that experience. There were members of that group whose relatives had actually fought in the war of independence in Zimbabwe, on the white side, and had left for South Africa as a result of Independence. There was one, who was of Portuguese extraction, and all she knew was what the Portuguese had said about Samora Machel. They went through that experience, and at the end it was so moving that Frelimo invited it to Maputo. It was performed in Maputo, and the way they put it, it was like light at the end of the tunnel! If young white South Africans could do that, they felt something would go right in the future. That was before the political change, you see.

I am just using that as an example to show that things are possible in South Africa in terms of working together, which had not been possible here. But having said that, I think I also need to say that of course there is still the same tremendous white arrogance that the Black Consciousness movement spoke about, which still prevails in South Africa and has to be tackled. So that, yes, there is a readiness to work together, but probably a readiness on the part of the whites to work on their terms. Things like that will have to be challenged, and how they will be challenged and what will happen is looking into the crystal ball, which I don't have.

Don't you feel tempted to go back and participate in that process? Or are the demands more urgent here?

Well, right now the things that I am involved in here are very urgent. That's why I'm saying that I am so busy that I wake up in the night and wonder how I can keep all these balls in the air.

Ya, there are interventions that I would like to be involved with in South Africa, like the untold tales you spoke about. One play I would like to do in South Africa is with some Umkontho we Sizwe ex-combatants, and tell the story of MK in Angola. That story has not been told. People don't know what our combatants did, how they fought. And there are some tales of heroism and sacrifice, which are very important I think, generally, for our country to realise, to be proud about, you know. There is a danger in history that our armed struggle be dismissed or reduced to blowing up some oil refineries and things like that.

Whether I am here in Zimbabwe or whether I am back in South Africa, I would still want to do plays that agitate and provoke debate on issues that are of relevance to South Africa and Zimbabwe: things like the IMF and the Structural Adjustment Programme. With most of the work we have done here in Zimbabwe we've found actually that you can eventually trace the answers to the problems here to their roots in South Africa. What happens in South Africa radiates out and affects the rest of the region. I was mentioning Mozambique and the Renamo gangsters or bandits there. At the end of *Simuka Zimbabwe* the *Muponesi*, the 'saviour', the embodiment of the Structural Adjustment Programme, is at the airport saying goodbye. And he makes it very clear that from Zimbabwe he's going to South Africa to do to South Africa what he has just done to Zimbabwe.

So in many ways the issues I feel I need to engage with are to be engaged with here as well as there. For instance what I feel I'd like to do here next, is maybe a play called *The Right to Strike*. Because right now in Zimbabwe, as a result of this Structural Adjustment Programme, the fundamental right to strike has been seriously diminished. Now, what are they doing in South Africa right now? They are out in the streets on precisely this: on making sure that in the alleged interest of economic stability and the creation of a favourable foreign investment climate, etc., the workers don't lose the right to strike, which they fought for under apartheid.

So, *ja*, I would like to do that play. I think that the one difference is that I must admit I would be very happy indeed to be working with South African actors. When I went to Tanzania, and I worked with the ANC in Mazimbu – that was when we began our play on Mandela – it was such a relief and so refreshing to work with South African actors. Because I am always conscious of the fact when I am working in Zimbabwe, that although I may know some Shona, I am working in somebody else's language, whereas in South Africa now I would be working with people in whose languages I am very much at home. And there is a whole history, culture – the songs, the music I am much more at home with. Yes, in many ways working in South Africa would be very refreshing.

Coming back once more to your socialist convictions: In your view, has socialism got a future in South Africa?

Yes, I believe it has. If it were possible I would like to work with the Communist Party in South Africa: have a kind of a cultural group that is involved in trying to popularise and raise questions relating to the whole problem of socialism in South Africa. That's why I am interested in the workers' theatre movement in Germany, the United Kingdom and the United States between the wars, and also in the workers' theatre in Natal.

Were you very disheartened when the Communist Empire of Eastern Europe collapsed?

Oh, yes, very disheartened! Totally devastated. One really feels that one has been pushed back so far, and that now we just seem to have so much further to go than we did before. Disheartened, in the sense of not ultimately having lost heart, and I think the reasons for that are that when you support something idealistically, when you support it with illusions in a Utopian way and things go wrong, you give up. You become disillusioned and you give up. But if you support something critically, you understand that the ways in which the things you support operate, will never be pure. And ultimately what you are looking at is a balance. You are asking on balance, what it is that is taking us forward, which is taking us in a direction which we feel is better. If you have that approach, it is not so easy to be disillusioned as such, although you may lose heart. So, yes, one was disheartened, but not ultimately disillusioned.

As to the next question, which is 'Well, don't you think now that socialism is bankrupt, defunct?' I always say, well, you can say that, because of your position in life. If you have a middle class position in life you are only too pleased to propagate the idea that socialism is bankrupt. But to me socialism is the ideology which expresses the struggle for a better life of those millions and millions of people in the world that do not have a good life. Really, you can go into all sorts of theoretical definitions, but ultimately to me socialism means the movement to make sure that *everybody* has a better life. And how can that be bankrupt? That *must* remain our goal, that *must* remain our objective. And if it means that we seek different ways, OK, but ultimately you can't give up on that.

So, my answer to that would be that yes, we have been pushed back. Many people now, on a much larger scale, are getting poorer and poorer and more and more wretched. But that doesn't mean to say that the struggle to reverse that can be abandoned. And that is what this play *Simuka Zimbabwe* does at the end. We say, OK, we see what is happening. Now the only thing we can do is try to make more and more people see it, and then make more and more people expose it, resist it. It feels very unfeasible at the moment because the odds are stacked against us. But to give up on it is really, in a very deep sense, to die.

Fatima Dike

Could we start by digging a bit into your past? What has led up to the Fatima Dike that people know today?

Let me start with my family, which was in business in the township. My sister was married in 1965 to Mr Vokwana. He used to run a grocery store in Punga, which was known as Dumisa, which means 'Praise the Lord'. There were several shops around, but the finest thing about this shop was that when it opened at eight in the morning, you would always find people standing up against the wall, waiting for this particular shop to open. And as I grew up it dawned on me that this was a man who was actually dealing with poor people. He had potatoes at four-and-a-half pence a pound: he had cheap, cheap food for everybody to flock to his shop. We worked in this shop, and among the most basic things we were taught was that we live in a country where black people generally are not respected, and since we are trading in the townships, we had to learn to give black people the respect they deserve.

So from an early age we were being 'conscientised' about who we were; not severely politically so as to say 'no, that man is white', or whatever. But as we grew older and more responsible in the business, we were taught also how to respond to white people when we were dealing with them in business. If you say something to a white person on the phone, you have to follow it up to the end. You must never accept anything inferior from him, whatsoever. If you are paying for it, you must expect quality. That was another thing I was taught in my home.

I am a qualified butcher. I am a proud person. I am a black lady. I can run a butcher's shop single-handedly. I make sausages, I cut meat. I do everything with my hands that men can do, that's how I was taught at home.

Then I went to work at the supermarket near my home. So I'm very well versed in that business also. And now we have a service station, selling petrol. When I was beginning to go into theatre as such, the policy in the family was, knowing that artists have a tendency to be ignorant about their value, or how to run their professions as a business, the policy was that I should work in the family business and then go out into my art and always be able to fend for myself out there, if needs be. And I have learnt to negotiate in a business manner and I can always fulfil my duties in a businesslike manner even in the art world. I worked in the township for many, many, many years before I went into theatre. I grew up. I only went into theatre when I was twenty-eight years old.

However, I went into theatre quite by chance, through my friend Sue Clarke. We have been friends since the late sixties. Sue Clarke was a poet, and she had a group of friends around her who were also into poetry. She used to take me around to poetry readings. She introduced me to Oswald Mtshali, Wally Serote, you know, all the poets in South Africa, whites as well as blacks. And when I was confident enough, I began to take part in poetry readings with them. I think my most famous poetry reading took place in 1972, when Brian Astbury, who was the founder of the Space Theatre, was raising funds to build the Space. One night we were sitting at Sue's house she said to me, 'Oh, Fatts, by the way, they are building a theatre just across from my flat.' I said, 'Oh, really?' 'Yes', she said, 'and I think we should go there and be involved. We should go and offer our help.' And that's how we started working at the Space right from the beginning, just as it was still being built.

In 1972 they had a fund-raising party in Constantia in a place called the Barn Theatre. So we went there. At first they asked me, who can read a black poet? And there was a gentleman by the name of Ken Bosman, who lived in Guguletu. He was a social worker. He was also into the arts. And I said 'The best person to ask is Mr Bosman.' We tried to get in touch with Mr Bosman, but he was unavailable for that date. So they turned around and said 'You read!' And I said *'Moi?'* And they said 'Yes'. 'But,' I said 'I have never read in public before.' They said 'That'll be perfect.'

Then Barney Simon came down from Johannesburg, and he brought a poem with him called 'Madam, Please'. And I was supposed to do this poem on stage. He said it was not really a poem. In fact it was a song from a musical called *Phira* that Barney had adapted from a

French musical. This musical was done in Soweto. They got people to write the songs, and Barney wrote the lyrics. And he brought this song along, for me to do as a poem. I looked at the poem and thought this was it. This was what I'd been looking for! It was a poem about a maid talking to her Madam, because in South Africa white people don't know black people, and black people don't know white people. This black woman was now sitting down to have a heart-to-heart talk with her Madam. I was, at that point, very militant, and I saw this poem as a militant poem to tell white people off, to let them know what I thought of them. So I went into rehearsal and I did this poem so militantly that I felt good!

At the end of the poem Barney didn't say anything. I was waiting for him to give me a crit, but he didn't say anything. Then I said to him 'So what did you think?' He just looked at me and said 'If I was the white woman, I'd tell you to fuck off!'

I was angry! I WAS MAD!

So I said, 'What did you expect me to do?' And he said to me; 'You talk to me like a person, not with an outburst of your hatred. Because if you talked to me the way you did just now, I wouldn't listen to you.'

Oh, I got hurt. I said to myself, 'Being a white you know that people like her are ill-treating us, so why do you expect me to talk to her like a human being?'

And this became a conflict for days on end. I totally refused to be subservient to this poem. And then he absolutely demanded that I should calm down and be subservient to the poem!

So it got to a point where it was either we do this, or we don't. So finally I realised that OK, if we don't, then all these people are going to be pissed off with me. So I said, OK, fine. I'll do it the way you want me to do it.

So I read it quietly and nicely:

> Madam, please, before you shout about your broken plate,
> Ask about the meal her family hate.
> Madam, please, before you laugh at the watchman's English,
> Try to answer in his Zulu language.
> Madam, please, before you say that the driver stinks,
> Come, take a bath in a Soweto sink.
> Madam, please, before you ask me if your children are fine
> Ask me when I last saw mine.
> Madam, please, before you say the last Saturday's funeral was a lie

Ask me how my people die.
Ask about my mother: Is she old? Does she sew? Does she still cook?
Ask about my father: Is he still looking for work?
Ask about my brothers: Are they improving?
Ask about my sisters: Are they in school?
Ask now what we want,
Ask now, if we live,
Ask now, if we breathe,
Madam, please!

And on the night I got a standing ovation, at their own venue. Then that old thing, that stubbornness, that militancy was here! Because when I arrived in the Barn Theatre in Constantia, I first saw all these rich white women in fur coats and diamonds, that's all I saw. And when I stood on stage, that was all I saw in front of me. I remember that my tongue stuck to the roof of my mouth. I couldn't speak. And after a while I just pushed myself in there, and everything went all right. I got a standing ovation from the same people that I wanted to teach a lesson, a militant lesson.

How did you react to that?

I was so upset, I cried. I just ran off the stage at the end of everything, went into the toilet and locked the door and cried and cried and cried, because I was so disappointed. Why were these people so pleased with my performance? They ought to be sitting there feeling ashamed of themselves, but they didn't!

That was lesson number one for me when I started writing in 1976, as a black person: reverse racism doesn't work. It was a good lesson for me. I joined the Space Theatre permanently in '75, as a stage manager. Rob (Amato) arrived in '75, and when he saw my poems in a book in my dressingroom locker, he asked me to resign from the Space Theatre, and we started writing *The Sacrifice of Kreli* together.

I realised from the beginning that this was the hottest era in South Africa, when protest theatre was really cooking. You know protest plays were written like nobody's business. Things were coming, pitiful things, ugly things, all kinds of things, but everything was protest. But funny enough for me: I could not see myself writing a play where I would actually stand on stage and point fingers at white people, in that sense, you know what I mean? These were naked, naked, naked, aggressive plays, that did not give white people a chance in this country. And it was difficult for me to stand there putting down all white people, because I had known white people who treated me like a human being, not like the officials, and the others. So I could not honestly stand there and put down every single white person in South Africa.

When I wrote, I used to write from a very honest place in my heart, which was really addressing the system, you know. Addressing the system.

We wrote *The Sacrifice of Kreli* in 1976. We had problems here, because it was a play that should really have been written in Xhosa. But we did not want the play to be expressedly aimed at a Xhosa audience. This was a play that was speaking about the land that we lost a hundred years ago, which we still didn't have a hundred years later. It was the Ninth Frontier War. But we decided from the beginning that to retell the Ninth Frontier War would be a waste of time. We should tell the people something new coming from the Ninth Frontier War.

What we did was we started the play seven years after. What was left of the Gcalekas went into self-imposed exile. Instead of giving themselves up to the British, they went into exile. Huddled warriors who were left over after their king, Kreli, had led an army of forty-thousand warriors against the British for thirty-two years of fighting. Finally, thirty-two years later, he had lost all of his men, there were only a few hundred men left. So he goes into the Hole, instead of giving himself up to the British.

If you are doing a play like that, it's a traditional play, it deals with African traditions, you are going to talk about an African king, very well known by many people as he was paramount chief of many, many tribes in the Eastern Cape at the time, then you have to know his praise songs, he has to have a diviner, he has to have a praise singer.

Now, the problem here was that you had to portray the diviner in as honest a way as possible. Because in the African tradition the diviner is the church. He is the man who communicates with the ancestors. He is the man who communicates with God through the ancestors. And because the African traditional religion was never given a chance by the colonisers. It was put down, even Africans put it down, because they didn't understand the whole concept of the African traditional religion. So I had to dig out all the things that are valuable, that made this religion what it was then. I had to portray Mlanjeni, the diviner, as somebody positive, somebody powerful, somebody who communicates with the ancestors, and give him that power, because that *is* really his power.

Then I used Mpelesi, the praise singer, as a militant man who did not believe in waiting for the ancestors to give them a sign: he was practical, he was a soldier who wanted the soldiers to go out and fight the British again. We now had a conflict between the two. I give Mlanjeni an opportunity to make a sacrifice to his ancestors. His ancestors give him a sign, and he makes the sacrifice. But then the sacrifice is interrupted by the arrival of a white man accompanied by Tiyo Soga. The king, now, thinking that this man has been sent by the British government to pardon him, stops the sacrifice and attends to the man, only to find that he is nothing but a journalist, and so the sacrifice failed. And so Mpelesi says, 'There you are. This man is a liar,' and Mlanjeni is sentenced to death.

But I don't want him killed immediately, because I believe this man has powers, this man is a messenger from the gods. So, as Christ is wrapped in a cloth, Mlanjeni is wrapped in the skin of the bull that was sacrificed that morning. It's still wet when he is sewn into that skin and placed outside in the sun. If the person inside the skin is a liar, he is crushed as the skin dries.

Then three days later, when the skin is hard and dried, the king commands that the skin be opened, and Mlangeni lies there, lifeless. Then Khulukazi, the oldest woman in the nation comes forward, and feels and tries to see if there's any breath in him. There is no breath, but his body is warm. And as far as our culture is concerned, if the body is warm, there's life. You can't bury that man. She actually tells them that the body is still warm, but there is no heart. So it's a stalemate. They can't touch him. He just lies there, with the skin opened.

On the fourth day he opens his mouth, and suddenly everybody rushes to hear what he's going to say. And he just says to them, 'I've been to the place where the ancestors live.' They say, 'Go back and build your homes, re-plough your fields, give birth, live, because there is a future.' And he dies.

And this is exactly what is happening in this country now: we are given a future. We had many of our leaders in prison for twenty-seven years, and never thought they would come out. Suddenly they came out and we were delivered.

I was talking to Rob Amato about this play recently, and told him how incomprehensible the play seemed to me when I read it. And he said that the play should never have been allowed to be published the way it was, without proper stage directions and commentary that would make it accessible for people who don't know these traditions. But after being given this introduction it comes across as a really fascinating play.

What I want to do now is to get in touch with Wits University Press and re-publish the play on its own, with everything. Because to me it is one of the most valuable plays in South African theatre today.

Well, that was the story. And then, after that play, I went alone, I was trying to walk alone, without my mentors, Rob Amato, Rob McLaren, Barney. This was such a major piece of work, such a beautiful piece of work that people are still talking about it today, nearly twenty years later. It was done in the Greek style of theatre, but with an African traditional theme, and it is also an historical play.

What I did in writing the play was to do some of the things in Xhosa. Some of the things were so beautiful in Xhosa that I didn't want to lose the richness of the language. So some of the verses were done in what is called literal translation.

In the African concept of time there is no hour, there is no day, there is no week, there is no month. It's just time. The African concept of time is three-dimensional. We have a past and a present, and a present past. There is no future. The future is born out of the past.

I did a monologue where the king goes to choose the bull for the sacrifice in the morning. And he goes with Mlanjeni, his diviner. He sees this particular bull, and he says to Mlanjeni, 'Mlanjeni, do you see that bull?' And Mlanjeni says, 'Yes.' He says, 'Do you know that bull?' Mlanjeni says, 'No.' So he gives him the history, the family line of the bull.

> The mother of that bull was a cow in my father's herd. The bull that fathered it was slaughtered by my father at a time when a lot of white people came across the seas, having run away from a war there (with the Russians, the Crimean War). That bull was a wonder. One day it went about the village butting everything and everybody that got in its way. It bellowed for five days, foaming at the mouth, till all the men were out of their mind trying to think what was wrong with the bull. When the new moon arrived, it was slice. On that day the British attacked us.

Now, what you find here, basically, is again the oral history of the African world. The bull and the humans each have a line of heritage. This bull has a line back to the king's grandfather's time. When *he* was born, the bull's grandfather was alive. He was a bull from that line. When the king's grandfather died, the old bull was slaughtered at his funeral, but the bull had already fathered other bulls or calves. The line continues. When his father became king, that line of bulls was still there, so the mother and father of this particular bull were alive when his father was still around. So there is what you would call a family line between the animals and the people. For each generation there is a bull.

Secondly, the time. When a lot of people had run away from the war – that was the Crimean War – you already have a date around 1854. In this way one can establish the time of the events.

When Khulukazi, the old woman, goes on the first night to visit the Thokai young men, who were watching over Mlanjeni's body inside the skin, the first thing she does is not to point fingers at them. But she makes them feel guilty, indirectly. She goes back, feels the body. It's warm but there's no heart. She takes a hair from her kaross and puts it underneath Mlanjeni's nostrils, but the hair doesn't flutter, which means there's no breath. She sits back, because she knows, now, that his soul has gone on a journey to the ancestors. If it comes back, it is only to say goodbye to the body, and then it leaves, and he can die. She is watching for the moment when the soul leaves the body. She sits back, and she says to the warriors, 'Do you know this man?' They say, 'No.' She says:

> Mlanjeni's father was the great diviner of the King. I was a new wife then. I had been brought from my home in King Sandele's country, by Mlanjeni's father. When I arrived there, he cleansed me, and told me all about myself. I have always been faithful to the Gcalekas till today. When it was time to reap, Mlanjeni's father used to ride his horse, which was white. He would go into the river; he would not be wearing anything, he would go deeper, and deeper, and deeper, till we could not see him any more. We would wait on the banks, frightened that he would not come out alive. But when he came out, his body would shine; it would have the colours of the rainbow. He would talk to no one. He would ride his horse through all the fields of the villages, throwing the blessings our ancestors had given him. When it was time to reap the fields, my son, Umhlo, would give us pumpkins as big as your two heads

put together. The mealie cobs were as long as my forearms. My head is not grey only because of my age; there is wisdom, too, that goes with it. I am used to death and all that goes with it.

She goes to the body, pulls out another hair, puts it under his nostrils, nothing happens. She says, 'The body is still warm, but there is no heart.' And she leaves. But she has cast a spell. As she leaves, the warriors begin to say, 'Did we do the right thing in condemning this man to death?'

This play is for me the most beautiful thing we ever created. Very simple, but very, very beautiful, and basically from Africa, inside me, from my heart. For every single word was from the African traditional culture. The way Khulukazi would refuse to say the horse was pure white when she was referring to the whiteness of the horse; she would say it was white-white, emphasising the whiteness of the horse. 'He was like the day he was born,' she would say, instead of saying he was naked. Because in Africa we also have a language of respect. You wouldn't say that he was naked, you would say he was like the day he was born, for your mind knows we are born naked. But you needn't *say* 'naked'.

When you went into theatre and established yourself as a writer, were you at all involved in politics as such?

No, no. I always felt that for me personally, as Fatima Dike, if I had belonged to a party I would have problems. I want to be loyal to my work, not be biased by the fact that I am ANC or whatever. That would have been a problem for me.

Foreigners coming to South Africa in 1995 get profoundly worried by the level of violence in the country. I am sure it must worry you as South Africans even more. How do you yourself face this problem?

Yes, it is very worrying. The people of this country, I believe, are not originally violent people. It must be viewed in the light of the deprivation of our people during apartheid, when we were subdued by the army and the brutality of the system for over forty years. The ANC tried, when they were still allowed to operate in our country, to defy the system in a non-violent manner. When that didn't work, they tried the violent way. Then we know what happened. Those guys went to Robben Island for twenty-seven years. After that the students took over. When universities sprang up which admitted blacks, the black students did not agree with what the white student organisation was saying. So they broke away from NUSAS, the National Union of South African Students, which was formed by white universities, and formed their own union, SASO, the South African Student Organisation.

And, of course, there was Steve Biko and the Black Consciousness Movement. Look at the history of America first, before we get to the violence. In America we had the Civil Rights movement in the 1960s. But that died when Luther King was assassinated. Immediately after that we had the Black Panthers, who were young, militant black men, who used guns to fight the system. The Black Consciousness Movement was in a way copied from the Black Panthers of that era in the '70s, modified to accommodate the South African situation. During that time there was no violence as such, up until 1976. What had happened was that the young people realised the only way to get rid of the government was to do what they did, and so violence took off. Their violence was pitted against the violence from the system.

What added to the violence of the conflict was that black people had been crammed into poverty-stricken squatter-like situations in the townships, where a lot of violent gangsters were operating. However, during that period, from 1976 up until the '90s, they were felt by the comrades not to violate black property and black people, but to work *with* them. But when the system realised that these two elements were working together, they then infiltrated the students' movement, and turned students into informers for the state, to avoid a member of their family being arrested or whatever. And so black upon black violence started in that manner. Also a lot of black people have been out of work, and many of them have turned to robbing banks and other acts of violence. The main aim of the Black Consciousness Movement was to render this country ungovernable. But then, of course, these other elements joined in and took over. And the violence escalated because we had a white minority that wanted to maintain an identity of their own in the country, and they also became more violent.

Would you agree with those who contend that artists and writers should no longer feel bound to look upon culture as a weapon in the struggle? They should be free.

Yes, it's true that we should be free to create, but I don't believe that the struggle is over. It is not over yet. But this is a beautiful time for all of us. For me, for instance, in 1990 when Mr Mandela was freed, I knew that this country was going to go one way, our way. And I said to myself, 'What am I going to do?' And I said to myself, 'Stupid! Do you remember in the early '60s when we still wanted to create a theatre of politics, so that we as artists had a voice to talk about what was happening in South Africa?' There were no writers in this country at that point who wrote for the theatre. We took plays from Europe and adapted them to the South African situation. And after that, people decided, 'No, we don't want to use the language of the Europeans to express our feelings about apartheid. Now we *are* going to sit down and write our stories about our situation.'

The playwright did this very successfully. I think without theatre very few people outside South Africa would have known what was happening. *Sizwe Bansi, The Island, Bopha, Asinamali!* went out into the world to say, 'This is what is happening in the land of our ancestors.' They made South Africa known internationally. And I keep saying to South African artists: 'We are at a crossroads again and we don't have a voice now even if the war is over. We are still at that same point where we were twenty or thirty years ago. We have to find that voice.'

But we must move away from politics; our voice must speak about social issues, which is what black theatre was all about in South Africa before we changed it into protest theatre: it was a social comment, about the situations we lived in. We should concentrate on social issues, for instance the rights of women. What is going to happen in the townships? Are we getting houses or aren't we getting houses? What is happening to the education of our children? Because housing, health care and education are the central social issues in South Africa today. And those issues are enough for us as writers to write on, as a social comment.

As for myself I was also looking at entertainment in addition to writing other stuff. When I wrote *So What's New* in 1990, I said to myself: 'I am a woman. This theatre has been dominated by men for over twenty-five years, protest theatre. We can count plays that were written by women or for women on my two hands. Now I, being a woman, have the time to sit back and start writing plays about women and for women.' So I wrote *So What's New*, which is a typical South African play. Three black women who used to belong to a singing group called

The Chatanuga Sisters, way way back in the 1960s. They felt at some point that they could not go on singing together, because they were not making money, and they had families to feed. So they broke apart and each went her way. Doris became a shebeen queen, Pat started selling houses and became an estate agent and Tandi, Pat's younger sister, started doing drug-pushing.

Then there is Mercedes, Doris' daughter, who is seventeen years old and doing standard ten. She is of the '76 generation, so she is still involved in politics. She's involved in a group who go out hunting for empty white schools in Cape Town, and then they find one school that is empty. They organise a bus-load of black children and go into the school and take it over. And basically it is still the same *angst*, the same anxiety that each parent has with children who are involved in politics. You want to say to the child, What are you doing with politics? Go to school! Study! Become something! And then, when you have finished, go into politics!

But it is stupid, because the child is suffering in school, she is not getting a good education. The school building is up to shit, overcrowded, and there are white schools standing out there empty. That's the reality. But it is what the parents want for the child, in contrast to what the child wants for itself and for the future for others, that creates this conflict between parents and children. That's *So What's New?*

How was it received?

In Johannesburg every paper loved the play. Because for the first time they could sit quietly and not be made to feel guilty. What I did to the play was I just concentrated on these women. Pat and Doris are avid soap fans; they love American soaps. Their favourite soap is The Bold and the Beautiful. So every day at five-thirty Pat and Doris are sitting in front of their TV watching The Bold and the Beautiful. And because they don't have love lives they live their love lives through the television, and they argue and fight over the characters in their TV set.

And in a way that is a good thing for me, for every woman in South Africa has a soap that she loves, so when they went and saw the play, the people sat there and laughed and laughed, because they were seeing themselves on stage. The black on black violence was happening outside their window. They would be watching the soap, and then suddenly the guns would go off outside, and they would duck under the chairs, under the tables, but after the guns died down they would still get up and watch the soap.

And, of course, there was Mercedes, who has a special relationship with Tandi, the drug dealer. She and Tandi love each other so much that Mercedes, being the child that she is, doesn't like the fact that Tandi deals in drugs. At some point during the play she and Tandi are left alone in the house. Tandi comes in and says to her, 'Where's your mum?' The mum has gone to Sun City with her boyfriend Willy. He is also a drug dealer, but he doesn't tell Doris. And, of course, he is Tandi's friend: they both deal drugs together.

And they sit there, and they have this one beautiful moment together when they can be on their own and talk to each other and open up to each other. And so Mercedes says to Tandi, 'Last night I saw Willy. I walked past Willy's house. He was sitting outside. I called out to him and waved, but he couldn't see me. He found it hard even to lift his arms, because he was so bogged on mandrax he didn't know whether he was coming or going. And do you know something? Willy was an A-student at school.'

The whole talk turns to Tandi's drug dealing business. And, of course, drug dealers always defend themselves. So, the last thing that she tells Tandi. is: 'Today we are fighting racial injustice. Tomorrow we may be fighting drugs. I hope when that day comes you'll be on my side, not on the other side.' In talking to people close to theatre I have found that there are two contrasting views concerning the function of the theatre in today's South Africa. One is that one ought to revive the township musical, which was so popular a couple of decades ago, and take advantage of its entertainment aspect in order to educate the disadvantaged masses, to 'smuggle', as it were, knowledge and education to the deprived generation in the townships. The other view is that this is not a task for the artists: 'Let didacticism look after itself, and concentrate on creativity.'

Where do you stand in this debate?

Fortunately the education in theatre is being taken care of in South Africa. We have people who are doing education through theatre, who concentrate exclusively on the educational aspect.

So that is again a parallel to the struggle literature?

Yes. So I don't see any problems. I believe in education through theatre in many ways, because we have a very big percentage of illiteracy in this country. And if we can help eradicate that through theatre, it's good. There are already things that are being done.

For schools do a lot of set books. Now I think they are reading *Macbeth*. So all the state theatres are doing *Macbeth*. And schools are given block bookings at discounts, to see it live on stage. You see, education in theatre in this country is helpful, especially for the black children. Black children don't get the chance to travel like white kids. It will take a black child that is born in a Cape Town township perhaps the better part of his or her life even to go to Port Elizabeth, which is about six hundred kilometres away. By the time a person gets geared to go out of her city or township, she will most probably be in her twenties. If you don't travel, your imagination becomes stagnant. Unless you have a good mind and can read. But our kids don't read. When I was twelve I used to read forty English books a year. I read all the English classics when I was twelve to fifteen. I did most of my reading during that period, because I was in a boarding school that was run by Irish nuns. And there were bookshelves in my classroom and I could read forty books in one class. That finished, I would go to the next class, read that lot and go on to the next again.

But today we don't have that advantage. We've got television. But I feel that television should play a role. In America they've got Channel 15 which is purely good stuff. It's got everything that is educational. So if we are going to pay TV licences in this country, television must give us back our money's worth by giving our children a basic education. The Government must also fund education theatre besides funding proper theatre. Ballet and opera are élitist theatre, which black children know nothing about. It has to go down to the grassroots so that people get to know what ballet is really about. It should also be possible for our children to dream of becoming a ballerina: they mustn't see the ballerina as exclusively a white person. A black person can be a ballerina as well. In America they have black divas in opera. It's not an empty dream any longer. But in this country those things are still seen as being far-fetched. There are opera performances in Cape Town, at the State Opera in Pretoria, but they are for whites. So the minute those walls are broken down and people are made to realise that all of this is available to them, then the country changes, and the people will change as well.

Could you see Gibson Kente recreated and produced in the townships for young people to get a feeling and a love for the theatre, thus paving the way for a theatre culture?

Do you know what my greatest regret is? It is that today Gibson Kente, the man, is not being given the full respect that he deserves in this country. There should be a theatre built for that man, named after him. Money is not the thing. Gibson should be given his own theatre, because you can go anywhere in South Africa, and you'll find that Gibson was there. He taught!

It is with Mbongeni Ngema as it is with me: I wouldn't be who I am today with my talent if Rob Amato hadn't come the Space Theatre and said, 'Hey, you can write. WRITE!' Mbongeni Ngema was a protegé of Gibson Kente. Have you ever seen him mention Gibson? Never! As for me, having grown up in a township, I wouldn't have been where I am today if it wasn't for Rob. And I say that with my heart. I cannot pay Rob for what he did to me, but I am paying tribute to him today because I am somebody. Every time he sees me or hears about me, I know he must feel very proud inside, because without him I would not be Fatima Dike, the person I am. I learnt a lot of things from Rob.

Apart from Rob Amato, who else has inspired you as a writer?

Wally Serote. When I first met Wally, it was one evening at my friend Sue Clarke's house. He just came there briefly. And I looked at him and I could see that he was like a coiled spring, ready to be unleashed. I read his work, 'Johannesburg, City of Gold', and then I remember – I've forgotten the title of the poem, but I think it was 'Ofay's mind looks back', but there are two stanzas that remained in my mind for, oh, twenty years, which say:

> White people are white
> They are burning the world
> Black people are black
>
> They are the fuel
> White people must learn to listen
> Black people must learn to talk
> Amen
> Hallelujah

Another poem that he wrote, I'm just ad libbing the lines, I can't remember them word for word:

> I saw a man come
> Walk
> Run
> Fall
> Like a branch of a tree being sawn
> People gathered around him
> I was amongst them

To me this is a typical township situation. I can see everything: a person was stabbed, people gather around him, nobody is helping, the police come. Did you see anything? I didn't see anything. But you were there! He just took that one incident in the township and put it down in such simple language that when I first read it I laughed, because it was so familiar. So he became my hero, you know, as far as poetry was concerned. All my life I had wanted to write like him, but that was impossible. Every writer has his or her style. But his style so impressed me because it was tight, it was tense and it was focused.

And Oswald Mtshali, *Sounds of a Cowhide Drum*. I read it. It was very simple, easily digestible. It opened a window in my mind, and made me look again, clearly, at myself and my surroundings as a black South African. I learnt something from him, the poem 'Boy on a Swing':

> Mother . . .
> When will I wear long trousers
> Why was my father jailed?

Black men's castration. But Tony Morrison is my favourite black writer at the moment.

What is there in Tony Morrison that fascinates you so?

Her stories – about families, about townships, about life. It's the poetry that gets me. It's her poetry. She never writes straight. She has a special melody:

> In that place down there, where the earth is bare, there used to be a place called Medallion, where men used to go into the bar and sit on

tall stools with the toes of their pointed feet hanging on silver rungs pointing downwards . . .

Reba used to cook with her hat on, because she could not remember the recipes without the hat. You know those people! And when she says that one day the construction workers came and pulled the house down, I saw District Six. There are similarities between her America at that time and South Africa of today. But I love the way she takes the edge off bitterness by the way she uses her language. Because that is the way I write. I do not like to stab the hearts with a spear. Instead I like to *pinch* the heart so that it jumps, and says, 'What have I done?' And I say, 'This is what you have done!' And that's what Toni Morrison also does.

That's what Barney Simon taught you, wasn't it?

Yes. When we wrote *Kreli* he said to me 'What I like about you is that when you write it's like you know those guys who work on the construction site in Jo'burg. What do they do at lunchtime? They come down to the pavement. They 've got empty jam tins. They put tea in and eat dry bread. That is South Africa.'

Who said that?

Barney Simon. I think that the quality he likes in my writing is that nothing is ever glamorised, it is written the way it is. It's like *So What's New*. It says to me, 'We know these people.' And what I like about *So What's New* is that these women are amoral, and you don't feel shy about them being amoral. It's the truth. The truth is most important to me. If a black man is subservient, as you find it in *The First South African*, who cannot cope with the fact that he married a black woman who has a child by a white man. The system hates her. The township people hate her, and he's stuck in the middle, because the system has castrated him. The fight is no longer there inside of him. He is dead. But she is alive. She is a lioness. She will fight for that boy, her son. And he sits there as an observer and sees her going through her life fighting the system to keep the white boy. Until the system eats the life out of her body and she dies. At the end Nhijema becomes mad. He is white physically, but because of the laws he is classified as a coloured. Culturally he is black, because he is brought up in Langa, and he is circumcised as a black person and all his relatives are black. So he has the three races in South Africa in him, he's black, white and coloured. To me, then, he was truly the first South African.

When he comes on stage in the opening scene of the play, the whole stage is in darkness, the theatre is in darkness and he stands there. He says, 'What would I be likely to do if I were in a free society?'

I would have had him standing on stage totally naked. But because we were living in South Africa in the '70s, we couldn't do that, we couldn't have him standing on stage naked. So everything was done in the dark. The only thing you could see was Frieda, his mother, standing behind him, and she had her hands like that, her black hands cupped, begging.

And he speaks a long monologue. I go back to the Bible again, I take from Genesis: 'God created man in His image, male and female, And the Lord formed man from the dust of the earth, And breathed into his nostrils the breath of life, And man became a living soul . . .' The father looked at his children one day, and found one different. 'This is not from Heaven, this is from hell,' he said. And the child was no longer fit to be called by his name . . .

So it goes on and tells the history of being ousted by society. But at the end of the monologue he asks one question: 'Am I not a man, then?'

What are you working on now?

I am working on a set of little vignettes called *South Africa Today*. The opening piece is from a cartoon called 'Madam and Eve'. It is just after the elections. Eve, the black maid, comes into the room, and she's excited: 'We are free at last! Free at last, Martin Luther King! Madam, we must shout it on the mountain tops, we must shout it through the windows, on the streets. WE ARE FREE AT LAST.'

Madam says 'Yeees. Don't forget the dishes.' So she sulks and goes and watches TV. Madam comes into the living room and says, 'Eve, don't forget the dishes.' So Eve goes, 'MARIA!!' Another black maid comes in. 'Don't forget the dishes, Maria!' says Eve. So Madam wants to know what is going on there. Eve says, 'I wanted to know what it feels like to be a madam, so I hired my own maid.' And so Madam says, 'No-no-no, wait a minute. We've got this wrong. *I am* the madam in this house, not you. You must fire her.' Eve says, 'If I fire her, then you'll have to pay her for a week's work.' The Madam says fine, and she pulls out a hundred rands, and pays Maria off. And then, of course, Maria turns around to Eve and says, 'Eh, Couz, that's the easiest hundred rands I have ever made in my life. A hundred rands for one hour! This is truly the New South Africa.' And as she goes out Eve shouts 'Say Hi to Uncle Joe!' And she goes off.

So you have a cluster of these vignettes?

Yes. Then I have a grandchild who goes to the German School up in Long Street. On this particular morning we didn't have a car, so I took her to school by train. We were walking down Government Avenue past Parliament. And I said to her, 'Do you know this place?' 'No,' she said. I said, 'This is Parliament.' She didn't understand. So I said 'This is where Mr Mandela works.' And all of a sudden she got animated, very excited. 'Can he see us through those windows?' I said, 'Maybe.' And this whole conversation as we were walking I made into a little poem which I called 'Walking Down Parliament Avenue':

> Mummy, Mummy, is that Mr Mandela's house?
> Can he see us through those windows?
> Can we see him?
> Can we go inside?
> I can't, because I'm on my way to school!
> What school?
> I want to see Mandela

How are you going to present them? Are they made into a book?

We are going to act everything out. They are little vignettes. It's like a review. Then I have this white man who used to be in the army, in 1976, who killed black school children in Soweto. He was talking to me about how brainwashed they were. They were told to kill blacks because then they were killing Communism, and of course the system was prepared to kill all blacks in this country, if necessary, in order to maintain apartheid. And afterwards, when everything was over, he began to realise that it was all a lie. And now he is actually having to live with his guilt. And he said to me, 'If I were black, I would be out there killing white people for what they have done to me. You black people have good hearts. You can forgive.' I said to him, 'Of course we can forgive, but we mustn't ever forget what the previous government did to us. Because a nation with a short memory will become slaves again.'

So I went home and wrote his piece down.

I have a piece from my third play, *Glass House*, where my son went out one night without telling me. He went to a students' meeting, and he was shot. I got home from work at nine o'clock in the evening. I was in the middle of having my supper when the phone rang. This voice said to me, 'Come to number 9 Mvambo Street, your son has been shot.' And they put the phone down before I could ask any more questions. You do not know the trauma!

When was this?

It was in 1986, during the state of emergency. The army was in the township, all the street lights in the township were out. I put my sweater on, and a beret, and I started running to this place. And as I was running there was a constant prayer in my heart, 'Please, God, don't let them shoot me, don't let them shoot me.' I ran across an open field, and I promise you, I won't say I will never do that again, because if it is my child, I will. But I would never ever want to go through that again. I ran down the road, through this open field praying that they won't take a shot at me.

When I came to the corner of Church Street and Mvambo, there was a saracen and a police van. And, of course, in a blind reaction I leapt across the fence into somebody's yard, without thinking, and I hid behind a hedge. After I'd done that, I said to myself, 'Oh, my God, I hope there are no dogs in this yard. Please, God, don't let there be dogs in this yard,' and God was with me.

When I saw the police van and the saracen move round the corner, I went out through the gate into the street. And there were no lights. I couldn't see the numbers on the doors, which means I still had to go into the yards, and I was still scared of the dogs. I was like one demented. At that point I didn't even care, I was just frantic trying to find number 9. Then somebody came out of the shadow and just grabbed me, and before I could scream they put a hand over my mouth, and I thought, 'OK, just relax, because if you fight, they'll kill you.' So I tried to relax when somebody said in my ear, 'Come this way.' And I followed, and this man took me to number 9. We went in through the back and there was a single candle in the back room that was lit. Then I did something that Africans don't ever do in other people's houses: I ran into this room and there was nothing. I ran into the next room and there were bodies all over. Of course I was mad. I lost my mind. I was calling my son softly, JiJi. Then a woman came up to me and touched my shoulder very gently and said, 'Go home, we'll phone you.' I was screaming, I couldn't stand it. But I had to go back, through the open field, the dark streets, and I'm the only person out in the deserted township.

I got to my house. My mother was looking at me, and I had really nothing to say to her. 'He wasn't there,' I said. 'They said I must come back. They will phone.'

The phone rings again. I pick it up. This time they say, 'Go to number 35 Moshoeshoe Avenue. Bring your car.' I don't have a car. But my sister has one. So I go to my sister's house, and I explain to her very quickly. And she says to me, 'You can take my Hi Ace.' Because of the state of emergency you couldn't just drive out of the township. And I wanted to be as quiet as possible. I was pushing this car alone, you know, towards this address, when two men came down the road, saw me, and they were a little bit drunk, and making noise, and they wanted to know why was I pushing this car in the street. I say, 'Don't ask me questions, please help me push the car.' We pushed the car past the police station, and then I started, and got to number 35. When I got there, the door opened and an old school friend of mine was standing at the door. I knew her. 'Shhh!' She came out and she said, 'Just bring the car into the yard.' We went inside into her lounge. More bodies! No, God, not again! I started digging again, and she said, 'No, don't. Just relax.'

She just said one word, and the bodies stood up and they all got into my van. And when they got into the van, they again lay on top of each other like dead bodies. And we drove. Somebody took the key from me, and we drove and drove and drove. I realised we were going down Modderdam Road, so we were going towards the squatter camp in Crossroads. When we got there they drove inside the squatter camp until we came to a clinic, that was well lit. And then the kids got out and were treated. They all had bad shot wounds and stuff: they were all injured.

And your son, then?

He was fine. He was shot at, but he wasn't hurt. The trauma of being a mother! Now, that was the monologue I recreated from that experience. It is part of the vignettes, next to the piece about the white man who had killed black kids, that I just told you about.

Then in Jo'burg I met another guy, who was in the camps in Tanzania. And he actually ran away from the ANC camps, and he had his own story to tell, you know. It was so funny. He would tell us about when Joe Modise, the Minister of Defence, came to the camp to visit, and what he used to say, and so on. So I take these three monologues and bunch them into one vignette.

When will it ready for production?

It is going to be done in La Villette in France in May (1995). And then there's another fine one that I did on 21 March, to celebrate Sharpeville Day, which has been renamed Human Rights Day.

We went to pick up somebody at the bus station in town. So my two 'keeps', who I call my 'coconuts', because they haven't been through Bantu Education, they have been to private schools ('Coconuts' are black kids who are 'white' inside). And they speak English without an accent and they are élitist, you know, which happens when they go to white schools.

So these coconuts drove me to the bus station to meet this lady, and then they parked where the buses park. Now this guy comes, and the whole thing goes like this:

- When is the bus from P.E. coming in?
- Seven o'clock.
- But I phoned before coming, and they told me the bus came at six.
- I beg your pardon, I can't park here?
- Aha. Listen: I don't want you to think that we blacks are tsotsis, or tsaras or disobedient people. But, you know, this is the New South Africa. And I can park anywhere I like.
- No-no-no, you don't understand, sir. You say this is where the buses park?
- Who cares? I can park anywhere I want. Do you know who I am? I am Winnie! Winnie Mandela. You don't recognise me because I am not wearing my wig. This is my friend Shani. You can call me Wee

> and you can call her Sha, and if you want to address us at the same time, you can call us ShaWee.
> – Now, listen. No-no. You've got it all wrong. Do you know what today is?
> – Today is Human Rights Day, OK?
> – So, please, don't mess with my rights!

Yes, it's satire on South Africa today. And I have a thing, a monologue, that I do about Mr Mandela, where he is beginning to reveal all his secrets over the past twenty-seven years – how he survived Robben Island, patiently, without getting killed. And his story is that he had an out-of-body experience with the leader of the Brhama Kumaris, Dadi Prakashime.

Who did you say?

Dadi Prakashime is the leader of the Brhama Kumaris, a Hindu religious sect which teaches Raja yoga. So Mandela claims that they taught him Raja yoga, so that he could supersede the human trivialities as a prisoner for all these years. That is how he managed to come out after twenty-seven years without going crazy. It is because these women, these Rajis, came to him in out-of-body experiences and every single evening they would come to him above Robben Island, and sit with him and teach him Raji Yoga.

As you can see, it's South Africa today seen from different levels – social, political – and it is laughter, you know, everything.

You mentioned briefly your play The Glass House, *which apparently was based on some traumatic personal experiences earlier on. Could you give me a brief run-down of the background of that play?*

Yes, it was in 1976. We were rehearsing *The Sacrifice of Kreli* when the student uprising broke out here in Cape Town on the 11 August. And so I recorded it on a daily basis. I was at home, and I would be there watching the marches, watching the students being picked up by the police, and when this first child was killed in Cape Town, I was there.

What happened was that on that day these kids came out of Langa High School after assembly. They unfolded this huge banner which said, 'We do not want to be taught in the language of the oppressor.

Down with Afrikaans!' And then they marched out of the school singing freedom songs, and carrying this banner.

I was in the house getting ready to go to the theatre when I heard this music. I ran outside to see where the music was coming from. It was coming from Langa High School and the students were marching. We had seen what had happened in Soweto on June 16. We didn't expect anything similar to happen in Cape Town, but it did.

When the boy was shot, what was happening was that the police would come and drive next to the kids, and they would pick four kids from the group and put them in the van. This went on and on until the kids got angry, and finally they decided to go to the police station and ask what were they being arrested for. But the police refused to talk to them. They just closed the gates and wouldn't allow them to go in. So they kept going back to the gate wanting to speak to the station commandant. But the policeman refused to let them in. That's how the shooting began, they fired teargas at the students.

Then there was this one boy standing on the pavement watching. Then he went over and said something to this policeman. And the policeman got angry. So he came out of the gate, chased him and caught him. But he just took his school jacket off, so that the policeman was left holding on to this school jacket. And the boy was in his school shirt and his grey flannel pants.

The next time when they went up to the fence, he said something to the policeman again, and the policeman came out and chased him, but this time he grabbed him by the school shirt. The boy got out of his school shirt, and the policeman was left holding his school shirt. And we were laughing, because it was like a game.

But the third time the policeman did not come out. He just pulled out his gun and shot him through the back of his head as he was running. So he ran with half of his head, the other half and his brains flying in the air. And he crossed the street, but when he lifted his leg to put his foot on the pavement, life went out of his body, and he fell back – wham! – you know. And when his head hit the street, what was left of his brains was spread there. Then there was complete silence, because now the people realised that these people meant business.

When the school children went to pick the body up, eight policemen came out with machine guns pointed at the teacher, and they cried 'Don't touch him. He's state property.'

And you were actually there watching this?

Yes. Phew! Anyway. Initially we did not expect the South African government to start killing children. But this was when we realised that the enemy was determined to go to any length, and that it was going to be a long and hard fight, and that many people were going to lose their lives. And these kids were not backing down.

And I remember going home after the – I mean a dog was eating his brains! I went home, totally empty. And I phoned the theatre and said, 'I can't work today.' I went to the theatre the following morning, and a strange transformation took place. I became so evil, so full of hate, I did not know myself. These were the people I had worked with in the Space Theatre all my life. They were white, and I hated them. Oh! I hated every one of them. Every single one of them.

I remember Cathy, a retired lady, who worked at the restaurant. She was an elderly lady. She called me and she said to me, 'Go and get my cakes.' She had tarts, you know, that she sold for lunch from the Vienna bakery up in Long Street. And I walked up Long Street, and there was a little coloured boy sitting on the pavement, begging. He happened to say the wrong word to me on that day: 'Kaffir, please give me ten cents.' He was ten years old. I picked him up and I was smashing his head against the wall. Ben Decker came at that particular moment and found me bashing this boy's head against the wall. He hit me. He said 'What the fuck do you think you're doing?' Then I said 'He called me kaffir!'

And for a long time I knew I had to get reconciled to all of that. Besides that I had to be myself again. I couldn't write. I just carried on doing *Kreli*; I had finished *The First South African*. I pushed it to the back of my head and forgot about it, but it was there, due to come up and say, Hey, I am still here, that memory!

And so in 1979 I wrote *Glass House*, because I had to get it out. I just did not know that I could hate that much. And do you know what I did? I wrote that character of Phumla exactly as I am telling you, in HATE. Do you know what it is to hate? Hate is one of the most vicious emotions any human being can feel and it can take your mind away. Totally make you go crazy. And I went crazy. I hated! People who I loved, that I trusted, that I had worked with for a long time, they were just so white – I hated them. And the poor people couldn't understand what they had done to me. In fact, my friends had to go and explain to them what was happening. Then they understood. And they forgave me. I would never want to be like that again, ever, ever!

So this took away your creativity from you, did it?

It did not. I just calmed it down, and I said to myself, *Kreli* has to go on. And we did *Kreli*. And with the success of *Kreli* it kind of evened out that experience. I forgot. But I knew that one day I had to sit down and take it out of my system and write *Glass House*. It's a play that I find difficult to look at, even now. I looked at it, in Jo'burg, and I was thinking I could cut here and cut there. But every time when I think about *Glass House* I want to cry. Because for me the question that bothers me is, what was it about us black people that made the Afrikaners hate us so much? If someone could answer that question, perhaps, perhaps? I don't know. I am still asking that question. What was it about us that made them do those atrocious things that they've done to us? My friends, my other white friends, now that they can be calm and think rationally about it, say it was fear, the fear of being outnumbered, of being swamped.

So it is a very complex country, and it creates complex souls, so that people cannot be rational at any given moment. Because when people look back at the past and they see the atrocities that were done to them in the name of apartheid, how can you stop the madness, the violence? And the question today is: should the government have public trials of the people involved in those atrocities? And we think perhaps they should. Even if they're not going to be sentenced. People must know what happened, so that when people forgive, they know what they are forgiving.

People are scared of violence. But we were violated! And the problem that we have to live with in this country is that now Mandela says, 'Let's forget, let's forgive.' What are we forgiving? There are many people out there who have lost families: people who were killed, people who were burnt in the burnt-out huts, people who were shot. People don't know what to forgive or who to forgive. How do we deal with that? We fear the violence that we are experiencing in this country, but people still want to know: Who did what to whom, when, how? Perhaps when that is done, people can say OK?

Could you see the recent public prosecution against ex-police Gen-

eral de Kok as a beginning of the process of getting some of the skeletons out of the cupboards?

Yes. We've seen ANC people's washing being hung out, literally, in public. We know who killed whom – McBride placed the bomb, the St James' killings case is coming to an end; those people are going to be sentenced. They are our people. They were fighting for our cause. But what about the other side? It is not enough for them to say to us, 'We were fighting Communism.' There was no Communism involved!

Has Glass House *ever been produced?*

Yes, at the Space Theatre, and they did it in New York, at La Mama and Off Broadway.

How was it received?

Very well. But after that I could not write in America, because it was not my country. I had no gripes there, it was the African Americans who had things to say in their country against their government. And what I did, finally, to remember home was to paint pictures about my home, and I wrote these poems. I wrote one called 'Me':

> I am the Siren that clears the streets
> As I bleed from the point of a knife's blade
> Toward the City Hospital
> I am the brains that spill in the streets
> The dogs that lapped them up
> I smelt blood with sand
> I am the pass-book in your back pocket
> The hand that reaches for it on demand
> I am the knife in your breast pocket
> The hand that reaches for it in a dark alley
> I am the smog that greets the dawn on my way to work
> The song on Friday nights
> The song that turns boys into men
> I am Sheba's breast rising from the hills of Xhosan Baba
> Because I am Africa

Then I wrote 'Langa, My Love':

> I was born in this township
> I grew up on this street
> The ten houses on this block
> Joined together like railway carriages
> There are peach trees and lemon trees
> Chrysanthemums and roses
> And low red stoeps
> That run from the verandahs to the gates
> Like long red tongues
> Stuck out at something or someone
> We used to play this pot-holed street into the ground
> When it rained,
> Gasoline water would fill the potholes
> With delicate rainbows
> We slashed them with our bare feet
> Spreading the puddles far and wide

It's just painting a picture of the street I live on. So basically that's what I did, I wrote poems.

Then I came back, and for five years I didn't work in the theatre, because I felt that for me the quality of theatre between '83 and '90 was going down the drain. People were just standing up and raising fists, and they wanted to be recognised as artists. So I refrained from writing, I refused to write. I stayed and worked in my family business for five years, without writing a single word. The only two things I did was to contribute to this volume of poetry, *Siren Song*. And then there was another book, a volume of short stories by black South African women, called *Women in South Africa: from the heart*, an anthology, where I wrote *Township Games*. That was in '88.

Julius Mtsaka

Julius Mtsaka, you have been involved in South African theatre for a long time. How did it all start?

It goes back some twenty-five years now. In the late sixties there was this wave of township musicals, and I must say Gibson Kente has always been in the forefront of that. But I was fortunate enough to be in Johannesburg during that period, in the late sixties, and I was exposed – not only to his productions, but to those of his contemporaries, as well as Basil Somhlahlo and Conny Mabaso while the former was still living in Johannesburg. Because I have always had a profound interest in the theatre, I decided to try out something. I had some ideas, but I lacked some skills.

And then I decided, since there were no opportunities like schools where black aspiring dramatists could go and train, let me just give it my best shot and see what I could do with the little knowledge I had.

So I scripted a musical play based on a story I had heard when I was young. What was uppermost in the minds of the township dramatists then was gangsterism. So my story was based on the actions and the practices of these gangsters who were making life unpleasant in the townships.

What did you call that play?

NkoNzombi, which means Bad Service in English. That was the name of the leading character and the name of the play. It was a musical, because it was very difficult to do anything in the townships if you didn't have lots and lots of music to accompany it. Even though the story line might be very strong, the people out there in the township wanted to be entertained. And music was thus a kind of a vehicle to entertain them. So from that moment I never looked back. We came together here in East London as a group of aspiring dramatists called Imitha

Players, and we performed under the leadership of Rob Amato. We did a production of *Oedipus Rex*, the Greek tragedy, where I was cast as the leading player, Oedipus himself. But by then I had already begun on the script of a new play. I gave it the title, *Not His Pride*. It was later published by Ravan Press at the beginning of 1978.

From there I moved on to a few other interesting things. In 1976 I was called by a group in Cape Town called Sechaba to take part in a production of a play called *Sacrifice of Kreli*, written by a woman called Fatima Dike. Rob again was supposed to be the producer of the play. In fact he put in some money to take it on a tour of South Africa. I ended up directing it, jointly with Rob, while I remained the leading actor and manager. I was a jack of all trades, which is typical of township cultural activity. You end up doing so many things, because of limited resources.

Again I got an idea, which I felt needed a lot of investigation, because I'd read about this in the *Drum* magazine. It was about a man who had been banished from Transkei, in Pondoland, by the Matanzima regime, because of his active involvement in what was called the Pondo uprising. He was banished I think in 1963, to a place which is a semi-desert area anyway, near Bechuanaland (Botswana). He lived there for about thirteen years. The man was called Theophilus Tsangela, and was one of the leaders of the Pondo uprising in the early sixties. When he got there he reared some livestock and thus eked out a living, using his own kind of native genius, and he was a very resourceful man.

So this story struck me, and I felt I needed to do something about it. I researched the story and travelled to the Transkei, and other places, trying to pick up information about this man. And I spoke to his next of kin, and some of them were in Johannesburg, in Soweto. I interviewed a number of people here in East London, too. In 1979 I produced a play, which I titled *The Last Man*.

This was a play once again which had significant entertainment value in it, music and dance, but there was no orchestra. It was just incidental music. But it was very entertaining, and I got some very nice notices from the press.

At the end of 1979 I enrolled as a student at Wits University and did a four-year degree in dramatic art. A year after finishing the degree I went overseas on a British Council scholarship to Leeds. I went to the famous Workshop Theatre and was there for one year. While I was in

Leeds I produced a play called *The Bargain*, because one of my major courses there was play-writing apart from directing. I produced *The Bargain* with my fellow students.

After that I went to London for two and a half years, where I wrote a play called *Bongi's Struggle* for three South African women who had gone over to England with *Ipi Tombi*, and had decided that they wanted to stay on.

In 1990 I decided to come back. When I got back here, I became very much involved with community theatre. Professor Mavis Taylor in Cape Town invited me to create a play for her students, because she set up a little school called the New Africa Theatre Project. I wrote a play based on gangsterism in 1990. When I came back to East London from Cape Town, I did a play with the residents of an informal settlement called Glenmore, between Peddie and Grahamstown. These people had been chased away by South Africa and were accommodated by Sebe, who created a residential area for them. Not that I want to speak well of him, but they were caught between Sebe and South Africa, between the devil and the deep blue sea.

Sebe was then the strong-man in Ciskei?

Yes, he was the so-called President of Ciskei. So when South Africa chased them away, Sebe seemed to take pity on them. But the community said, 'This is not Canaan, the Promised Land that we were invited to.' I was invited there to create a play, because these people wanted to enjoy a decent life out of their experience there, and I created this play which addressed their problems, based on their day-to-day survival.

Back in East London at the end of 1990 I wrote a play called *This or Nothing* and produced it for what I call the Mdantsane Community Theatre Project. Mdantsane is a black township about twenty-five kilometres from East London. Again it was created as a result of the Group Areas Act, when people were driven away from the old Duncan Village in East London.

At the end of 1990 I got a job as a community theatre consultant with the health department of Ciskei. The health department joined the education department that I worked for. What I did was to go to the clinics, work with the nurses and doctors there, asking if there were any problems there, related to health and population development.

And, on the other hand, the education department was enjoying my services too, because whenever there was a need to produce and stage a play based on the set-work for matriculants, they would contact me. For instance, I became a so-called expert in dramatising Shakespearean works for black kids in the Eastern Cape. So I served that dual purpose in the border area from 1990 till the end of 1994.

At the end of 1994 I was invited by the Fort Hare University rector to consider joining the staff as a visiting lecturer in the English department, with a view to giving me an opportunity to set up a travelling theatre company at the university. And I am hoping that this year, or the beginning of next year at the latest, I will set up such a travelling theatre company.

At the present moment I am busy producing a play called *Member of Society*, which I wrote for a local group here, in the wake of the political and social transformation in the country. The idea is to say to people, 'Here is the opportunity for you to become a member of the society that you have always yearned for'.

So you see theatre as an instrument to address the problems of the New South Africa?

I think so. I think theatre can significantly work as an infrastructure for education, formally and informally. Theatre has definitely got a role to play in socialising people, so that they can become members of the new society, so that they can have pride in their own country, take control of their own lives, become responsible: they can stand up and be counted. Theatre challenges not just the audience but also the maker. The theatre is that kind of a double-edged sword. In the days of apartheid in South Africa we were mostly involved in Protest Theatre, and were always too happy to criticise the regime here, and thus took ourselves for granted.

But at the same time we were investigating our own selves and our own lives, we ought to have been equally critical of our own perceptions of life here in South Africa. What role did we play in helping the regime to oppress us? Theatre is that kind of tool.

You know John Kani, of course, who is now Director at the Market Theatre. How do you look at the established theatre venues in comparison with the township- and travelling-theatre groups?

Well, the established theatres will not in any period of time meet the needs of the township audiences, because they are exclusive and because you have to travel to get there if you live in a township. Not everyone has got transport. There is also the fact that good theatre shows are held in the evening or at night. There is a built-in mechanism to exclude people, so there is no way that those theatres can meet the needs of the people. What they can do, of course, is to tantalise people and say, 'Look, what a gem of theatre, but maybe it is not for you until you've got a car (laughing).' That's a problem at the moment, you know. There is no way in which we can imagine that the established venues are going to come to our rescue. Government has got to try and create community art centres, so that people can feel that they are not left out in the dark. They've got to have a home to try out their own talent.

It is not enough for the local people to utilise that venue, but the theatre managements from this established theatre must come to those community art centres and see what is going on there, because so long as there is a gulf between the theatres that belong to the affluent society and the theatres that are at the disposal of the poor artist, there never will be a chance of transforming all this energy into something that is going to service everyone. The townships have been used for a long time as kind of a workshop by everyone for things to be tried out, and when they are ready, they are taken to the Market Theatre. As soon as they are shown to sophisticated audiences there, and acclaimed critically, there's no way the companies responsible for the productions are going to look back or be bothered about their obligation to improve townshiptheatre.

So, really, it's a terrible situation where you're going to watch your own experience being made into something artistic, and as soon as people come and see it, and say, 'Ah, this is a terrific play', they kiss it goodbye. What it leaves in its wake is a series of frustrations. People become frustrated because some of those who have been left out there thought they deserved the opportunity. And this is terrible, Rolf, this is tragic! The township audiences will have been introduced to this venue in town. Try as you might, to come up with something very good in the township and put it on in one of the township halls, people are not going to come there because they're used to going to the Market Theatre. So it really is tragic that townships have been largely responsible for creating a theatre which has been acclaimed worldwide for being representative of South African talent, but those audiences that were directly responsible for offering the material for those productions, don't want to come and see those finished products in their own back yards. They travel all the way to town, a) because in town the venues are good and, b) it is the status thing: they get a certain satisfaction from being seen watching a play in the so-called multiracial theatres.

So what is one to do?

I think one has to go to the government, which is largely representative of the aspirations of the people, and make the government create companies which must service the townships. And I think a mechanism has got to be created that operates, perhaps, along the lines of a rotational pattern, to attract the good critics to come and see the same productions in different venues.

Are you aware of Matsemela Manaka's work along those lines?

Yes.

What do you think of his ways of approaching things?

Well, I must admit I haven't been to see any of his theatre productions since 1991, but I think he is a man with very good ideas. And the work he did at Funda Centre when it started was phenomenal in terms of creating new awareness in the townships. The only thing was that in his case it was just one man who didn't get enough support from all of us. So again the problem was how in black theatre we tend to want to work in isolation from the rest of the people. Sometimes it is because I guess we are interested in advancing our own careers. But at the same time people tend to create rivalry out of nothing, and say, 'Look, that's Matsemela Manaka, he's doing his own thing' – instead of throwing in our lot with Matsemela, and creating something jointly.

It seems that Manaka and others are looking for a fusion of committed or communal theatre and the old Gibson Kente tradition. What do you think of that proposition? Any comments on practitioners who are working along those lines?

Ja, I think it has become a conscious thing, because whether you like it or not, living in a township you'll be tuned in to what people want. And you will end up doing what people want even though you don't do it consciously. But it is part of your own make-up, part of your subconscious thinking. But at the end of the day – as a writer you like music, you like to dance, so you end up including those things in your theatre, even though you know it has been, perhaps wrongly, associated exclusively with Gibson Kente.

But you know that's your theatre too, because art in black communities is not really perceived, or even practised in terms of isolating it from other disciplines. You dance within a context, you sing within a context, and you act within a context, and that context is dependent on music, dancing, praise-singing and divining as a *sangoma*, – all sorts of things. So what I am saying is that art in a black community context is the fusion of so many things, so many practices. The conclusion is: Yes, that particular orientation may dominate, but surrounding that there will be many other instances which you may not even have thought about, which suggest that art is not practised in a cultural vacuum. It is a combination of so many elements.

When you look forward to the development of South Africa now under the new dispensation, do you see any particular trends, any particular themes that are likely to be on the theatrical agenda?

I suppose what we are going to be seeing in the not-too-distant future is a trend of different racial and cultural communities coming together in a production that is going to reflect that diversity of people. It may be a bit too contrived for a start, but after a while it is going to be a norm.

Do you see this as a reflection of the stage where you started with the Imitha Players, which was a combined effort of whites and, I suppose, coloureds and blacks?

No, not really. You see, and I'm going to be very cynical: white people have always perceived themselves as directors, directing black companies, black artists, and never wanting to be part and parcel of the acting business. They've always been directors, writers and, of course, producers insofar as money is concerned. During the time of the Imitha

Players and whatever other groups were operating at the time, it was a matter of a black group transferring their power into the hands of a white person in the name of learning. So the relations cannot be the same.

Couldn't you see that as being a consequence of a lack of trained black personnel at the time?

Ja, to a great extent it was. But at the same time I could not find any reason why white directors could not say, 'Look, I've trained you. Here's an opportunity for you to take over and direct.' Yet again we were directed by people who had no theatrical background, except a strong mission. None of us have the Ph.D. qualifications they have today, based on African experience.

Wasn't that done? Weren't you given such opportunities to direct?

Well, certainly not in the Eastern Cape. I cannot think of any plays where . . .

You mentioned earlier the Sacrifice of Kreli, *where you took the leading part. Didn't you say you were invited to join in the production? Or did I misunderstand you?*

No, I acted the leading part, and I also directed. *Ja*, I directed because there was no director. The people concerned tried all over to get a director to come, but that director would have required payment. Now, it was cheap to use me. Mr Amato came to assist me after 5 o'clock as he was a businessman running factories during the day. It was a lot easier for him to come and take my hard day's work apart when everyone was tired already.

Oh, I see.

Ja, because I never demanded any fee of a director. So I acted, I directed, I managed for very meagre money. Of course I was not bitter. I didn't feel that I was being robbed or exploited. Because I felt it was something I just wanted to do. But the fact of the matter is that historically in this country, artists have had a master-servant relationship with white directors. Ultimately it's up to the present generation of actors to reverse this legacy, and earn themselves a bit of respect.

In the context of your own personal situation, will you pursue this combination of commissioned writing and acting? Do you do much acting these days?

I don't act any longer now, I don't. I miss it. I miss hearing my voice on stage and reading about myself in the newspaper columns. I don't do that any longer because there is so much to do as a writer and a director.

You mentioned this crossroads between the provincial ministries of health and education. Will you be developing that any further?

I would like to, informally, because at Fort Hare, as I told you, I've been asked to set up a theatre company. I am going to have to address problems that relate to education, formally and informally, health, development of large economic projects – just about everything. So it's going to be a theatre for development in the true sense of the word – health, education, economics and politics will come into it.

Have you accepted this invitation?

Yes, I have accepted it, because I spent the whole of last year teaching in the English department, with a view to sensitising students to this theatre project.

So you are going to pursue this now?

Yes.

Sounds very interesting and challenging. Any other plans, any other projects on your slate?

I've been approached by a returnee international celebrity to write a play on some of the early Eastern Cape Xhosa leaders. He's promised to score the music. He wants me to try and recapture that history and put it on stage. So far we have been writing in the vein of protest, but now it's about time we remembered that we have a past, a history prior to apartheid, and that history must always be reviewed, in terms of what was good about it and what can still be practised.

Before we wind up this talk, is there anything else you would like to bring up?

It's a great pity that there's no Truth Commission set up to investigate any irregularities in the sphere of arts and culture. We've been insulted in the past by our liberal friends. Just to quote from my personal experience: while I was producing *Meko* in Johannesburg in 1972, a well-known theatre director of that time had just come back from the UK with some funds for his predominantly black company. He then 'took pity' on me and offered to donate to my group R500, but on condition that all fourteen of us were willing to live together under one roof, I mean in one of these 3-roomed houses in Soweto . . . Of course I rejected those conditions, and so the money could not be forthcoming.

Rolf, this man had been accused of being a wolf in a sheep's skin by some of our township friends. Were they wrong? That's the kind of man who believed that for a black man to go to Britain was the highest honour he can ever enjoy. I am naming no names, but he said that to a fellow actor. *Sies!*

Rolf, there is another thing as well which has always sickened me, and that's the attention the Johannesburg art and theatre companies are getting from overseas theatre managements to the exclusion of what is going on in places such as ours. Yet over the years the Eastern Cape has always ferried to Johannesburg, not only material, but also actors and other artists of note. The next thing we hear is that there is a festival happening in Norway, or in Denmark, and no companies, no groups from the Eastern Cape have been invited. And I find that very frustrating.

Let's hope this is the turning point, then. It has certainly been very interesting to hear voices also from the Eastern Cape in this series of interviews.

Ronnie Govender

Mr Govender, could we begin with a few words about the early days? Would you care to reflect briefly on the events that set you on to a theatrical career?

I will have to go back to the 1950s. Theatre was then non-existent for blacks in South Africa – I'm talking of formal theatre. And belonging to a minority community in the sense that I am a descendant of the 1860s settlers, who came here to work in the sugar plantations, so-called indentured labourers. I am a descendant of that community. And apart from their own folk theatre which they brought along from India, there wasn't much else. There wasn't much else for me as South African, because I was third generation and very much a South African.

I got attracted to the theatre because of various influences. My mother used to take me along to see the epic Tamil songs, where the good guys were good and the bad guys were bad. Very early in life I was exposed to these things. Much later, at high school, we were treated to a 'special' performance for non-whites of a production of *Oedipus Rex*. I was transfixed by the performance of André Huguenot: you have probably heard about him as a great Platteland actor. And this was at the City Hall, which wasn't a theatre. We were seated right out there in the gallery, and it was a stirring performance.

When was this?

Oh, this was in the early fifties. I wanted so much to be part of the theatre, but there was nothing for us, and I decided not to just sit back and do nothing about it. I started a little group and we put on the first production of a South African adaptation of *Antigone*, which at the time was very relevant to South Africa. We attracted the attention, of course, of the Special Branch.

We went on, nevertheless. Eventually we formed a group called the Shah Theatre Academy which trained a number of people: among them were Welcome Msomi, Kessie Govender, Saths Cooper, and Benji Frances, now in Johannesburg. Alan Joseph (now a major figure) came out of this initiative. And this is how we started our own theatre.

So I was involved in training people, which we did without any grants, without any remuneration. My writing was done on a part-time basis. I got a job as a teacher until I got into conflict with the system because of my political views. And then I branched out later as a sales representative for a brewery.

But in that time I wrote several plays. I experimented quite a bit, and eventually I wrote the play called *The Lahnee's Pleasure*, which was, I think, one of the first plays that transcribed Natal Indian patois onto the South African stage. It was one of the first South African plays that really dealt with South Africans of my community.

The play was a runaway success. We played in a makeshift theatre, in the Himalaya Hotel in Grey Street, a six-hundred seater. It was L-shaped; we had a stage in a corner and constructed the stage ourselves; we did everything from writing the play, training the actors, directing the play, producing the play, putting up posters, etc. On opening night we turned away people. Couldn't believe it! A six-hundred seater!

What are we talking about now, the early '70s?

We are now up to 1974. I am not talking of the intervening years when I did other work. So in 1974 we did *The Lahnee's Pleasure* and it was amazing, because it ran for twelve weeks, every night except Sundays, with capacity crowds. We were offered a sizable amount of money to play in a hitherto white theatre in Johannesburg. The management told me that they would apply for a permit, and the permit would allow only Indians and coloureds. They obviously felt that they had offered me a nice carrot. And I said, 'Go jump in the lake!' I was stupid enough to do that, to turn down such a lot of money. But seriously, what else could I have done?

And we went along to the Market Theatre where we played four weeks running, capacity crowds again. We would have run longer at the Market, but our guys were only part-time actors, and they had full-time jobs, so we had to make the choice, and, of course, I left the choice to them, and understandably they came back home to start working again.

Who was in charge of the Market then? Was it Barney Simon?

Barney was at the Market, but he wasn't in charge, it was Mannie Manim.

Did you have contact with people like Gibson Kente and his theatrical activities in those days?

Not direct contact, but it was about this time that Gibson was doing a lot of work in the townships. And I met him very briefly, and I doubt whether he himself will remember that.

Do you reckon he has been as important for the development of South African theatre as some people appear to think?

He was important in the sense that he did work. He worked in places where there was no theatre at all. He reflected on the lives of people, and they easily identified with his plays. So they were major box office successes.

Whether in fact I agree that the stuff he's done is of any real worth, I don't know. I think there were far better writers, if one may say that, in the black community than Gibson Kente. I think that the bottom line was that Gibson Kente was working to a formula. His last play was panned by the critics, more because it poses naive political solutions than for any other reason.

When was this?

At the Grahamstown Festival about two years ago, I think.

Have you been in touch with the so-called serious, 'committed' black writers/dramatists from the late seventies onwards?

Yes, I would say so. I have been in touch with them. However, many of the serious writers have been scattered throughout the country, and more particularly in Johannesburg, so contact hasn't been all that close.

Manaka was saying that in his experience, Kente's work has created such a strong tradition, that he himself and people of his ilk find it difficult to break through it.

But I think this is the challenge. We mustn't assume too much in terms of our audiences. We tend to underestimate them, we do that, you know. We once did a play called *Riders to the Sea*, by J.M. Synge, for a festival in Johannesburg, at that stage run by Union Artists. The festival was to culminate in Soweto. We had a mixed cast, which was illegal at the time. One of the players was Welcome Msomi, the creator of *Umabatha*. We did it at the so-called Bantu Men's Social Centre in Beatrice Street, and in those days we used to call people off the streets to come and watch theatre. And we managed to get a fair-sized crowd. It wasn't a theatre, of course, it was just a hall, a community hall.

We staged this play, just wanting to see what the reaction would be. I think we ourselves were rather surprised. We had the arrogance of youth also, thinking that these people wouldn't really appreciate this 'foreign' play. And then we had a meeting afterwards, where we allowed for free discussion. We were totally amazed at the kind of responses we got from the audience. It indicated quite clearly that although they were deprived of theatre, they certainly had a keen eye for works of art, and had opinions about it, sound opinions.

You are now in charge of the Playhouse Theatre, the major theatre next to the City Hall, aren't you?

Yes.

I know there are mixed opinions about the relative value of the permanent city venues and the experimental community theatres. Have you any views on that?

I would agree with the view that in the past these theatres actually worked against the interest of the people. And, in fact, against the interest of the art. Because what was being done here was all bourgeois Eurocentric stuff. While the rest of the world was breaking away from that kind of thing and was looking at life as honestly as possible, we weren't doing that here. We were just stuck in our little mould. And there was a danger of the black bourgeoisie following suit. I would say that in the past that was the case. At the same time I think that there is a place for the city theatre, while, of course, we must put in a lot more effort, a lot more energy, and a lot more money into fostering community theatre. It is not as if we must emphasise one before the other. We must, of course, address the imbalance that there is at the moment, and, as I said, promote community theatre.

I talked to Zakes Mda about twelve months ago. He is sceptical when it comes to the city theatres in general, because in his view they are perceived by playwrights as stepping-stones towards Broadway. A view which seems to be borne out by Mbongeni Ngema. Any comments on that?

Yes, certainly. Again I think the emphasis is wrong. Broadway will always be there, and it isn't as if to say that nothing good is being done on Broadway. I mean we understand that commercial theatre, the establishment theatre, dominates in London, in Paris, in Toronto, on Broadway, anywhere. However, we can't deny that good theatre occurs there. The whole point, I think, at the end of the day, is to look at the administration, to look at the orientation of these places, and say, 'How can these places now be returned to the people,' as it were? And to get greater participation along those lines. I know it is a difficult battle, but on the other hand, if we adopt a scorched earth policy, we will in fact be depriving ourselves. These structures are there, and skilled people are employed here. I think it is for us now to say that these centres must be returned to the people while still being centres of excellence. This would help greatly in fostering a true South African theatre.

How could you envisage theatre being reintroduced or expanded into the townships?

I think it is a holistic problem. I think we need to look at it in all its different aspects. We have to look at formal education. We have to look at services being rendered in the townships. All these things will impact again on the cultural life. And while that is happening we mustn't just neglect the cultural life and take for granted that things will happen the moment the standards of the people improve. I think, as I said, that this is a holistic thing. Theatre is life. There are no fixed formulas. However, if we remove the old limitations on the growth of an organic South African theatre, if we remove those limitations – in the townships, in the rural areas, wherever – we will give theatre the opportunity to flourish.

Do you see the money coming forward for that kind of expansion?

No, I think because of the years of apartheid devastation we have an immense backlog in social terms. And there are major priorities, although as a writer, as a cultural person, culture to me is just as big a priority as anything else. However, one must understand the fact that you have to have a roof over your head, you've got to have education, policing – all that.

I think that those are priorities that of necessity will cut into the piece of cake that is set aside for culture, however little. The necessary funds won't be forthcoming from the state, understandably. But I think that the corporate sector could play a major role. As, in fact, some of them are doing at the moment.

Can you see education through theatre being used as a lever in order to open up coffers in various cities, and for taxes or other moneys to flow into this?

Rather than as a lever I think what must be brought home is the fact that a city, a country without theatre, without culture, is a city or a country without a soul. I think we must bring home this perception, and in fact I think that is happening to an extent – this consciousness, this awareness that theatre like other kinds of art or culture are there to enhance one's life.

You are talking of consciousness. What is, in your view, the aftermath of the impact of Black Consciousness on the theatre?

I think as long as you have people who are exploited, as long as you have people who are being subjected to the abuse of power in one form or the other, you will always have the necessity for people to be given that sense of dignity, and that can only come about with belief in oneself. There are overriding powerful forces at work at the moment

– in all honesty we must accept the fact that there are very dominant cultures. It will perhaps take a different form. Black Consciousness arose in the face of jackboot repression. I think the focus has now shifted. But this shouldn't be confused with the kind of ethnicity that is tearing many parts of the world apart. I think it's quite important that we have a responsibility to assert the dignity, self-worth, self-esteem of all people.

Do any of these things come out in your own work?

I hope so, I sincerely hope so.

Could you say something about your own work as a playwright and as a producer?

When my last play, which was *At the Edge*, was invited to the Edinburgh Festival and to Toronto, *Stage and Television Today*, which is an authoritative magazine in London, regarded it as 'a hymn to humanity'. It certainly won much critical acclaim. I think these plays have been acclaimed by critics for precisely that. That also goes for plays like *The Lahnee's Pleasure*, which was staged in 1974.

And then I did some political satire at a time when political satire brought forth heavy-handed action from the security police. All forms of political protest were being crushed. At this time I did a play called *Offside*, which was a musical satire on the tri-cameral parliament. Indians and coloureds were brought into parliament to show to the outside world that there were steps being taken towards democracy. And of course the real leaders of both groups were all banned and organisations that sought to educate the people were banned. *Offside* was staged before thousands of people – in tents and make-shift venues in the townships. And I followed that up with a satire called *Inside*. That was, to my mind, very, very political, although there was a good deal of entertainment in it – it was a musical satire.

Do you operate a lot with music, dancing, like people in the Kente tradition?

No, well – I think there has been a fair mix. But it doesn't dominate in my work. But I have had some works that have had music and songs.

One thing that surprised me a bit in the Manaka interview was that after having in a sense collided with the Kente tradition, in having had near-riots at a performance of Pula, I think it was, which had been advertised at the end of a Kente show, he realised that they had to take the Kente tradition into account. He seems to be suggesting that the coming together of the Gibson Kente tradition and plays like Mbongeni Ngema and Mtwa's Woza Albert, *may initiate a sort of fusion of 'committed' Black Theatre and Gibson Kente's more popular brand of theatre – into what seems to be the present line of Ngema. Could you comment on that?*

I am surprised that *Woza Albert* is regarded in that light. *Woza Albert* in itself is an outstanding piece of work. It stands on its own. I don't know, really. In terms of form, shape and content, I find it hard to realise that Kente had some kind of influence on the formation on this piece of work. Is that what he is saying or . . .

No, not he, but his contention seems to be that the popular genre of theatre, fused with this 'serious' theatre of people like Mtwa and Matsemela Manaka, might be a 'new' genre to take to the townships.

For me *Woza Albert* had much of the spontaneity of folk theatre. And it was profound. It was given much shape, of course, by the fact that it was put into a formal theatre. But that didn't kill the spontaneity that it had. And I found it exciting from that point of view. So I would disagree.

How about Ngema's recent successes abroad with pieces like Sarafina *? Is that a line of development that will bring any joy to South African theatre, or is it a sort of dead end? These were things I would have liked to put directly to Ngema, but he was too busy to give me an interview.*

Well, it depends on what one wants from life, from theatre.

If one sees it now in terms of the establishment of the New South Africa?

Look, it's working for Ngema, and I suppose that's where he is heading for. But whether in fact that is good for South African theatre is a totally different matter. I don't know. While there is a place for Ngema's kind of theatre, as there is for all kinds of theatre, I think the danger would be for that kind of theatre to be dominant. We must guard against that. We must be vigilant in the sense that we must work towards a situation where we provide for the other forms of theatre and be as assertive about it as we can.

I listened, you see, to a talk given by one of the professors up on the hill, who seemed to suggest that maybe it would be a good thing now to look more to popular theatre than to 'serious' theatre, maybe because he was looking at the issue in terms of bringing theatre to the people, to the dispossessed, and using it as a source of empowerment and uplifting of the masses, the educational role of theatre.

I would say there is some sense in that. Obviously when you've gone to a place where people have never seen theatre, and you've made this accessible to them, you are providing a service. Again, one could perhaps say the same thing of the American video, which you might find played in some forlorn place to first-time viewers: one could hope that this would lead them on to better theatre. I don't know whether that kind of thing works, but to say that it doesn't have any effect at all is another matter. I think as writers we all have a responsibility firstly to ourselves and to our work, to ensure that what we're doing we're doing honestly, and that we are not in any way being influenced by factors such as crass commercialism. One has got to live, and one has got to earn something out of the work that one does. But when crass commercialism enters into it, that's another matter.

What do you see for yourself as a writer and dramatist as important themes that you might wish to pursue, or that you are pursuing, seeing it again in the light of the struggle that is over and the new country that is in the process of being built?

From my experiences and from the kind of perspectives that I have, I write from deep feeling. If I am moved about something that is happening, I think that is the impetus for me to write. Art must challenge us, it must challenge life, challenging and looking at life as honestly as possible. So I think my themes will come from that kind of perspective.

Would you be backward-looking or would you be forward-looking?

I don't really know. We grew up in the apartheid situation – it has affected our very psyche, it has impacted on our lives. And while you may not directly write about apartheid as such and those years, you cannot ignore it. If you are writing such a play set in the fifties or the sixties, and you are writing about a person then, you are writing about a person who is in an apartheid situation. So from that point of view you cannot ignore it.

But politically?

I don't know. Human nature with all its complexities. Except for something as overtly political as *Inside* or *Offside*, which were specific to a political cause.

In satire?

Yes. Even in satire – the starting point has been people. In those times, I've written about people. And I think I've got those kind of responses from reviewers and critics, who have pointed to that.

And that will also be your course in future?

Yeah.

What are you working on at the moment, if I may ask that?

I've written a series of short stories on Cato Manor. The collection won the prize for the short story category in the Martel V.O. Literary Competition (Skotaville).

But prior to that I'd done four of the stories and dramatised them, and that made up the play *At the Edge*. It was about the people of Cato Manor, the first area to be destroyed by the Group Areas Act. And I subsequently dramatised four more of those stories which will be staged in 1996.

Here?

No, not here. I am very careful about staging my plays here at the Playhouse. I don't want to take advantage of my position here. I will be doing this one play here, that is *The Lahnee's Pleasure*. But I am not going to do another play this year in this venue. I'll be doing it outside, in a community venue or somewhere else. This is different from my job as a director of this complex, you see.

Before I joined the Playhouse, they commissioned me to do a play on Gandhi. However, I have had to put that on the back burner for a little. I've done a lot of research and I am very excited about what has come up in that research.

There have been many attempts to do something about Gandhi. Having done this research I feel there is so much about this great man. My only problem is I don't want to contribute to the building of an icon. He himself would have been totally against that: but there is rich material for me as a writer in response to a request.

Approaching the end of this interview now, let me ask as a final question: do you hold any specific views when it comes to South African theatre and language? Some dramatists appear to be for the use of indigenous languages in all sorts of mixes depending on the township or area in which they happen to be performing, rather than falling back on English as lingua franca.

Of necessity I think these languages must now be given their birthright. I think it is important to do that, and I am all for greater encouragement to people writing in different languages. However, I think, while that's being done we mustn't do it at the expense of any other language, even English. While I agree totally that we must foster all these languages and give them their place in the sun, which they didn't have in the past, I personally have always written in English. I come from a Tamil-speaking background. To my great shame I cannot speak Tamil. And I think those people who are Tamilians, they should also be given the opportunity of getting their place in the sun. But for me I find that English as a language holds so much possibility for a writer, but that's purely personal.

Kessie Govender

Kessie Govender, how did you get into theatre in the first place?

That is not something I could easily put my finger on. It was something that evolved from the time I was a little boy. It's like in the Christian institutions where singers begin in gospel choirs and eventually break into the music world. Being a person of Hindu leanings I belonged to a Hindu Shivite temple organisation, and part of the tradition there was singing, dancing and drama. These are worshippers of Shiva, the sun god. As part of the culture you sang and you enacted the various roles in the religious calendar. That started at the age of about, say, six. And from there on it simply evolved. Something inside of me just made me continue with it. This was a vernacular Tamil school. And then I also attended English school, where I did quite well, and my English was pretty good. Together with that was my interest in reading. I couldn't stop reading. Even now I am a compulsive reader. That inquisitiveness in me – and also the whole concept of appearing on stage – pushed me through, and I stuck it out. I gave up formal education at a very young age, though, and I served an apprenticeship as a builder, a bricklayer.

During my apprentice days the urge to get on the stage was very strong. Then I met a group of high-school students in 1960 who were preparing a variety concert which they called 'Christmas Nuts'. I asked if I could join them. They were all strangers to me, but they said, 'If you can sing a song or play an instrument you are welcome to join us.' I didn't know any songs that I liked, so I went home and wrote one, and came back and said, 'I've got a song.'

That group remained together. There was a woman called Muthal Naidoo who was a lecturer at the local tech, and she sort of formalised the structure. We got down to workshops at the weekends, and we eventually decided that we were going to make a play. At that time one of the most recognised writers was Arthur Miller. For some reason or other she went for American plays, and I did my first major role in Arthur Miller's *All My Sons*. And you can say that it then began. I just couldn't get out of it.

What was Durban like as a theatre city at the time, in the early sixties?

It was not a theatre city at all as far as the black sector was concerned. Well, there were productions going on, and there was a period when I got involved with the Durban Academy of Theatre Art, where they did a play once a year. It was mostly professional people, meaning people like doctors, lawyers, the academics. It was sort of an elitist club. They used to produce a Molière – one of the French farces, or one of the Elizabethan farces. I was involved with them for a while, but because I was an apprentice bricklayer they thought I didn't want to get involved on the stage. All I did was to help build the sets and move the sets about. They would call us stage hands, and assistant stage managers and that kind of stuff.

Coming back to your question what the theatres were like during that period – there was no theatre, really. In the Indian vernacular sector they would have these occasional variety concerts, or one of those historic epics related to Indian mythology – once a year, perhaps.

But theatre addressing the needs of people as such was actually non-existent. In productions like the Arthur Miller ones, you rehearsed the play, you put it together, you got the posters sorted out and the stage set – you did everything that was necessary for the production itself. You weren't just an actor. At any rate it wasn't so with me. Because of my building skills I also got into building the sets, and because I am also a bit of an artist I contributed towards creating the posters. Lighting was pretty crude in those days. If you could get sufficient light to light up the stage there wasn't any specialised lighting as such.

Sometimes you had a demo-board to fade in and fade out, or you would just snap off and snap on, whatever the case might be. And after doing all those things you would then also go out and sell your tickets. You'd go door-to-door and sell tickets! The tickets in those days were generally about a rand and fifty cents. That is how the theatre went on.

A couple of years later Ronnie Govender joined us. He also wanted to formalise and get the necessary committees and get a formal structure created and a name given to this group of people, and he called it the Shah Theatre Academy, which is named after Krishna Shah. Ronnie also introduced the concept of indigenous writing. He wrote some plays, and I took part in some of them. This went on all the way up until 1972. But in between I would break away and join up with other theatre groups and get into plays with them. It wasn't that I wanted to be 'loose' in any way, but I thought that the experience of being under different directors was necessary, different plays were necessary – approaches like that were a necessity. Ronnie was, of course, very annoyed at this, because he felt that if you belonged to a theatre organisation you owed your allegiance to it. I didn't in any way break my allegiance, but there was this need to experiment, to know more. And I did that from about 1962–63 right up until about 1972–73.

Come to about 1969–70, the situation in the country itself was beginning to foment in a manner of speaking, so that the black people were getting a lot more frustrated round about that period. There was a sense of growing political awareness. It became necessary now to look at the people around us and look at their ignorance as far as the political situation was concerned.

What was also very noticeable was that there was this element of complacency among the general mass. But there were those groups of people that took on the responsibility of becoming 'representatives' of the Indian community. They were working quite closely with the government itself – they were collaborators with the government, trying to get a bit here and a bit there. And there was also the element of becoming 'Indianised'.

From our side we felt that we were not 'Indians', we were black people. And whatever was happening to the African community should affect us also. With the whole concept of Black Consciousness, with Steve Biko coming into the picture, and with Strini Moodley, Satch Cooper, Dennis Potter and people like that coming onto the scene, we became a lot more politically conscious. And, of course, unwittingly, the government itself was pushing us in a certain direction because they were beginning to show a certain amount of interest in the artists and the theatre people in the city. They created this Special Branch, as they referred to it, of the police force, and the bulk of it was concentrating on activists. And if you belonged to the theatre spectrum you were branded as being an activist until you sort of proved yourself otherwise. This pressure from the Special Branch – they were trying to question us, to be around where we were and just lurking there – made us a lot more conscious of what the government was trying to do.

The government in its own way was looking at these people involved in the arts as people who had the ability to communicate with the masses. We didn't really look at it from that point of view at the time. But when you are under pressure, and you are more conscious of what is happening around you, then you realise that there is this avenue that is available, and you've got to make the best use of it. This meant now, that when you were choosing plays, you had to be very careful. And if you were writing plays, you had to make sure that the kind of play you were writing was going to say something to the people. We weren't going to just discuss mundane activities. The situation at that time was such that we were very divided. And as Indians we were not exposed to that many African people.

Did you think of yourself as a spokesman for the specifically Indian part of the community at the time?

No, we didn't look at it that way. You see, quite a number of events were meshing themselves. I must say that I was pretty young at that time, and also I was not devoting all my time to theatre. I was a builder during the day and an actor in the evening, and my exposure to the arts spectrum was more in the evenings and during productions. But reading played its role, and friends – there was a process of influence that was going on. When the Black Consciousness Movement was created and launched, all theatre companies in the country were asked to contribute towards the launch, meaning you had to come up with some kind of production or other, or with poetry, or write an essay for this particular launch that occurred in Cape Town.

And you were a Black Consciousness person, were you?

Yes. Through our exposure to this whole new spectrum, and strengthened by what was happening, we were demanding a lot more of ourselves. Of course, lots of people were telling you to move cautiously because the Special Branch didn't ask any questions, they just brought you in. At this time there was an element of arrogance from our side also. They could lock you up, or the worst thing they could do was to kill you. There were a lot of people dying in prison at that time.

It was because of that process, and when I saw that the right kind of scripts were not forthcoming, that I decided to start writing. The awareness among the masses was now being strengthened: more and more people were coming to the theatres. It wasn't in its full thrust in any way, but people were more conscious of the theatre. However, I could see that we were not getting through to the masses themselves. We were addressing a sort of semi-élitist kind of community, especially academics. And that wasn't good enough for me. I found that to encompass the whole thing, plays had to be written where the central characters were not necessarily teachers and lawyers and students and university people.

So that launched you into writing?

Yes. And I decided that the central characters would have to be people from the street – street sweepers, garbage collectors, factory workers. And I put the play together with these kind of people in it, and also wrote the spoken language for the stage to a point where anybody could understand it.

How would you define this language?

At the time I wouldn't say I was consciously aware of it. But it did seem that the writers of the period were trying to show how clever they themselves were by the choice of the words they were using – words that the layman doesn't use – in order to show that they were a bit more intelligent than the other person. I think the writers were guilty of that sort of thing. I told myself, if a person is coming to view a play, there mustn't be a process where he has got to start thinking about the language, he's got to start *absorbing*. It's got to be direct. And for you to get direct communication and avoid that sort of thinking you have to speak his language. You must speak a language that he will understand, from the person on the ground level, for lack of a better description, up to the academic level. And obviously, if you can reach this person, you're certainly going to reach that person up there. And that's when I decided we'd have to start changing the language structure, the English itself would have to be toned down, be made accessible.

So I started writing. I didn't know that I could write, because when I first started writing, I wasn't handy with the pen. But I had people around me who would write while I dictated. And that's how we got my first play put together.

Which was . . .?

Stablexpense. It spoke of the Group Areas Act and what it was doing to the people, and also of the destabilisation process that was happening – the building of townships on the outer fringes of the city and people being displaced, as well as the role of the Special Branch in this process of making people toe the line.

It was also about the attitude of the Indians towards the white person – the 'Yes Baas' mentality was still strong at this time you understand – that the white man couldn't do any wrong as far as the Indians were concerned. And I wanted to break that myth. It was a very, very strong attitude which they hung on to, especially the older generation. And I must admit that one of the nicest things that came to my notice after writing this play was when I met a person living out at Stanger, which is about sixty kilometres north of Durban, who was working for Clover Dairies. I met him in town and he came up to me and he said, 'Mr Govender?' and I said, 'Yes?,' and he said, 'I came and saw your play.' I said, 'Good.' Then he said, 'I waited till it came to Stanger and I brought my father along to see it. He's an elderly man, and I am twenty-six. And for the first time in my life my father and I sat across the table and spoke. We debated and argued after viewing your play. My father was against what you'd written, and I had to try and explain to him why it was necessary to write a play of that nature.'

They had spoken well into the night, and he said he wanted to thank me for that. That prompted me to go for writing.

Because of my involvement with theatre I couldn't work for a firm at that particular period – from about 1967–68 onwards. So I had to create a little firm for myself, where I took on building cottages. That allowed me sufficient freedom to engage in theatre activities and also to earn a living on the side. And by 1972 it had really flourished. It became quite a massive business. Then I had to make a decision. Well, unfortunately for me it wasn't I who made the decision. One of the people I built a house for made the decision for me. He cheated me, you see, to the tune of about R42 000. He did it in the smartest of ways and there was nothing I could do about it. And I said, 'That's fine, I'll concentrate on writing!' I would take on little jobs, but I concentrated on writing.

The exercise was so exciting, and the world it was opening up for me was so beautiful that nothing else mattered. I didn't even grieve over the loss of the money that this man had taken from me. Inside myself I thanked him. If he hadn't done that I would probably have continued being a builder.

As a theatrical practitioner did you have any role models that influenced you or that you strove to emulate?

I just started writing, and I didn't go by any convention. I was careful not to be influenced by other writers. I was very guarded about that. I always told myself that if there is a situation, let's look at it from another point of view. And I always looked at things from another angle. Of course this did get me into quite a bit of hot water, because the plays had to be portable in that we weren't just playing in Durban. We were going to all sorts of places into which theatre had never ventured before – hotels, and restaurants, and even using marquees and things like that.

The other thing that was happening was that the Special Branch was still hovering over this whole thing, so they pulled us in whenever they felt like it, and asked questions about why I had to write about *that* thing, and what did I know about this person or that person. They would always throw in names of communist leaders abroad, Black Consciousness, people from America and people around us. It was very fortunate that I did not ally myself with any particular philosophy or anything like that. I remained quite independent. I like the freedom of thought and not being influenced by anybody. The Special Branch themselves added impetus to my writing.

The more the Special Branch harassed me the stronger I felt about what I was doing. And I had to rely a lot on myself. I had to take the responsibility myself, even when it came to the casting for my plays. It was difficult to cast in those days, because most of the people were scared to take parts in a play that was supposed to be radical or political. There were quite a number of occasions. I remember that even in *Stablexpense* some of the guys who worked with me withdrew because of the interest of the police. *Working Class Hero* was very,

very provocative. It is very critical of the Indian and his involvement in the political structures, and also of his personal prejudices – he was equally racist at that time. Now, the fellow that was doing my lead role was in the teacher training college at the time, and because he was going to apply for a job in a government structure, the society that he belonged to told him he should withdraw from the play, and about two weeks before we were going on stage he retired.

But we worked really hard and got the play put together. It was condemned outright by the Indian community, and later even by the newspapers, again because of the language that I was using. My play was set at a building site, you understand, and I used the language of the building site. There were lots of people who walked out half way through the play!

As it happened this was the time when the Natal Critics Circle met – these were newspaper critics in Natal – and made an assessment of plays, and *Working Class Hero* won an award as the best play of the year. It was then that people began looking up and taking note of it, and then they started to come and see the play. Of course when I went to places like the Transvaal, the critics of the day again really went to town with me because of my attack on the white community and the Indian community. They didn't like it. Now, I wasn't the kind of person who was going to go about writing plays that were popular, and the critics didn't bother me much. I mean – they *did*, and you did feel a bit slighted. They said, '*Ag*, this play is loaded with deaths, and the language is foul,' – and what have you. But by and large you were getting across to people. When people came back-stage after the performance, they said 'Thank God we are not like that!' – that made you feel a lot stronger. When people said they didn't feel like the characters on stage, then you were making them think. My plays were not money-spinners!

How would you yourself characterise your genre?

Well, I didn't characterise it in any way, but they called it Protest Theatre. I didn't really care what genre it was.

It is satire, basically, is it?

There were elements of satire. Yes, satire gave you the flexibility to get away with quite a lot of criticism, and satire also provokes laughter, and it is with laughter you can say what you've got to say.

Was music and dancing part of your style?

No. Some way or other I don't like those unnecessary frills. The dance drama had not evolved to the point yet where it could say something vital. To date it hasn't really evolved to that point – where it could give out a story. It is there as an accompaniment. Even the music is a sort of accompaniment, and people don't write lyrics strong enough to say what they really feel. That is why I have avoided extensive use of music and dance. But what I would really like to do when it comes to dance or music is to go for the traditional stuff, but weave it in such a way that it becomes part of the play.

In *Stablexpense* I had these people going into a shebeen, and after having had a couple of drinks one of the characters says, 'How's it if we throw a song?' And this guy says, 'Buy me a drink and I'll give you a song.' And then he sings. And he turns to his friend and asks him to give a song, or maybe a dance. This friend plays a bit shy, and he wants to get out of the situation, and the guy says, 'Hey, d'you know what happened the other day at our depot?' – they are both garbage collectors. And here I bring out a situation that happened in that depot. It was the white man's birthday and for that occasion they had hired one of these strippers, and all these workers, the carriers themselves, were entertained with a certain amount of alcohol and they were outside. What was going on inside was not for their eyes, because it was a *white* woman stripping.

It was one way of bringing that situation out, because the same kind of situation was existent in the South African theatres. We had no access to places like theirs. We had no theatres at all. And if we did get to a theatre it was under segregated circumstances. Your audiences had to be Indian, not black: Indian! And if you wanted to have a multi-racial audience you had to have separate facilities for the Africans, for the Indians, for the whites and for the coloureds – separate entrances, separate seatings, separate toilets, everything separate.

For my own part I just sold my tickets and whoever wanted to come, came. There were no separate facilities provided. It was this situation that forced the Special Branch to create a document forcing the people who hired out these venues to ask us certain questions. They insisted that we sign the document, which said that there would be only Indian audiences. If we accepted Africans, we had to provide special facilities for them. And if we weren't prepared to sign that document, that place was not given to us. As we were not prepared to sign such documents, the halls in the city were now closing up for us. And that was what pushed us into hotels and restaurants, even the libraries – the Gandhi Library on one occasion – to perform in the city. It was necessary for us to perform in the city, for if you performed in a city you'd get the newspaper critics to come crit your show and put you in the papers, and the people outside the city would read it, and then you were asked to come to various other places with your plays.

Could we come back to the question of the need to conscientise your people?

Well, fortunately when I wrote *Stablexpense* I didn't know what it was – perhaps it was the language structure itself, because it was an Indian colloquial way of speaking English. They came in masses, they really did come. And they began to speak about the plays. Theatre now was something that people were really looking forward to. How much I contributed I couldn't really evaluate. You did what you had to do. You had to withdraw from everything to get down to the next play. In most cases while the play is still going on, you're already looking at other themes. So that as soon as this particular run is over, you'll start another production.

I would say that theatre, not necessarily my theatre, but theatre as a whole, did contribute towards conscientising the people. It did do that. What you must understand is that every other avenue of communication was stifled. The newspapers themselves would not take the chances and say what the theatre people were saying. The radio was run by the government – there was no independent radio at that time – and there was no television either. And when television did come in, it was the government-run television station. And you could not go on to a political platform – that bores people. So the only way you could do what you had to do, was via the stage. And the stage did contribute in a large way in terms of conscientisation.

The entertainment element of theatre would be important, I suppose?

Very very important. You had to keep your story line in such a way that it didn't get lost. To me it was very important that you didn't go up there and give a talk on apartheid. What you did do was that you *showed* apartheid, and you let the people decide. To quote you an example of how I did it, in *Stablexpense*, that first play of mine, this guy has got to go to court. He was the one that loaded up the trucks. The driver was a white man. He sat in his truck, he read his newspaper, he drove a distance while the guys brought the dirt and stuck it in. The fellow at the back there was keeping charge and would blow a whistle. As soon as he blew his whistle the car started moving. On this particular occasion, when he blew his whistle and the car started moving, he didn't know there was a little child in front of the vehicle, and the child was knocked down.

To protect the white man he goes and he tells a lie in court. That is something that is made very clear, it's blatant – that he went there and wanted to protect the boss. What I did was, I made him tell what happened in court:

> 'I went inside the court house. I sat over there, and I was waiting and I was waiting – d'you know what I was waiting for? I was waiting for the Lahnee to come – (Lahnee is an expression for the white boss). But he didn't come, man. I was frightened because the Lahnee had got scared, that the Lahnee wouldn't come, what's going to happen? You see, he's guilty. Hey, then I turned around and looked aside there, and the Lahnee was sitting over there, man.'

Then the other man asked him, 'How come you didn't see him arrive?'

> 'You know, man, I was stupid like you too. What I forgot was they have got another entrance for the betters right outside there, man. They don't use the same entrance as we do. No, they've got another entrance on the other side over there.'

In that way I brought out the fact that there are separate entrances without labelling it as an apartheid structure thing. These were the kind of things I was working on.

I've got the impression that the township theatres are gradually losing out. Is it a correct analysis of the situation that after the dismantling of apartheid, the people in the townships do not get the same amount of attention from playwrights and theatres as they did before?

Part of what happened after the dismantling of apartheid was the integration of communities. I wouldn't say it was taking place on a large scale, but there is that integration. Together with that we are faced with the violence that's going on in the townships. It has led to a situation where people don't want to enter certain townships because of the violence. In addition venues like the Playhouse are now more accessible for people from the townships. That is playing its own role. Another point that you've got to look carefully at as well, is that because the Playhouse is available with its own sophistication and its technical structures, taking a play into the township doesn't have the same attraction and impact as it had in the past.

And we mustn't forget that there are a lot of other contributing factors, such as the influence of television, which is playing a pretty ugly and damaging role in this whole set-up. And the younger section of society that we should be catering for, is caught up a lot in Americanism. If you can come up with a production that has a lot of breakdance in it, and has a lot of rap music in it, which inevitably makes it into a kind of musical, then you're going to get your crowd coming in. Otherwise it's not going to happen. And those people that we catered for in the past, during the apartheid era, going six or seven years back, are people who have greater responsibilities. Let's look at it this way: these people are now married with children. They've got their homes, and the constant battle to keep head above water is taking more time and energy than goes into any kind of entertainment. And in terms of entertainment, any play that you'd want to produce now has to be different from the play you did in the past.

But the fact that these people are now under economic pressures, and are unable to go into the cities for entertainment – doesn't that mean that they are actually still depending on something to be provided for them, on their level, in the township?

They are, they are. But the dismantling of apartheid gave rise to quite a number of other areas of entertainment for the people. Well, let's take casinos, for instance. If you take the daily intake of the people who go to casinos and put them into the theatre, you'd need four or five performances per day to cater for that crowd. Casinos have now become a medium of entertainment.

Then the video shops. With the disappearance of censorship in this industry there is an abundance of such material – arses and titties have gained prominence. And this is bound to go on for a period because of the newness of this concept – the looking at nudity and sex and things like that. And until these matters themselves have run their full course, you can't compete. And people won't look for alternative methods of being entertained.

Then you've got this new genre that has presented itself recently – the dance and music where the storyline doesn't matter as long as they've got lots of bodies there, loud music and dance – I'm thinking especially of the Indian sector now.

Would this be something along the lines of Sarafina?

Not necessarily along the lines of *Sarafina*. *Sarafina* made its own impact and it had its own message against apartheid. Here the storyline doesn't matter at all. Or you've got stand-up comedians. As long as they can go and mouth four-lettered words and sex terms, they are drawing the crowds.

So where do you see the real theatre going now, if the situation is as you are describing it?

It's got its place. The question now is how well you're going to balance yourself, with entertainment and, let's say, a certain amount of conscientisation. You see, now it's not political conscientisation. It is now looking at people and life itself in a broader context, and even asking certain questions about our existence on earth – purpose, concepts like truth, and time. These are now areas that should provide material for the writers, which is, from my point of view, a very advantageous position. I just don't feel that it is a disadvantage at this time, because the removal of apartheid has unshackled us. We are freer to roam this whole spectrum of life itself. And our writing could be of more true relevance to human society.

So no more agitprop?

No. And the interesting thing that has happened also is that while there was an influx of writers during the apartheid years, now there is a dearth. There are less writers around. And there are those also, who, for the sake of survival, have opted out for arses and titties! Well, personally speaking I think it is to their disadvantage that they have done a thing like that. I know there is a place for it, but having been a serious writer – even if you did write satires you were still in a serious mode – you could not afford now, all of a sudden, to go and do things that have absolutely no relevance at all to what is happening around us.

So now the pure propagandist is dropping out because he has got no more to say?

Yes. And there is also the element of fear. The situation in the theatre world in the past was that you were part of the struggle – without being politically involved in any real way – because you were articulating what the people wanted articulated. And once the ANC government was installed into place there were very few people wanting to take the responsibility of criticising it. And that is the dangerous part of it. If you are afraid to criticise the government, then you don't belong to the writers' fraternity. You need to be bold enough to say, 'This government is not beyond criticism.' You've got to go along and forget your survival, forget being politically correct. A writer cannot afford the luxury of being politically correct. He's got to have the guts to say what is actually happening. It doesn't necessarily mean that because racism was perpetrated by the white man in the past it is OK for you to attack him. And if racism is now practised by the black man, you should feel equally strongly and speak out against it. And that is the sad thing about the writers of the past: they are not prepared to adjust to that situation. They are not bold enough to say, 'ANC, you're fucking things up!'

Are you casting your critical writer's eye on any particular issues these days?

Yes, the very last play I wrote was highly critical of what's happening with our structures at the moment.

What is the title of your that play?

It's called *Affirmative Action*.

And what is it about?

What I am doing in the play is I'm criticising that whole policy. Affirmative Action doesn't necessarily mean that you've got to be black to get a job, to enjoy a position. It doesn't mean that you've got to be of African stock to warrant Affirmative Action.

I am also discussing the violence that's going on in this country. And I am discussing the rise in white collar crimes, the kind of scams that are being pulled continuously – especially insurance scam, the looting, the raping. You pick up a newspapers any day of the week, and that is all you are reading about. And the drug trafficking that is going on. And the educational system and what is happening to it. It is in a very frightening state.

And these are things that have got to be addressed. Unfortunately, with Affirmative Action there are so many areas for me to address, and I do feel guilty at times that I am putting too many things into this particular play, but these are areas that have got to be addressed and I don't think I have that amount of time to go into detail and discuss specifically the educational structure, or the health structure, or the political structure, or the crime problem. So I am forced to bring everything into a singular melting pot, create a play with all these things I have brought up. Even if they cannot be dealt with in depth, they are being broadly discussed.

How was it received?

It was received quite well.

And how long did it play?

It played for a year in Durban, and then went out into the suburbs. I didn't have the time or the marketing skills to exploit it any further. It went on until the end of last August. Then I went to Jerusalem for five or six weeks, and by the time I came back and could begin to rejuvenate the marketing process, we were coming into the festive period, and my plays don't play well during the festive season. People want to be silly, they don't like to do any serious thinking, and so I stopped it. But now that the holiday period is over, I will remarket the play again.

I love acting, and I also act in my own plays. But now I've got to withdraw from it and find a replacement for myself, so that I can tackle another play. I've got another one working in my mind and I want to get it down on paper.

And there are other plays that I have written in the past which have not gone on stage yet. I didn't feel it relevant to put them on stage at that time, but they could be produced now, I think. Today they would be quite relevant, because now people are free from the frustrations of racism. We've got to discuss things like the existence of time, and what the thing we keep strapped around our wrist is doing to us and our lives; what it is doing to the matters around us. How much are we in control of time? Or is it in control of us? Is that the Big Brother we have given human physicality to?

What did you call the play?

I called it *Tramp You Tramp Me*. The characters in the play are all tramps, with Champ, the newspaper seller, being the person who sort of represents society as a whole. But the rest of the characters, or cast members, are all tramps. What I was contemplating toying with is how horrendously our minds are shackled with responsibilities, and how much strength it requires to unshackle oneself. And the Champ has, in a way, reached that level. You've got the sea, as an image of the uncivilised society, and in the midst of it you have a couple of drops of oil, which are the civilised society. And the mass, the indoctrinated lot, are dictating the terms. The squalid surface self that is attached to the tramp is what comes first in our minds, not his inner clean lines. That's what I was reviewing when I wrote that particular play. I wrote it as early as 1975, and never got the chance to produce it earlier.

It's high time, then.

Yes it is, and I now intend to do it. And then I've got an anti-war dance drama, which I felt at that time had a universal appeal. It is something I would like to take on a worldwide tour. I called it at that time *O'Kali*, and in that one I am discussing this whole concept of people creating wars. There is a war going on as we are speaking now, somebody is being shot now, somebody is creating monstrous weapons at this particular moment. And masses are being drawn from society itself, and recruited into the army.

Somewhere along the line there is just a group, a handful of people, that are making these decisions, and they are prepared to sacrifice millions of lives. Look for instance at recent debacles like the war in Vietnam, or the Saddam Hussein situation. There is no justification for any kind of war. This body here was not meant to be destroyed the way these people are destroying it. I therefore felt I'd like to make a play on that, and a dance drama was what I was looking at.

Kali – *has the word got the same connotations as in Kiswahili, meaning angry, or mean?*

That's the Swahili sense. Then there is the Hindu concept of *kali*, where one loosely refers to kali as the *mother of destruction*. But the deeper meaning of kali is *disillusion* as opposed to destruction, and also *mother of strength*. So I use that word, because in my play I look at the masses reverting to tradition, or ancient customs, and seeking help from nature itself. We are moving swiftly away from nature. And nature is the force that can decide the fate of mankind. Kali in my play personifies nature itself. I create some weird situations where she tells the women who come to her for assistance, 'Make love with your men, but don't produce any male children.' When there are no hands to hold the guns at the borders, then there will be no more wars to go to. Eventually, when the absence of males is noticed in the population, the army itself takes notice and says, 'Who's responsible for this?' And that is when they say, 'Kali.' The army people then go and question Kali, and say, 'This must stop.' But she says, 'No! You stop it! Mankind was not intended for the kind of situation you create for it.'

You see, the old Hindu conception of man being half male half female is not given due recognition by our society. It has given recognition more to the male half. So I am trying to restore that balance, and I am seeking to create a mythology for battle between the army representative and nature's representative.

That is what I have done with *Kali*, which I hope will go on stage pretty soon.

Maishe Maponya

Maishe Maponya, you are obviously wearing a number of different hats: you are an actor, a playwright, a director, and you are also a teacher, I suppose, since this is Witwatersrand University Drama Department. And aren't you also an essayist? I wonder if you could start by giving a brief outline of your past and of your theatrical career?

Generally I started off in the theatre with an untrained history. I was not formally trained as a writer or as a performer, so the greater part of my writing and performing was self-taught. The inspiration came from a number of activities and sources that were taking place especially in the early seventies. In the mid-seventies I belonged to a group of writers called Medupil Writers Association, which was a Black Consciousness kind of organisation of writers, or who were more Black Consciousness orientated. We did a lot of performances of poetry to a large extent, which was published in magazines, and the most popular one was *Staffrider*.

So a number of people like myself who had not initially written anything or had not had any training, had some sort of a platform from which to begin to test one's creativity and creativite modes. And so in interacting with those kind of acclaimed or known and established writers like Sipho Sepamla, Matobi Mutloatse etc. one became confident and gained a lot of experience in terms of writing.

So it is from that time that one developed this kind of a feel for creativity, and I wrote my first play in 1976, *The Cry*, which was just basically a kind of a collage of readings I had done in various places, and then trained myself and got friends to begin to perform in this particular play.

I was also inspired at that time by a play that I had seen done by some reverend, called *Give Us This Day*, which focused on a Black Consciousness leader called Onkgopotse Tiro, who was a student of the University of the North, and a member of SASO (South African Students Organisation). He had given a speech during the graduation, which was very scathing, on the regime and the education system in this country. The speech was so heavy that the security branch closed in on him, and he finally went into exile, where three months later he received a letter bomb and died in Botswana.

So from that moment you realised that you could begin to mix reality with, you know, the kind of imagination you would have as a writer, to be able to create something that was concrete enough for people to begin to relate to. And it was then I did this play *The Cry*, which was performed only twice, and which had to close because of the unrest.

Then I wrote my second play, *Peace and Forgive*, which was performed in various townships and at the Market Theatre.

The third play came at a point when I'd had a little bit of formal training in workshop performance in the township and the UK. The township workshops were run by Sam Mhangwane, who was a protegé and a contemporary of Gibson Kente. He was running workshops at a venue in DOCC in Orlando, and I attended those and began to grasp a little of the dynamics of performance.

This was in Soweto, was it?

Yes, it was. And I also travelled with a community group to Europe, and at that point I asked the British Council to sponsor me to observe the theatre in the UK, and they agreed for me to do that. So I attended few workshops and courses on script writing and directing. I mean, even though I did not understand much of what was being done, because it was very British, I think it gave me some kind of inkling and an opening towards the writing of *The Hungry Earth*.

When was this?

It was in 1978. And when I came back from that trip in Europe and the UK I then proceeded with the writing of *The Hungry Earth*, which I completed the same year, and started performing the same or the following year. And that's when I got a break, because at that point I had also established some friends in the UK, and in organising performances here, I also organised performances with these friends that I had already established in the UK. So in a way that gives an idea of where I've actually come from.

And maybe to sum up that period I would say that the performances that we did and the tours that we did with my group, which was the Bahumutsi Drama Group, we basically funded ourselves, which was quite an interesting concept of self-reliance.

You were the director and the one who started that group?

I was the director and initiator, and, basically, performer. So we came up with that concept, and we performed quite extensively abroad; in a way funded by ourselves, no public or private funding at all, you know, we paid for our own tickets, we didn't have any money. What we did was we asked for guaranteed fees from the box office, which was a step towards self-determination. So all of us were prepared to make those sacrifices, so that each one of us paid for their own ticket from the box office, so we got guaranteed performances, and from those guaranteed performances we would work out what we would make in a week so that we could get our salaries and pay about £25 back a week from each performance. Because we were getting the Equity minimum. So that was very important. And for many of the following years I had to rely basically on that concept of self promotion in our own works. We did that for quite a long time.

And finally my most formal kind of training was when I received my Master's degree in Leeds, in Theatre Studies. That basically sums up my kind of education and expertise in the theatre.

Your political leaning is, I suppose, towards the working class?

Yes, yes, to a very large extent. Yes, that's where I am rooted, and I feel most confident when I am dealing with that.

From what you have said, and from the pictures on your wall it also seems quite obvious that you have been influenced by the Black Consciousness Movement?

Yes, I usually don't make any bones about my being an Africanist, and I come from the Black Consciousness kind of mould and philosophy. And those are for me what has actually shaped my confidence and my self, and for many years I think that will remain so. It's not a philosophy for me which is kind of strictly dogmatic. You might find ways of actually analysing concepts of Black Consciousness or Pan-Africanism and end up with a sense of dogmatism, but it does not carry weight for me.

Where do you draw the line between Black Consciousness and Pan-Africanism?

Well, the line can be drawn in the sense that the two operate slightly differently. The Black Consciousness philosophy has to a very large extent addressed issues of race. The Pan-Africanism has to a very large extent addressed issues of heritage with regard to the continent. So there one can draw a line between them, although many of us have argued that there is not much of a difference between the two. They should augment each other, you know, and each should begin to give some sense of power to concepts that we believe in – self-determination, self-reliance, self-definition. Those concepts are most important to the two philosophies, and we define ourselves in terms that we deem fit for ourselves, and we don't want to be defined by other people. The two philosophies are non-apologetic about where they come from and who they address and where they stand. So *that* for me is most important: that I cannot be apologetic about who I am and what my philosophical position is, concept of life and so on.

So you see yourself as a militant Africanist?

I am not sure, because I wouldn't know what you define as militant.

I suppose I mean exclusive.

No, you see that was what I meant when I talked about dogmatism a moment ago. To me it is not a very dogmatic kind of principle, because once it becomes very dogmatic it means that one to a large extent cannot develop beyond what one believes in. You become located in a kind of cocoon, which is much more dangerous, I think, and tends to become more like fundamentalism. And I don't believe in that.

How does it agree with the ANC?

Wow! I suppose one should rather ask how does it *not* agree with the ANC! It does not agree with the ANC in the sense that the philosophies of the ANC would be more accommodationist, and to a large extent they would be more apologetic.

More pragmatic?

Maybe the ANC philosophy is more pragmatic, I'm not quite sure. It's quite an open issue. I would think that for us to develop a sense of the self, to understand our values, our culture, we would need to be given the space to be able to go into those aspects ourselves. Not to let others do it, or even be concerned about where others are at this moment. But we have been the most under-privileged; we have been the most denied and deprived. We have lost the land. And for us to be able to regain that confidence that was lost we need to be given space to develop that self, instead of beginning to look outside. The struggle begins *here* for me; it begins with *me*. It doesn't begin with other people. It begins with me. Who am I? Where am I? What do I want? How do I relate to other people. How do I fight to regain control and ownership of the land? That's where all else begins. I don't begin with other people. I don't define other people. I don't want to begin even to attempt to define other people. Let them define themselves and deal with their consciences, and with their philosophies – with who they are, where they come from etc. etc. I will also do the same. So that we can be able to meet each other somewhere and create a sense of equilibrium.

Have there been other major forming influences in your early life?

There haven't been any other influences than the Black Consciousness and Pan-Africanism which I have continued to uphold, because that's what creates me and keeps me alive. I think also spiritually I have been enriched by those philosophies. I may be poor materially, but this is what keeps me going spiritually.

Were you ever in contact with the Junction Avenue Theatre?

No, no direct connections. I have never been influenced by their principle and philosophy of work. Actually I have been kind of a critic of their principle of work. For one thing they had whites and blacks operating and creating work in a situation which did not allow the kind of equality between races at that point, and I tend to think that a lot of the things that I believed in as a black person were compromised. And when one looks at those black practitioners in that group, they were not really very political. Not that they needed to be political – we are dealing with the arts here, we are dealing with a craft – but I think that sense of consciousness was not instilled in the minds of those people. What they basically were seeing was themselves participating in an open kind of society, which was not open at that time.

Their works were inclined to appeal to a liberal consciousness, which was, to a very large extent, that of the whites. Not that their works were bad, I have to admit that. There were works that really impressed, works like *Dikhitshineng*, a play about the experiences of domestic workers and their white masters. Those were interesting pieces that they came up with. But I just did not believe in that concept of work. Somewhere someone had to be the boss, and to a large extent the boss was the white person.

I gather they were also more focused on class than on race, isn't that so?

Yes, that's right, the issue of race was to a very large extent compromised. And, obviously, each one of us would decide our route, so they were entitled to that. The race issue was addressed from a white perspective.

How do you regard the more popular theatrical genres, Gibson Kente's, for instance? Has anything of that rubbed off on you?

No, not at all. I guess some of what has made it difficult for me to adopt that genre has been the costliness of Gibson Kente's productions – especially when you had to have a band, large casts, and to have to depend on the music to be able to carry the performance and the production through. So that has been difficult.

I'm not saying that I could not be in a position to write that kind of stuff, but it is not the genre that I am really at home with. I feel I could do more without the large casts and bands and so on.

So music and dancing are not really part of your style of work?

Well they are, but they come in a different way. When I talk about their music and dance, they use instruments, you know; whole bands with a drum kit, guitars, saxophones, trumpets and things, and that's not easy to cope with especially today, because you are working under financial constraints. I use a lot of song and dance movements in my productions, so that element is not absent.

Between scenes?

Yes, and also within scenes themselves. I do write music, too. I have done two albums, and I have done a number of tracks of music, so I am well conversant with that.

How do you think Gibson Kente will go down in history?

I think he has reached the pinnacle of his success. He has stopped being creative, being productive. The major obstacle within Gibson Kente is that he is an egoist. He is a very self-centred person. I have to say that. He does not believe in collective, collaborative work. If he ever attempts to get into collaborative work, he assumes the position of the boss, of being the leader within that, and he would often want his own ideas to predominate. And that's where the problem is. I don't see him achieving much more than he has already achieved. So he has actually reached a point where he has stopped coming up with new ideas.

I have had some kind of communication with him. I guess his major disadvantage was that he was – I must say that he was not really influenced by the politics of the time. His interpretation of the politics was always wrong.

Wasn't there a period in his writing when he got himself politically involved and attuned to progressive thinking?

Yes, he did have a brief spell, but he never opened himself to be more analytical, to be more objective. He basically took a dismissive attitude, to a point where that basically misled him. And therefore that's where his failure was. I remember at some point he had gotten into some sort of negotiation with some department of the old regime to be able to get funding for one or two of his projects that he was intending to do.

What happened was that when Gibson started doing those kind of communications with either ministers or officials within government, those became rather dubious set-ups. I can say this because at that point I was trying to communicate with him to create a collaborative venture between himself, myself and Matsemela Manaka. And I remember well that we tried to get Sam Mhangwane involved, and he didn't want Sam Mhangwane involved, he wanted only the two of us, Matsemela and myself, to be part of this. He kept mentioning a source he expected to get money from, and when we tried to investigate this we found that it was some minister or some official in the Department of Information, which for me was not on. And we cut ties from that moment on.

So, for me his interpretation of politics was skewed. I remember at one point at the DOCC we were talking, and he was saying to me something like, 'If you look at that man walking up there, in the centre of Orlando diocese, he's from work. That man is concerned at the moment with where he will get his next piece of bread, where he will sleep etc. He's not interested in politics. And that girl down there, has not seen Mandela, and does not know who the man is. You cannot force that person to begin to believe in Mandela, because that person has not seen Mandela. We must stop imposing leaders on people.'

And that interpretation of the politics of the day for me was kind of skewed, and made me feel very uncomfortable about where the man's politics were.

What does tradition mean to you in terms of South African theatre? I understand that Credo Mutwa's theories about the origins of African theatre are found to be interesting?

Yes. It was fascinating and inspiring to see an African developing such approaches and analysis. His works were more towards the continental African historical and cultural background. Anything that relates to written material about South African theatre should not be taken at face value – it should be queried extensively, because we make references to those people that have written before us.

We know that there are certain things and practices that are still carried through, over the years, over the decades and centuries, that are basically what you then might define as traditional or dramatic performances, without the people themselves defining them as performances for theatre purposes. They are performances of the ritual, you know, during birth, death, weddings or whatever kind of celebration. And those are quite important. I don't really need to go into the books to find those practices. They still continue today.

Would story-telling come under the same category?

Yes, it does, because the young people, the children, need to be told about those traditions in order for them to understand where their parents and grandparents and relatives came from.

I suppose you welcome Gcina Mhlophe's endeavours to resuscitate the tradition of story-telling, then?

Yes I do. She does something which I don't do, but which definitely needs to be further developed with more people getting involved in that sort of performance. I think it is a valuable contribution. And by the way – Gcina started theatre performances with me, in my production.

I gather, but without having as yet had the chance of speaking to Matsemela Manaka, that he takes a special interest in the educational side of theatre. That is part of his involvement in theatrical work, isn't it?

He may have got involved in that in recent years, but I think his theatre was also about the raising of the consciousness, of sensitising our people, so one may say it is educational in that sense.

One young drama student I talked to in Durban some time ago had just produced a dramatised musical version of Dikobe's Marabi Dance, *and he suggested that one way of raising the level of consciousness among the dispossessed might be to take popularised versions of literature and theatre to the townships – in the shape of musicals for instance. Any comments on that idea?*

Ja, that's quite an interesting one. But it should not be stuck to that period, the 1930s or so, which would mean romanticising the South African situation. These works also need to be critically re-assessed.

But could it not be taken into our day and age and treated in the same way, like Sarafina, *for example?*

Yes, it would need to be developed in that sense, so that it could be seen to be a more realistic and more contemporary and topical thing. Maybe, on one level, it would be felt to be important also to dwell on that period, also to see that there was a great American influence that rubbed off on the South Africa scenario in the thirties – the musical, the dance patterns, etc. The movies that were sent through to this country at that time had a great influence on South Africa, which was influenced by those patterns, and they were to a large extent Southfricanised. You can look at the way they dressed and the way they danced.

So how do you regard Mbongeni Ngema, then, in that context?

Well, in a way one would say that Mbongeni's contribution is valuable. It is also largely influenced by the Gibson Kente kind of mode and style of performance genre. One can also see that it is geared to being acceptable on Broadway. It does work for South African audiences to some extent, but its creation is geared towards some kind of a commercialised international market.

So one needs to be aware of the dynamics of such influences.

One thing I would like to ask you about is the relationship between young black theatre directors and producers like yourself and the old regime of white theatre moguls – people like Barney Simon, Athol Fugard, Mannie Manim and others. Have you met any of them, have you at all been involved with them in your theatrical career? Or have you dissociated yourself from them?

I have not dissociated myself from them. And I have not encountered them in creative work. I would guess for me it has been a very deliberate position. I was in the process of redefining myself, rediscovering myself, which at that point I had not yet really achieved. There was no point for me to go into the other, for then one would get swamped by the other which was fully developed, whereas I was not. I am not saying that their contribution has not been valuable – it has been very valuable in its own context. But my own contributions and direction were even more valuable to me, perhaps for those who cared about the ethos of African philosophy.

Do you think South African theatre should remain political? Do you see theatre as an agent in the shaping of the New South Africa?

Yes, I do. It should remain an agent. For those who don't want to make it an agent, that's OK. That's their business. For me it cannot be otherwise. We have inherited the legacy of apartheid. We were the dispossessed. The situation is more complex today. We need to address that issue of the land. We need to redefine our position in the new dynamic that is taking place, that is shaping our lives, and theatre needs to be an agent within that, what has happened to the African values of life, morals etc. These have to continue to be a backdrop to our struggle towards a new sense of identity, if you wish, for those that want to look at that – and a new sense of direction for those who wish to find a new direction for themselves. And therefore, for me, those concepts and those principles are not dogmatic, they are much more open.

Have you any views on theatre and gender?

I think that those who have the sensitivity and the expertise to address the issue of gender in their work must be given the space to do that. We cannot continue to impose our male conceptions on women's issues. We need to be much more sensitised about the whole issue of women's roles without actually imposing ourselves – we must give support and encourage women writer activists to come out and find space for themselves in order to redress the sexual imbalance. We need to be more open to those areas.

But one thing that I keep discouraging is for men to write plays about women's issues. It must be the women who take charge. And they must be given the platform to project their strengths much more than they are doing now. And there needs to be a co-oporative of women who are in the arts, to address these things, people like Gcina Mhlophe,

Christina Qunta, Sibongile Khumalo, the Nokwe sisters and others. But they should not be isolated: they should be integrated with some of us. Not integrated for the purpose of lending support to us, but to exert their strengths and gain more strength in that sort of a collaboration. In this way we could both be able to recognise our own weaknesses and gain strength from each other in order to support each other.

We need women directors in the theatre, we need women writers and administrators, so that is very important.

How about your own work? Anything in the pipeline now?

Well, I have a lot of ideas of what I would want to do, but one is faced with financial constraints. I have a story that I have just written which I would like to turn into a play. It is called 'Give Them Fire'.

Matsemela Manaka

Mr Manaka, would you mind giving me a brief account of your development as an artist?

I think I have a typical South African background in terms of my involvement in the arts. I wouldn't say it's unique – it is what most of us have gone through. I didn't have plans to become an artist, it just happened. I didn't go to school to study art. It was after '76, when some of us were activists. I was restricted, I wasn't allowed to be at the school where I was studying. I could not even communicate with my fellow students.

Then I started using art as a tool to find my way back into the education problem that everybody was facing in this country. And most of the time I was working more as a painter than as a writer. Then I did an exhibition, not long after I started, but the exhibition was to try and expose myself to more of the artists. And then I met a lot of writers, and the interest in writing poetry started developing. In doing praise poetry or live poetry performances at funerals and other congregations together with people like Maishe (Maponya).

Now, as I said earlier – this was a typical South African experience – that you don't work in the arts because of your training or your background. Several of us haven't been academics, or haven't had an interest in education and valued the need and the right to learn. We studied on our own. We had to range into the whole theatre business, into the art business through informal education, because at that time there was no education in South Africa due to the total crisis.

Then I started painting. I had exhibitions, and had the frustration of being prevented from having my paintings exhibited where my people lived, you know. Because in my mind I have always believed in exhibiting for the very people that I paint about, for these people who are my creative resource.

I then did a theatre piece with members of the Creative Youth Association in order to try and expose the paintings on stage, since there were no galleries in Soweto. So we used the theatre stage as a vehicle to exhibit the painting. And that's how I moved into the theatre business, and started writing for the theatre and began being more actively involved in theatre.

Now we began moving into creating educational situations in order to try and teach black people informally, and to say there is a need to learn the skills, there is a need to become an intellectual in this area. It is not just a question of an accident. If you realise that an accident led you into this, you take advantage of that accident and begin to develop something out of it!

We had courses, and a lot of writers and actors of today have been through our programmes. And then I personally felt that having trained so many people with no practice opportunities, this was a time to create a company that would create practice opportunities for them. One of the dreams – and it is still a dream – was to establish a theatre in Soweto, where there isn't yet a theatre. We had a small theatre space at Funda, where we had performances. But unfortunately, with the eruption of violence in the country, or using that as an excuse, people are scared of going out at night.

And that's why there is a lack in terms of support for theatre in this country. And for the past two or three years I have shifted back to visual arts. I have produced very little for a long time.

I started publishing my own works. I decided also to create a space for artists to exhibit their works. I had two galleries in this space. Then things also worked out, because you realise it takes a bit of time to educate your people to become part of the support infrastructure. You depend on tourists coming in, as the government depends on tourists. The reason why I put it here, and the reason why I transformed my house into a museum, was to make my people have access to this base. And in that way, if we can create a market in the majority, we as artists will survive. But if we do not create that support structure within the majority, we're not going to survive. And I think this is the dilemma facing artists in South Africa today.

You were a staunch supporter of the Black Consciousness Movement from the early days, weren't you?

Yes, I was, and I still am today. I believe a lot of black people in South

Africa need to go through that consciousness process that is also required to liberate the white man in this country. As long as black people are not psychologically free, the white man in South Africa will never be liberated, because the white man will still be seen as the boss – or the *baas*, and as superior to black people. For me that is the philosophy – given the history of oppression in this country, given the history of black deprivation – Black Consciousness is a philosophy for life. Our children and great-grandchildren actually go in a circle, for we see today with the interaction of integrated schools that when black people go to white schools, they become 'white'. And that's why this philosophy is a very important philosophy for the survival of black people, black tradition, black history and the black heritage. Otherwise we're just back to recolonisation – we're being recolonised in the modernised version, where there is a black man who is now in charge as President. Yes, Mandela is the president. A lot of us are very impressed and we're saying that the Old Man even changes certain traditions. He begins to wear shirts. He's not restricted to always wearing a tie and a suit – he has the freedom. And that is what Black Consciousness has been advocating, that you have the freedom to dress the way you want to dress and so on.

And I am sorry, but in this country we still have a lot of white domination, in many ways. It could be in education, in the advertising industry, it could be in theatre. If you look at the theatre of the seventies it is still run by white people. If you look at art, the galleries are still run by white people. And the media, the media are still run by white people with white traditions.

So for us to survive as a black people, we need to become very aggressive, and we need to reinforce this philosophy. Not as a reactionary philosophy; I've never seen Black Consciousness as being reactionary to white. I've seen Black Consciousness as a philosophy that says you as a black person, you are as human as any other person, and you can become part of the greater society, black and white society, without you diminishing yourself. But black people in this society continue to diminish themselves to nothing, because they do not understand the importance of this philosophy of Black Consciousness. They think that Black Consciousness is racism. It is *not* racism. It is a struggle to say 'You as a black person, you are still oppressed.' It is not only in South Africa. When did America declare the freedom, the independence of black people? But you go to America today and you still find racism. You still find Harlem. Harlem is still there! Not far from the forum of the United Nations! And I think this is why some of us as cultural workers still advocate the philosophy of Black Consciousness. Not from a party political point of view, but from a cultural point of view. And this is what we still want to see growing strong, and because that philosophy is dying, black people are becoming more and more colonised. What we call the decolonisation of the mind of black people is not happening, because that philosophy has been kind of suspended.

I suppose that is what Fatima Dike talked about as the coconut syndrome being brown outside but white inside.

Ja, it's like the CocaCola culture, you know. It's very painful when you see that happen. And now, today, we talk about the dilemma of the black artist, the black artist who used to write, or the painter, the sculptor or playwright who used to come up with creative work that would challenge the system of oppression during those days of apartheid.

But that oppression still exists today. And the black artist is faced with the fear of speaking out. There is silence.

You have written quite a bit about communal theatre in connection with the situation of the dispossessed in the townships. Could you say something about that?

Ja – firstly I would like to say that when we started the school and we were basing our old world experience around the 'theatre of the dispossessed' – because I wrote a lot of articles about that topic – we said, 'We first have to acknowledge that we *are* dispossessed, and what we are dispossessed of. Are we dispossessed of our own culture? Of our heritage? Our own languages? Our own religions? Of the land? We are dispossessed of all these elements that constitute a *culture*.'

Then we began to say, 'We need to understand the world around us. We need to understand Africa around South Africa, you know, and to turn the world into a global village.' We made students study first South African theatre in order to know the people within South Africa, be they black or white. Then continue to actually study theatre *around* South Africa, and then go to the rest of the world, and understand what the dispossessed peoples of the different parts of the world were doing. That's where we picked up a lot of inferences from Grotowski.

But that was also through people observing what we were doing at that time. And they said we worked like Brecht, we worked like Grotowski. We didn't even know these people! It just happened that coming from the same conditions of struggle, one creates the same way.

So you weren't actually directly influenced by Grotowski and those others?

No. Beckett, Brecht and Grotowski were just cases of given situations. Look, the way I can put it is that I was influenced by the tradition that influenced all these people, and the political situation that influenced these people. I was not influenced by them directly, because I would only talk about Credo Mutwa when I started looking at environmental theatre, saying that for theatre to become communal we must look at the concept of 'participatory theatre', where the audience becomes part of the performance. And this was the concept that we studied when we were reading about theatre. We would pick it up from Credo Mutwa, talking about environmental stage – like this is a theatre space – it could be this room, there is a stage here, there is a stage there, there is a stage there, and there are people all over. And then we took it further and said it's like a football ground. The mesh is the central stage, and if there is a festival at the football ground, there will be musicians performing, and there'll be another person dancing, in another space, and having his own audience.

And already you are creating an environmental performance, it's all over the place. This did not come from Grotowski, we didn't even know about Grotowski. And the story-telling tradition did not come from Brecht. We had a story-telling tradition in this country, and we picked it up from our own parents. That's why, when we do theatre, we always tell stories.

And we then began to ask how do we integrate other forms of theatre? For us it came naturally, and I think it also came naturally for Brecht. I don't know where it came from in Brecht's case, but I believe that when a person is confronted by certain conditions, the conditions dictate to you how you create. If you are poor, the conditions of poverty dictate to you how you create theatre. It's determined by your own poverty. Just like Grotowski doing poor theatre in Poland.

We moved into the concept of communal theatre because we realised that the rural areas were denied the opportunity to experience the work we were creating. And they were denied the opportunity to create work themselves within their own languages. And I must say also that I borrowed a lot of Soyinka's ideas and some of his concepts, and when I started my own theatre company, we said that we honoured Soyinka for his contribution to theatre, even though he was writing in heavy language, heavy English. And that was always my kind of vision. I was basically just an academic myself, you know. I loved to write in good English, what I called English with kind of memorable lines, so that you can remember the lines and say, 'Phew, this is a very pregnant line!'

And then I read a lot of Soyinka's stuff. I struggled to understand him, and I felt it was a challenge. If I felt it was a challenge to read Shaw, or Shakespeare, or Beckett, it was also so fulfilling to read a black person writing in that kind of style.

And then we began to say, 'We need to change this, we need to make him accessible. He says things that are very interesting. How do you make him reach the community that he wants to talk to?' And that's how, somehow, I wanted to start moving into his work.

When I first met him, he made a very strong statement about the problems of theatre in South Africa, saying that there was too much emphasis on protest, on resistance, on challenging the system. There was a need to integrate, or to fuse, protest and tradition. We had lost the sense of tradition. We never created tradition, plays that deal with the celebration of the South African cultural heritage. And for me that was a confirmation of the path I was following.

After *Egoli*, which was agitprop theatre and a strong statement about the fact that we are oppressed because of economic problems, I did *Pula*, which became a cultural celebration of our own heritage. People thought it was kind of watered-down. Writing is not just making a statement of principle. It is also making a cultural statement, reminding people of their own cultural heritage – where they come from. So it became very fashionable in South Africa during those days to make a statement against Vorster or Botha or de Klerk or apartheid. But for me I said, 'I create work that is beyond apartheid, that will still make sense even beyond apartheid.'

Some people thought, 'You are not politically correct! You are just escaping. You were creating political work, but now you are escaping from what you started.' I said, 'It's not an escape. You wait and see – after Independence!'

And that's what's happening. I can still create work. I did *Goree*, which is about the abolition of slavery, and comparing it to the abolition of apartheid. And I said that slavery was never abolished, it was merely polished, just like apartheid. And it is true! It is happening now. It was written in the eighties. And it is true, it is happening now, because the South Africans were trapped within, reacting to, apartheid and not reflecting *beyond* apartheid.

I said, 'Look, we're going to have this problem beyond Independence,' and it is happening now. You are seeing it, you are seeing the dilemma that confronts the black writer today, the black dramatist, the black actor. It's a total frustration, a depression. Because the anticipation and the expectations were too big. They thought the government would be in place, and the Mandela government would begin to uncover the big pot. They would come with the plate and say, 'Here's your food.' And that's not possible. The government is confronted with a lot of problems they inherited from the past. They need to change those problems.

So we tried to serve the idea of communal theatre in the sense that the very community must begin to address their problems through theatre. They must begin to use their own languages. And this is what we did in the rural theatre project. We would send some of our graduates all over the country, and say to them, 'You are not going to teach those people, you are going to learn from those people. You'll make the people express their own frustrations and their wishes.'

And the other thing we emphasised was that today we are young revolutionaries in the arts, making statements. Tomorrow we'll be very successful, and it is good to be successful. But we must not forget where we come from!

Have you been influenced by Mazisi Kunene at all?

Ja, I have read a lot of his stuff, and I have quoted him several times, about the ancestors and the whole concept of the heritage, and the history and the myths, and the myth of success, where success deprives you of what the community wants you to deal with. Like all our successful dramatists, the big ones, even John (Kani), my friend you know – he knows, too, that he performs less in the townships now. It applies to almost all of them . . . And that for me is a frustration, because that's our creative resource. We should be fighting to have theatres now, in the townships. I am being accused of being a die-hard Africanist. I am not a die-hard Africanist, I am a realist. I am saying, 'I live in this space in the township.' I mean – the people who live in this space say I am a lazy bastard, I'm not working, I am always at home . . . They don't understand my profession as a writer, or as a dramatist, or as an artist. Slowly it is beginning to grow in them, as they see a lot of other writers, a lot of other artists coming here. Because I insist on having people to come here – Stan Glizera, Denis Glover. I want them to meet at home so that my people get the opportunity to meet these names. That for me is very vital, like when we go to the rural areas and create communal theatre we say, 'We must not forget where we come from.' We might go to Broadway, we might go to the Market Theatre, to all the big stages, but we must go back to those people that we need to take from nowhere to somewhere.

And unfortunately, in this country like all over the world, when an artist becomes successful, the artist forgets where he or she comes from. And that's why I say that sometimes success becomes an enemy. We become very complacent, and then we suffer, because we miss our goals.

I've had discussions with John, who has directed some of my shows, and I have always defended him when people have been critical of him. And I have said, 'Look, there are certain great things in that man.' And he would be prepared to make certain sacrifices, although he would not admit that outright. But we would struggle together to do a show with no money and a senior director, and the show would take place and he would not be paid as a director, and neither would I – we would be worried about paying the performers. And we are beginning to ask, 'What does it mean to be a producer in this country?' Whether he be black or white, he'd work for the performers.

Taking this view of educational theatre, do you see the need to popularise the theatre in order to attract the township audiences?

For me the concept of popularising theatre won't necessarily mean to commercialise it. You don't have to reduce its standards. You've got to sell the very high standards to people. Theatre that is popular doesn't mean it has lost its value or its standards. You have to market it so heavily it's like fashioning ideas with the people. Any political party would do the same thing. You fashion the ideas of the very people you are talking to. That's why when theatre only happens in Johannesburg – forget it! It'll never get popular. It becomes an élite profession.

But when you take it to the people you will do it informally. You will sacrifice, and perform informally at funerals, at weddings, at parties and gatherings. You are performing without even thinking of being paid. You are popularising the concept. By the time you do a show that people must pay to attend, you pack the hall!

But now we have lost the tradition of performing at gatherings. For as soon as you have performed, the question is, How much? It's a problem.

For me popularising and commercialising are two different things. But some people are confusing that.

Where do you see Gibson Kente in this picture?

I must say that Gibson played quite an important role in the development of theatre in this country, and that role has to be read in a certain perspective. OK. Certain things in Gibson's way of making theatre were problematic for us as professionals. Because it was becoming 'opium'.

What kind of theatre were we to pursue? It was what we call bubblegum music today. If it is in, and you are not into that format, you are out. And we have been struggling to say, Gibson's not a problem, he is an important part of – or another 'leg' in theatre. And theatre needs to be supported by several legs.

But let me tell you one experience to show you what the Gibson tradition is: I was still working for Ravan Press as a co-ordinating editor of *Staffrider Magazine*. Then I said to Gibson, 'I am going to interview you for the magazine. I am having a show soon, and you are having a show this week. I would like one of your boys to announce that we are having a show next week. We are doing *Egoli*.' It was a two-hander – actually a three-hander at the time. It was two guys and a woman . . . So the show was advertised at Gibson's show, and I did the interview with Gibson for *Staffrider*. And Gibson is a nice person.

After the announcing of the show we packed the theatre for the first time. It was an experimental piece. But I tell you we had hell. The audience expected something very different – Gibson style! They were asking questions during the performance: 'Where is the band? Where are the dancers?' You know we did no music. 'We don't want recitations.' If we have a monologue, it is 'recitation'. It is English – high-flown English. In moments when we had darkness – like when these guys were in a dark mine-shaft; the light was very dim, and there were only torches on the stage – people shouted 'Where are these people? Where is the music?' There was a war, you know, in Sharpeville, in Vredenville. They broke onto the stage, they demanded their money back, they claimed they were being robbed!

This is what we've been through. I mean we've been through a situation due to the tradition that Gibson had created. Maishe (Maponya) was told 'A man can give birth,' when he did *Umongikazi* in Bophuthatswana. There was an actor who played a woman, a male actor, and people were furious. They couldn't see that this was an experimenetal piece – because Gibson had created a tradition. It is no exaggeration. And it was very difficult for us to survive under the tradition of Gibson.

And we struggled, along with John Kani, with *The Island*, and *Sizwe Bansi Is Dead* – these shows, which is also the realist touch which influenced me strongly; I mean – these plays, *The Island* and *Sizwe Bansi*.

And then there was Zakes Mda's *We Shall Die for the Fatherland*, and also *Shanti*, written by Mtuli Ka'Shezi, who came from a very strong Black Consciouness background in the seventies. A very strong movement.

And for me it all had a very strong impact, because I grew up in a Black Consciousness family. And we went to see these pieces. People couldn't follow, but I had been through this kind of revolution, in contrast to Gibson. But I tell you, those shows could not be popular. Gibson was in fact dominating the scene. Until people like Maredi and *Workshop '71* slightly changed the scene with *Survival*. And then, later on, we had *Woza Albert* with Barney Simon. And I suppose with proper marketing and the support and background of the Market Theatre, *Woza Albert* became very popular.

But this country then made a mistake again. They said the latest kind of theatre that had come out of South Africa was agitprop, which is rubbish. It was done long before. It was done in Port Elizabeth by the Serpent Players. They had long since started the tradition. *Workshop '71*, and even some of us had started to do the same thing. *Woza Albert* basically popularised agitprop theatre. Other people would struggle for some time. Then someone – we didn't know who – would crack the scene.

And so Mbogeni (Ngema) and Percy (Mtwa), coming from the Gibson tradition, had learnt the tricks. They introduced the tricks by fusing Gibson and us. And that's how they cracked the market, and that way serious theatre began to grow, and began to be popular. So everybody moved away from the Gibson approach, into this kind of theatre that we had initiated.

Then we had to start moving away, now going back to musicals. And then I started doing musicals, big shows, because I felt it is good to pioneer changes within society.

You feel that musicals are a legitimate mode of theatre in the future as an extension of what you have been working for?

Ja. We were saying various people have not experienced African opera. Now we want to do an African opera, with the link of African poetry; visuals, I mean like painting and sculptures. So I am doing an African opera piece now, for sports, like *Ubuntu* in Sports, using a musician to tell the story of a boy in South Africa. It is a multi-media approach, because things are getting so sophisticated.

And also we as writers, we are victims of modern technology. We are getting more and more trapped by the technology of modern media, of television. People are beginning all over the world to be too lazy to read, people are too lazy to listen for a long time. People are wanting something with a rhythm; it has to be so dynamic, it has to have so many kinds of magical effects. Like this Italian writer who says that the world has commercialised advertising in such a way that people cannot even dream without adverts. It is five minutes of dream, then an advert, five minutes and another advert. The society is so messed up. We cannot watch a show for three hours. Adverts! Look at television.

So it seems the multi-media approach is beginning to dictate to a lot of us, that if we still want people to listen to what we have to say, maybe the multi-media approach is what we have to resort to . . .

We are threatened by violence. The neighbourhood where I live here is seriously threatened by violence. And if we do not begin to use theatre, or art, as a form of dealing with violence, we will have big problems. Our parents, our family, our relatives live here, and we have a responsibility for that social transformation. It is not the responsibility of the government alone. It is our responsibility as artists. So that is why

I don't see the beauty of being trapped in town. I'd rather be trapped where the problem is. And I begin to see myself being functional, dealing with problems that confront society.

Johannesburg is a great problem to me; Soweto is a real problem. It is like Harlem. And this is where we see the role of theatre used as as positive and functional and revolutionary theatre; theatre that transforms society, theatre that empowers society, educates society. Not just entertainment. You entertain, but you educate and inform society in the process. And you actually effect changes. You make people participate, and you make theatre teach people.

James Matthews made a nice statement, saying that if you create a revolutionary piece to a number of people who are revolutionaries, that is a true revolution. If you take a revolutionary piece to people who are just audiences to a revolution, there is no revolution.

And this is the way the previous government suppressed us: when we were intrrerogated for our works, in the past, they would tell us straight, 'We know experimental theatre is revolutionary theatre, because you are provoking people to go and throw stones.'

And now here, today, this country needs revolutionary theatre more than ever before, whereby you can create theatre among the people who need the change, and the people who *see* the need for change. Theatre is not like a museum, where things are frozen, within four walls. But theatre is something that says, 'Transform society!'

How do you transform society? I am not just an entertainer. I am like an educational institution, and I am a custodian of the past. I educate my people. And I cannot educate my people if I am far from my people. The rest of the world will benefit when we take the production on tour.

But my target is not the world. The target is the people. If the work we proffer is good, it will be relevant all over the world. It has got the whole concept of the universality of art or theatre. To be universal, I do not need to use a language that communicates with the whole world. No, no, no! I can write, surely, in Pedi, in my mother tongue. And if it's good, it will communicate with the whole world. If it's good . . . And if it's no good – so good! I've been watching pieces written in German, French, in any language, and if it is a good piece of theatre, I won't understand the language, but I will look at the visuals, and it will talk to me.

How do you relate to Rob Mshengu Kavanagh's views on theatre?

Well, I was very young when people like Mshengu were working here. I've read a lot about him, and I had the opportunity to be with him in Nice, at Anne Fuch's place, and we kind of began to know each other. And I also met him in Zimbabwe. But I haven't worked with him. I appreciate people who can deal with issues of criticism beyond party politics, because I am not into party politics. I want to be free from party politics. I don't want to be the carrier of any political slogan. But I may be a slogan myself, of a particular party, without being conscious of that. And I saw that element in Robert. That making out requires courage. Making out is like a public confession of yourself and of problems within yourself, within your society, and even the ills within yourself and ills within the society you live in.

But I haven't had a working relationship with Robert. We've just had discussions and sharing thoughts about what is going on within the arts world. The only thing that I've always wanted to raise with white people in general, not only with Robert – with all white people – is that I haven't experienced black people who work with white people, being empowered to be in a position to do things themselves. I don't know if this is typical of Robert, but I've seen a lot of this. I've seen white and black people working with Junction Avenue. But I've never heard of any black person in Junction Avenue being the one who has produced a theatre-piece. And that for me is a problem.

And people used to say that I am saying this because I believe in Black Consciousness, and Black Consciousness is racist, Black Consciousness is exclusive. It is *not* exclusivist, it is *developmental*. When we talk about reconstruction and development today, the government is talking particularly about black people, who need to be reconstructed, because they were destroyed. And we need to be developed because we were underdeveloped. What the government is concerned about is what we have been talking about all these years: that you need to develop black writers and black directors and black producers.

If you talk about producing black theatre in this country, you tell me: which black producers do you know? There are no black producers. Black people are working for white people. They are working for white institutions. They are working for white theatre companies. They are working for white agents. If I am looking for an actor today, I talk to a white company – to get a black actor! So are we going to continue to be a fund for white people? I refuse. I totally refuse! And I say, and you can ask Rob Amato. Rob Amato is a friend. Rob and I struggled here in Johannesburg when we did *Egoli*. We were doing a show at the Box Theatre, and Rob came – we didn't know that Rob was in the audience. And I told the performers, whether there are five or four or two or one persons in the audience, you must give them a full performance. And they gave a full performance all the time.

Rob saw the show, and he came round after the show and said, 'Look, I want you guys to come to Cape Town. When can you come?' We said, 'Yesterday! We'll take the train tomorrow.'

Because we were running away. In those days it was a struggle. And I made arrangements with the actors, and they said 'OK, we're going.' I was working for Ravan Press, and Rob was establishing the Space Theatre in Cape Town. The guys left, and soon I also followed them. We sat down and worked on the script, and I must say the exercise I went through with Rob was very helpful for me in terms of editing. And with my experience at Ravan Press, I'd learnt not to be scared to cancel three of seven pages of your text in order to give it focus.

And we fought with Rob several times. You know, coming from Black Consciousness and now working with a white person . . .

At the back of your mind you think, and when you sleep you reflect, and you begin to see that the issues he was raising were quite valid, about the piece needing focus. And he then hyped us quite a lot, and for me personally it was good, as a writer, because I sat and worked through a lot of things with him for a long time, and I said, 'OK, I've changed a lot of things in my script based on your criticism.' But I was still going through the actual writing.

And this was a very good therapy for me as a writer. And when you do that now with some of the young writers today, you are like a pain, you know. They don't understand that any work of art has to be criticised. That's how it develops, and that's how it grows.

And that was very good with Rob. We were obviously criticised being Black Consciousness artists and then working with a white person. But I said, 'Look, being Black Consciousness does not say that you cannot work with a white person.'

But it does say you must be in a position to assert your own values and your own ideas. Working with a white person does not mean that you've got to be oppressed, or your views must be oppressed, or your culture must be oppressed. It was quite an experience working with Rob at the Space Theatre. Then we came back to Johannesburg and took only that performance to the Market Theatre after we'd done a run at the Space. Then we wanted to close the show, as we had an invitation to go to Germany.

And now, should we change the show, should we adapt the show to a German audience, what do we do? We decided to show it as it was. The two guys were very good performers. And the script was so tight. You could trust yourselves to go anywhere in the world. So we went to Germany, and people were giving us all kinds of definitions and names and theories and references that was when I started becoming very vulnerable, because I was young. I didn't know anything about theatre, so I started studying theatre then. I was reading about Mshengu, all the theatre theoreticians in this country. I also wanted to study about Brecht, and went to the Great Theatre of Brecht in Berlin.

When was this?

It was in 1982. From '82 to '86 I was studying in Berlin. One was not allowed to enter East Berlin. But I went in illegally, and I went to Brecht's grave. For everything we were doing was revolving around Brecht. I said to myself, I had to inform myself about this man.

But I must say I was also haunted by fear – for not having been to school, and about people asking me questions about our academic background and so on. People thought, with the kind of work we had produced, we must be very well informed and educated. And, you know, you get scared – you don't want to embarrass yourself and look like a fool before the whole world. At the time the two actors were not that much bothered – they were having a good time.

But I was not having a good time. I had to face all the interviews, and that's when I started educating myself. I started studying theatre on my own. I was being asked to go and deliver lectures at the universities, and I'd have to read the subject. And I'd have to speak from my own personal experience, like a person who has done a degree in theatre. And that was very scary, but at the same time it was very fulfilling.

Then there was Ian Steadman, who was a friend, who helped us survive in this country by writing and talking about us all this time in the university, and even in debates – about myself and Maishe (Maponya) in particular, because our position was seen to be anti-white or anti certain people who were in charge of the theatre scene in this country. And he was the one who said, 'No, no, no! These guys are talking about what you have been talking about, namely the need to assert black people.'

I would then struggle to study the syllabus of Wits when I was developing the syllabus of the school here at Funda, and I'd come up with concepts comparing different syllabuses. And for me that was like an educational process that somehow or other empowered some of us to be seen as academics within the profession. And each time I said, 'Look, I went through informal education, but I don't believe people are self-taught. You learn from other people, and from people around you.' When people like Professor Es'kiah Mphahlele and others came home, we would go and harrass them for information, do interviews to find out about the role of theatre in society, and different ways of creating theatre – mobile theatre – what were the experiences elsewhere in Africa? African theatre in general, not just South African theatre.

Then I would begin to expose black students to a Pan-African kind of theatre. Black students must be exposed to the whole continent. That was sort of taken up by people here, who'd begin to say, 'That's what even Wits University needs.' We did what we call community development theatre, through Wits, and we would fight for some of the students, who were not matriculants, to be accepted at Wits. And we said, 'Look, they must go for a degree.' But what is a degree? If you look at the education institutions in this country – it's a disaster!

Then I did a degree programme. For the first time I tried to study for a degree. I had started about four times to do a degree. First it was the B.A. It didn't work, because I was already working for Ravan Press as an editor. So when I did literary criticism, I would write my essay based on my experience. And this professor would tell me straight, 'You must stop writing what you know from your work – write what we are teaching you!' I said, 'But what is education? Education is supposed to inform in terms of what I already know, in terms of what is in practice.'

Then I gave up my literary studies. No ways! I wanted to go and do a degree in fine arts. In the second year I had already written a book on the history of South African theatre. I had problems with some of the lecturers. Some of them were even younger than some of us in terms of experience. I said, 'What is it I am studying here? I have to come and endorse your Eurocentric syllabuses. I have to study first about Europe, before I begin to study about Africa. Must I follow this process that almost brainwashes you?' After that you will have a degree or a paper, and then you have to go back and start to kind of bring back your mind!

It has been a struggle in terms of having papers. Maishe even had to go to Oxford to study drama for him to be accepted as a lecturer.

When they suggested the same thing to me I said, 'No, I am sorry, but if you want me to come and lecture, accept me as I am! Tell me which subject you want me to lecture in, otherwise forget it.' Educational institutions work on the basis of papers. And this for me is not acceptable. We need to educate society. We need to come up with an education system that will ensure that people really learn, and that the institution learns from the people. If the institutions cannot learn from the students, there is no learning. The educational dilemma is that it is teacher-based.

Phew! It is a problem.

And who are the teachers? Professor Mphahlele always says, 'You go to a white university. When you see a black person there, you'll know that person must be a student. You go to a black university and you see a white person there – that white person must be a lecturer. You don't expect a white person in a black university to be a student.'

And that is what this country deprives itself of, even up to today, in the new system. That's why you find the 'Maghoba problem', the new Vice-Chancellor at Wits. For us it's not surprising. We find it's about time we begin to talk about these things.

It is about time we begin to ask, 'How does so-and-so become a professor? What is a professorship? How do you earn a professorship? Do you earn a professorship by being associated with Mr Solberg? If you are an associate of Mr Solberg's, then he has the powers to say, Matsemela, now you can be Professor Manaka.'

Nonsense! But this has been happening for some time.

Now, this Maghoba thing – he's still young. But he has been a source of inspiration for a lot of young people, and people who are confronted by some of his thoughts. And most of the things he was raising were said earlier by Professor Mphahlele and some of the other elderly people.

And then he was saying that they will see us as Black Consciousness, as revolutionaries, as Pan Africanists, racists. So we would get dismissed. But now these things are coming up again. And I now want to see how Wits deals with it, as an educational institution.

How do you see this problem resolved? Will he be chased away?

No, they'll have to make the other people resign, I think. They have a big problem on their hands; it will create a revolution in education in this country. It is actually beginning to say, 'Where is education in this country going? What is the situation in the established educational institutions which used to be white? Or were pretending to be liberal? What is happening within educational programmes?'

Because I used to say to Ian (Steadman), 'Look, Ian, Wits looks very progressive, but your syllabus is not progressive. When I look at the content of your syllabus, I'd rather deal with a conservative Afrikaner university with a progressive syllabus.'

For me it is not the way the lecturers of the university look in terms of black and white. It's what they are lecturing on. The continuation of the colonial process! Transform the syllabus, not the outward image of the institution. They have black lecturers up there, and a lot of black students. But what are they studying? That is what is critical for me. I can have an institution where the lecturers are all white, if they are studying the right thing! That's what is important. It's not how it looks.

And I think it is the same thing that is happening with theatre in this country, that you see certain institutions that used to be white institutions or white dominated, bringing in black people to give it a facelift. But the institution has not changed. It's Fatima Dike's coconut thing. If society and the world are to survive racial animosity, we have to be honest and open to each other.

Where do you see the theatre moving – in concrete terms?

I think there is a revolutionary need in this country to take theatre to the people. Until we take theatre to the people, move it from these heavy institutions, it is not going anywhere. We've seen it in America, the Broadway tradition; you need to put in a lot of money. You see it in the Market Theatre today, at the Windybrow, the Civic Theatre, at the State Theatre, or Napac, or in Bloemfontein – all over the country: They are all dead! Why? Because they have left the people behind!

The majority of the people in this country are black, and the black people are not part of the superstructure of theatre. Peter Toerien in Johannesburg, has got his own subscription: people are subscribers, white people who support him all the time. That's why he is around. He has dealt with his people, he has created his own market. And he is one of the few people in this country who survives. And I totally respect it. He knew exactly what he was creating. He has survived beyond apartheid, beyond independence. It's the only place where you can see the theatre packed. The rest? They have left their target market behind. They will suffer like the rest of the world, like Paris, like New York . . . You go to galleries – only tourists support the gallery. People who live in the area – dead.

So until the theatre goes back to the people, in the true sense, and the achievers, like John Kani, all of them, go back to the people, nothing will happen. Not until the theatre goes back to the people and performs in a space amongst the people. And when I say the people, I mean the black people who are in the majority. Because you cannot destroy Soweto. It's a reality. You cannot destroy Port Elizabeth, you cannot detroy Pretoria. It's a reality. But we cannot take everybody to the city and say, 'Let's all move to the city.' That will be the end of it.

I think we need to learn from what has happened in other parts of the world, and how other people have experienced the decline of support in theatre. And even with movies, too. It's becoming the same problem. There was a time when we used to come up with theories about the theatre versus film. With theatre you can smell the performer, which you cannot do with film. Today it is television. You need not even go out, and be exposed to violence. Violence is real, but if a big name comes along, they pack the venues for ninety rands per ticket. So nobody can argue that it is a money problem or a violence problem. Yet they can go out to shebeens at night, and get pissed and drunk. They go out to a shebeen!

So there is something wrong with the theatre tradition in this country. It is a matter of focus, of target, and until we begin to create consortiums and stop becoming little monsters who run certain spaces, things won't get better. Not until you create consortiums that take theatre to the people and forget about the money.

Yes, money is a problem, but money is not the only problem. The problem is about focus. We have lost focus.

Yes, interesting times ahead, and lots of work to be done . . .

Yes, lots of work to be done. And the other monster to be transformed is the South African Broadcasting Corporation, SABC. We need to begin creating films of a high standard, to show drama on stage through the media to make people want to go and see proper theatre, drama on stage. The TV programmes in this country are appalling. They are terrible! How do we transform the SABC? They are the biggest providers of 'opium to the people'.

Is Sisulu delivering?

Sisulu is a policy maker. He can come with his theories and ideas and transformation strategies, but he is not handling programmes. He cannot from up there permeate, straight through, everything that must be produced. Sometimes he hardly knows what is produced. It's just like Aggrey Klaaste, the editor of *The Sowetan*. Sometimes he hardly knows what is being published in his own newspaper. He cannot read every article. And Sisulu cannot see every SABC programme that is being screened on the box.

What we believe is this: We need many Sisulus on the ground, hands on.

Sadly, Matsemela Manaka was killed in a car crash before publication of this book.

Thulani Sifeni

Thulani Sifeni, you are a young writer and theatre practitioner. Would you mind giving me a brief sketch of your background – your childhood, your youth?

It was a difficult childhood. I was born in Bhekuzulu, Vryheid, in Natal in 1963, but I grew up here in Johannesburg, in Soweto. I came here as early as 1965–66, and like all the other youngsters I attended school in Soweto, until 1977, and then boarding school. That was the time when I really started to be aware of theatre, since there was no school. One teacher invited us to get involved in a play. That was in '77, and the urge kept on until I completed matric. But I wouldn't consider myself an intellectual. I don't know the doors of universities. For me it has been more learning from experience.

So you were fourteen and on the threshold of adulthood when Soweto exploded.

Ja, ja, I was part of it.

What sort of development have you been through during these years with regard to theatre?

I became aware that theatre was something quite different from the radio plays that we used to listen to when the teacher asked us to do so. Gradually I became involved in school productions and in creating our own plays up to the time when I completed my schooling. And after completing matric I decided that I was going to do theatre full time. Since then, since 1982, I have been in theatre.

Were you also involved in the school boycott during the Soweto uprising?

Oh, yes, I was one of the ringleaders.

How did you manage to complete your matric, then? That must have been difficult!

Yes, it was not very easy, I must say, because there would always be those hiccups. But it was easier after 1977, when I started attending boarding school.

I understand that much of your work is community oriented. Would you like to comment on that?

If you look at those who have been influenced by the '76 era, the idea has been to try and reflect what is happening in the community, or to correct or to encourage certain directions. For us, doing theatre meant starting from there, and I think that influenced even some of the works that I was to do afterwards. Because you don't do a play simply because you want to do a play. You would always want to reflect problems within the community which you feel need to be challenged or need to be exposed.

Mainly I've been doing education programmes. The second play that we did when I started really to become a fully-fledged practitioner was *Burning Embers*, which was more a political thing, predicting the manipulations of politicians and all that.

After that it was *Top Down*, which was looking at the relationship within the African teaching profession, and the principals, and how they are being manipulated by the situation, and students would see teachers as a problem, whilst the principals and inspectors and the education department would also see them as a problem. So the problem was lying within the teaching sector. They see themselves as professionals, whilst on the other hand where they are supposed to be recognised as professionals, they are only seen as workers.

Did you write Burning Embers *yourself?*

Yes, I co-wrote it.

How many were you?

We were four.

Has collaboration been the pattern throughout your work as a script-writer?

Not throughout – off and on.

Do you have special political leanings? PAC? ANC?

I am a staunch Pan-Africanist.

South African theatre seems to be in a kind of limbo these days, if we are to believe some of the gurus. Do you see any new developments under way in South African theatre today?

Well – theatre in limbo – both yes and no. It is what people have created that has been in limbo. If you look, for instance, at works that have been promoted by institutions like the Market Theatre, you'll find that the works it has propagated have tended to serve certain needs, a status quo politically: they have started to suffer, actuality is not going in that direction.

But if you look at people who have promoted community-based theatre, they always have ideas they want to explore. It's just that the political climate really did kill the audience somehow – people couldn't attend theatre at night and so on. But if you do your theatre in a well-organised manner, you can work very well.

So you go out into the townships with your theatre?

Yes, that's where we perform, basically.

In Soweto?

Yes, in Soweto and throughout the country, I must say – in rural areas, urban areas. And throughout the eight years that we have been in existence, there hasn't been a single year that the Bachaki Theatre has been fully funded. We've never had real funders.

But we have run workshops, we have done performances, we have taught throughout the country, down to Cape Town, without any assistance. We have been surviving on what we get from door takings and we have continued doing our work. I think this has to do with a certain commitment. It is 'What we are preaching must reach the people,' rather than 'How much is coming in? Can it take me from point A to point B?'

And it is also a matter of age. Because now that we are growing older we are beginning to realise that, 'Hey, by the way, I am really supposed to have a roof of my own. I can't always be under my parents' roof.'

Then you are starting to scramble around to see what you can piece together to give you funds, you know. But throughout the other period, really, you have not minded much as long as there was something coming which would give you bread, and that you are able to leave some of it at home, and you just continue working.

You see that theatre as a didactic media, do you?

Ja, ja. Very much so.

How do you take care of the aesthetic side, if you squint back to Albie Sachs' 'heretical' paper on the Struggle and the ANC's cultural programme?

Theatre grows, you know. There was a period when you got influenced by certain ideas from outside. But at some point you realise the bigger role that theatre plays. For me entertainment becomes the bottom line. I've heard people from all sectors, white people, Africans, coming and watching some of the work that we've been doing to acclaim, because it is what you do creatively and what you preach that becomes relevant. For me that is the bottom line. Even now you have the kind of influence and the kind of direction and perspective that you would like people to view. They are daily experiences, but there is always the creative side: how much can you do to make what you are doing acceptable to people – for them to enjoy what they are watching, and to educate the people?

So education and entertainment must go hand in hand?

Yes, definitely.

One young man I interviewed in Durban, Jerry Pooe with The Marabi

Dance, claimed that the musical might be the best way of educating a township public, to make them acquire theatre awareness, because the enjoyment factor would be highlighted to a much greater extent in the musical compared to proper theatre. How would you look at that?

Well, for me it is a matter of style. Because you can do a boring musical and you can do a relevant musical. But for me it is not really the musical as *style* . . . There has been a dominance over the years, whereby certain kinds of theatre have been put on for the people to watch, as pure entertainment. But all the time you have to educate the people.

And people are not really dumb, you know. You can come with very serious productions, and if there is message enough and it is creative enough they will be able to listen to that attentively. So I do not really categorise: I've done a musical piece, I've done a theatrical piece like the first production of the Bachaki Theatre, *Top Down*. There was no singing there. It was strictly theatre. And we have taken it to schools, we have taken it to halls, we have taken it to community centres, and it has come out tops! I mean, we even performed it at the Market Theatre. *Top Down* was for us a launching pad. After *Top Down* it was as if we had been long in the field, while it was in fact the first production of the group.

Do you have any older, established playwrights that have in a sense been your models, ideals?

Well, I think I have been more influenced by the history of the country. I have read quite a lot. I like what Ngugi writes, and I like what Sembene Osmane writes. With the local writers I think I appreciate Dukuza Maku's works, and I also appreciate the work of a friend of mine, Angifi Oladla. I have seen some of what he has written and I think it is quite good. But I have a lot of reservations concerning some of the works – *Woza Albert*, *The Island*, all the other big super stars, the famous works – I have really big question marks, because the press writes about it so much that you think it must be something out of this world. And when you go and watch it you expect that definitely people should be going beyond what they have done. Maybe it is because of the extent to which it has been portrayed. And I always attend a lot of grassroot works, and

I think that when some of those are fully developed they would make the Market Theatre look like child's play.

So you look at the development in South African theatre with great optimism?

Yes, I do.

How about financial support: do you envisage any financial support coming your way from government? – From the Ministry of Art, Culture and Technology?

So far there hasn't been anything worth talking about. What we've had so far is just promises and a bit from emergency funds. I still hope that there could be a move in that sort of direction, but the government has in the beginning concentrated on bigger structures like the Civic Theatre, the Market Theatre. I think it would have been better if they had started by supporting the grassroots activities, because there are quite a number of groups throughout the country that do better work. But I think they are now more interested in the image. If they give money to the Market Theatre, everybody in the world will know, but if they give to Monde's group in the township, who will know? So that has for me been somewhat disappointing, but, well, they say it is a slow process, but we don't know how long slow is.

So there are, in fact, a fairly large number of travelling theatrical groups in the townships. How many would there be? Could you make an estimate?

I think there are more than twenty only in Soweto. For some of them you would find that the standard of work is not all that good, but you would also find that others are quite good.

When it comes to your own personal work, I understand you don't write only for the stage. What have you written so far?

I have written some poetry and short stories. But I write mainly poetry and plays. Presently I am teaching myself to write film scripts and stuff like that.

Have you had anything published as yet?

No, not yet. I wanted to publish my poetry, but I found to my disappointment that you get only seven percent of the proceeds as a writer, and thought, well, then I'd rather keep my work to myself. Because I really sweat when I am writing. I read a lot, and I have read how some of the people work on their things, and for me that has been quite a learning process. You read, you experiment, and you try and think what it is that is missing. So this, for me, has been my sort of growth.

But, of course, I haven't got enough experience on the administration side, because in theatre, especially community-based theatre, once you are a director, or lead that kind of a theatre group, you have to do the production writing of whatever material is at hand, and you develop at the same time both on the creative and the administrative side.

Actually, now, that I look back over the last eight years, I realise that some of the limitations of this is that some of the works are left half done because you've had to concentrate on one aspect at the expense of the others. I feel that we now have to take other steps, not only my group but others too, to inform each other about some of our experiences. That's why I would like to sit down and write down my experiences with big theatres, with community groups, and the responses – all the experiences that we have had in developing and creating our work, the styles of acting and writing and so on.

How about the language issue: do you write in your own language, or do you write mainly in English?

That's a tricky question. I think that poetry I write both in Zulu and in English. In theatre I use mostly the township language, which is a mixture of English, Zulu, Sotho, etc., so while a few plays are in fully-fledged English, most of them are in this township mix. I have not yet written a full play in Zulu.

Do you envisage doing that, or are you trying to get out to a larger public by using English?

It depends a bit on where we are performing. Since we are not performing a lot in Natal, Zulu is not an obvious choice for me now. Sometimes you have to take a play to Qwaqwa, for instance, where the larger percentage of people speak Sotho. Still, I feel it is important to write in Zulu, and with the present trend of translating into other African languages, it will be possible to write in any of the African languages and still be read by a larger public.

When I started writing poetry it was English that was important because of the politics of the time. If you were politically conscious, you had to know English. If you knew English, we knew that, oh, this one is politically conscious, because most of the political stuff is in English.

However, most of the young kids today who are politically orientated, don't know how to communicate. They hardly know how to construct a sentence. The political trend is moving in the direction of this new township lingo, which is dominating now, and also towards talking in the African languages. That, I think, is very important at this moment.

How many African languages do you speak yourself?

Oh, I speak a lot. I speak Sotho, Xhosa, Zulu, Swazi; I speak Pedi, Shangaan – most of the African languages.

And you are fully conversant in those languages?

You haven't learnt them at school, but you can easily communicate in these languages, whether you are addressing the audience after the play, or whatever. What we usually do, is we have workshops after the plays with discussions about the relevance of the work, what we are doing, and about the environment and stuff like that.

As a Zulu, do you see as hurtful any of the problems that one encounters in Natal these days, for instance the factional fighting, the black on black violence etc.?

Well, I prefer saying that I am a Zulu-speaking African, not that I am a Zulu, because there is this trend that people would say, 'Hey, this one is Xhosa,' or 'that one is Zulu,' which I actually think is what is propagated by Mandela and Buthelezi. I think on the ground it is totally different, and also to many people around the townships. We are not really very much affected. It does hurt you because you have relatives down in Natal who are actually manipulated by politicians into killing each other for the survival of the politicians. That does really affect us, but you don't automatically accept that when people say Zulu that means IFP, or that Xhosa means ANC. Not all Xhosas or Zulus are in that sort of ball game. Presently I just see that what the politicians are doing, is they are depoliticising the people for their own ends. Because, honestly speaking, all these people who are being used by Chief Minister Buthelezi, had they been conscious politically, they would not have been involved in that sort of game, because they would know that at the end of the day *he* benefits, and the same with all those people who are being used by Mandela on the other side.

It may seem that this is a present-day problem, but for some of us the problem is very old. Now it is like the IFP is on the 'wrong side'. But if one looks at the kind of political games of forcing political doctrines on others, if one looks into history, one finds that the problems arose when those Zulus from the rural areas came to the towns and were put into hostels. They were used to young people respecting the authority of elder people, but now they found that there in the townships the politicians were using kids, especially in the politics of the mid- and late eighties, to propagate whatever they wanted. You'd find that there was this kind of friction. Now the Afrikaners taught the IFP that if the others hit them, hit back!

So eventually the media propagated the idea that the violence was due to Zulus or the Xhosas as such, and because the people are uneducated it gradually became an on-going thing. You go to the Transkei, a person tells you, that 'Hey, the Zulus have finished us! You see that family? They lost one, they lost two members . . .'

And you go to Natal, and you get the same story in the reverse: 'How do you survive with these people, the Xhosas? Those people are killing us!' So when you sit back and reflect, you realise that it is all a political game. People are not given political education so that they can develop themselves and their society. They are only told political 'squares', you know: You are here, in this corner or in that corner, and you cannot go beyond there! You realise it is a game. That is why I believe so firmly in Pan-Africanism, the Sobukwes and the Lembedes, because for me those were people who actually lived what they were preaching: they never sacrificed people just so that they could benefit themselves. But their sacrifice was for the benefit of the nation, which for me is a very relevant and important thing.

I asked Wally Serote recently if he is still under the influence of Black Consciousness and Pan-African dogmas. His reply was that the majority of his generation moved in with the ANC, and, as one would expect from a person high up in the ANC hierarchy, his Pan-Africanist leanings are a thing of the past. Now, what is there in the Pan-Africanist Movement that you still find attractive?

It is the first principle that Sobukwe talks about, and the Nkrumahs of the past, which is African Nationalism. If people understood and practised African Nationalism, we wouldn't be talking of infights within the African masses, or the so-called black-on-black violence. There wouldn't be that kind of thing, because in Pan-Africanism tribalism is shifted aside in favour of unity of all the African people, so that we can be talking of Xhosa-speaking Africans. We become one nation and don't see each other as different peoples. That for me is still very relevant. I think that pillar, which is the continental unity, has been downplayed. Europe is now talking of Pan-Europe, but when Africans talk about Pan-Africanism, it is as if one is talking of a dream. But to me this is still very relevant, for the benefit of the continent and for the benefit of the whole world.

But you have dropped the 'colour clause' of Pan-Africanism? In the early stages the PAC was for blacks exclusively, wasn't it? Are you now prepared to look at South Africa as one nation, with all the colours that there are?

Well, there is a confusion about Pan-Africanism in some spheres. I think we talk more of the problems and the solutions that we foresee.

Problems, what problems?

For example the land dispossession problem. For me those are some of the ingredients. There is a first step and a final step, and I think that is where the confusion lies, politically, between ANC and PAC. I am not talking of the PAC of Makwethu. I think those ones are no longer PAC. Because they have actually lost their direction. If you know some of its history, you will know that originally the PAC was actually within the ANC. In fact, if you look at the programme of 1949, that was adopted by the ANC, that was a Pan-Africanist programme. And come 1955 it was lost. For me it is not really the question of colour, but it is really the question of interest. You will for example find that some people still hold two citizenships, while they are still in this country. But we need to come to a stage where we can say to our people, 'Hey, can you see that now we are really free?' And the people themselves will realise that this is really freedom.

In my view it has never really been a problem of colour, but it has been a problem of the needs: the basic needs, and the secondary needs. The dispossession has been the real problem. And now the question is how we actually go about redressing that problem.

For me the history has really been down-played in favour of positions. I think that the people who are in the leadership of political organisations actually jumped to their positions – the First Minister of whatever! But the people at the grassroots have not really been considered. They have to wait. Rather the leaders should have started by solving the problems within the masses and leaving their own positions to wait, but they started the other way round.

So that became a problem for me, because if you read the speeches of Robert Sobukwe, he talked of some of these things as early as 1959, when he talked of what is actually happening today, in 1995, saying that the revolutionaries of yesterday will become the betrayers of tomorrow. The workers are told: 'No, you can't be jumping around now: we'll send you to court!', while it was the workers that were exploited, that were used, being told, 'Liberation first, Education afterwards'. And when that is put into practice, Sobukwe was saying: 'We must actually fight colonial education, so that whatever you learn now must be relevant to the country and the continent.'

For me that becomes much more meaningful than the other dogmas. I think somewhere, somehow, there has been a political game going on. When you start to reflect, I think that basically politicians are the same throughout the world. Look at Kenya – it's the same thing. Look at the East – people have been going all out for the East, and you go around Soweto, and you see the KGB and stuff like that.

But when you see what they've done in other countries, then you realise that it is not a matter of hero worshipping, but it is about finding out what is good in socialism, and how you practise what is good in socialism. What could we borrow or steal from it, and what is it that works in the capitalist countries, what is it that is relevant to our situation? I think for me that is the bottom line.

Does that mean to say that the PAC of today has become much more pragmatic than in the early days, say, in 1959, when they broke away from the ANC?

Well, I think that the PAC that is led by Makwetu is the same as the ANC. It's just that because of positions they wouldn't want to say that, because I think what was the problem then between the two organisations is still there. For me it is OK that an organisation like the ANC stands for whatever it stands for, but it is very important to have the principled PAC, which will actually reflect whatever is actually being down-played by the ANC, and therefore I support the PAC. Some of the people within the PAC have probably forgotten about the principles of the party and done the same thing, but they have run more for positions and personal gains and stuff like that.

Returning to the theatre again, what do you see as future themes, if any, for the theatre and for the playwrights to pursue?

I think that for the present *development* is for me the most important theme, as it was during the times of the Vorsters and the Bothas. People need to develop and get rid of inferiority complexes: they need to develop within the health sector and in all areas necessary to put our country on a par with the other countries in the world.

Also the emphasis on self-identification and self-knowledge is very important. There are traditional matters that were practised before which need to be brought back, so we need really to research some of our past.

Look, for instance, at the problem of Aids, which is spreading among the youth. We used to have practices before called *ukusoma*, where you don't penetrate a woman in the love play. Such practices are very relevant under the present conditions, and the young people need to be enticed to practise these things, such as *ukusoma* – to have a publicly known boyfriend when you are at a certain age, so as to avoid the spread of VD and Aids. For me such things are of relevance and need to be explored also through theatre.

Talking of tradition: do you see the story-telling tradition, the communicative traditions of your culture as something worth cultivating for the future theatre?

Yes, yes definitely.

In what ways, would you say?

I think the form on its own, and also the content of some of the story-telling, those are definitely going to be adapted and will create new styles. But what interests me the most, actually, is what has not been fully explored or fully recorded for the use in theatre. You have things like *Umabatha*, which explore, maybe, one eighth of the whole area. But there's quite a lot of different styles, but more important for me is what message is being transmitted. Because people enjoy story-telling, so you are able to play around with and bring out some of these stories as something they can easily identify with, and also give them the urge to create as well.

You know, of course, what Gcina Mhlophe has been doing in this field. Do you approve of her way of approaching the story-telling tradition?

Yes, I have great respect for what Gcina has done. Well, there are some others who are doing the same thing. It's just that it's actually practised in the rural areas where it used to be practised together with other activities.

We were discussing with some traditional dancers, comparing the traditional dance with ballet and stuff like that, which is practised by PACT, looking at the standard of some of the groups that are doing traditional dance. Traditional dancing needs to be really uplifted. The government must fund the traditional dancers as much as they are funding the ballet dancers. Looking at traditional dances – in form, in content – I think it must be realised that when we do our dances they should not be looked upon as merely dance, but as dance that tells a story. That was there before, but I think industrialisation actually killed traditional dancing, when it became only some form of entertainment or merry-making, and fixed. So now we need to develop that to become part of the developmental programme.

One theme that has come up frequently in connection with the question of future themes, is that of gender: how to try and change the trend of male chauvinist behaviour, which clearly has also been part of African culture. Have you got strong views about this issue?

Well, I have actually discussed the gender issue with a lot of people. I don't really think it is a problem associated with African culture. I think it has been the abuse of African culture. Men and women in Africa had roles that they were playing. Because of colonialism and industrialisation some of the roles that the males used to play within the family have been changed by them having to go away to seek work, whereas some of the roles belonging to the women remained. That has actually destroyed the whole culture. If, for example, you were to beat up your wife, that was a taboo in African culture. Now, it has actually been practised by some men, but I don't agree that it is part of our African culture. I think African culture had definite roles for all to play.

So now what we need to do is to concretise some of those roles and develop them, and give them the status that they deserve. For example, I don't see why we have a male minister of finance. Because, honestly speaking, in all the houses, especially in the black community, the minister of finance and minister of housing and caretaking is a woman. So once you have a male minister of finance you may have a problem, because he may relate to some of the matters according to the books, but looking at the country as a family, it would be natural to have a woman finance minister. We need to develop some of the good things according to the old family pattern and do away with the bad things, with the abuses. Women's Liberation in the Eurocentric sense, for me, doesn't work. It is actually out of context, because all it does is it causes more divorces. We need to look at what it is that is good in the old family role pattern, and maybe use that as a pattern for the whole of society. I think we have to look into that.

I am actually working on another play which is called *Weemen*, where I am trying to reflect upon some of these things, the relationship between a couple – what is it that causes problems? I know it is industrialisation and money that are the bottom line, but I'm trying to explore it to find out what is important and what is not.

John Kani

John Kani, The Island *is currently running at the Market Theatre. How many times do you reckon it has been performed?*

It opened in 1973 at the Space Theatre in Cape Town. Then it could not be called *The Island*, because the authorities would have known we were talking about Robben Island. So we decided to call it *The Hodoshe Span*. The Hodoshe means the green carrion fly. My brother spent five years on Robben Island, and there was an infamous warder who was referred to as 'the fly that brings death'. He was so surgical in his procedures. He broke every person. You never survived Hodoshe. You would walk out saying 'Yes, Sir', 'Ja, Baas'. But those who survived were heroes. Hodoshe is in the play. And the play is about two men who survived Hodoshe. The way they survived was by keeping themselves busy rehearsing some extracts from *Antigone*, to present in a prison concert.

On the 26 May this year we invited the President, Walter Sisulu – all of them, about three hundred of them in the audience, and we did the play. It was laughter, anger, tears, and silence – heavy, heavy silence. And at the end the first person to stand up was the President, and they applauded for about ten minutes. I don't know whether I enjoyed it; it's just flooded with memories. But it was a wonderful evening.

How was the play actually conceived? It was a collaborative effort, wasn't it?

At that stage Athol Fugard, Winston Ntshona and myself had actually begun a process in the sixties which we called an Experiment in Play-Making, where together we would find, through trial and error, a subject that we wanted to deal with or to talk about. And then we as actors would improvise situations in the investigation or exploration of the subject. And Athol would be making notes of what had happened, and at the end of the day we would discuss it. And then take it up again and try to move the story, following exactly where the idea was developing, discarding where we felt it wasn't sticking to one theme or it was beginning to disperse in various directions. And after fourteen days we began to settle. It began actually by the limitation of space, and identifying that limited space as being that particular prison cell on Robben Island.

At that time my brother was on Robben Island. Four members of our group, the Serpent Players, were also on Robben Island. And when I performed *Antigone*, straight from Sophocles and directed by Athol Fugard, the man who played Haemon, son of King Kreon, Shark Mguqulwa, was arrested three days before the first performance, and he disappeared to Robben Island for seven-and-a-half years. So he never performed. I stepped in to play the part, which was my first speaking part in the Serpent Players.

Then we received letters from my brother on Robben Island. That Shark, who never knew his lines, because I prompted him all the time, was now performing a one-man performance of *Antigone*, while working at the quarry, trying to do all the lines himself and messing things up. That's where the idea of a play within the play came up. And that's when we began to work to make *The Island*.

Would you mind going back a bit into your personal life – your childhood, your development as a person?

Well, I was born in 1943 in Port Elizabeth and my family were about eleven. My father at that stage was a policeman. He was in the war, came back from the war and went straight into the police force. And in 1952 he got an early retirement at the age of 48, because he arrested two young white boys who were breaking in at the back of a jeweller's shop. As a black policeman he wasn't supposed to put handcuffs on them, and he arrested them because they said to him 'You're a kaffir. You cannot arrest us because we are white!'

My father wasn't very sober, and he was six foot eight inches; he was about two metres broad! So he handcuffed these two white louts and marched them half a mile from where they were, past two black bus stops, and it was like a comic scene, they were laughing. He put them into the police station. They were immediately released for 'wrongful arrest'. And father was furious. And a month later they said he was sick. He had a bit of an ulcer, of course, and they gave him an early retirement, which made him very angry.

My father was an incredible man. Being a policeman at that time, in the forties and fifties, was a very important place in the community. He was like the mini-magistrate of our little township. People came to him with their problems: they came when their children had been arrested and he found out why. A son is misbehaving at home: he'll go with his shambok and discipline him. Somebody is getting too drunk and is messing up somebody's party, and they'll call my father in the village. It wasn't like in the later years.

He instilled in me the sense of right and wrong as opposed to legal and illegal. I remember in 1956, when the ANC was campaigning very strongly in the Eastern Cape he bought two ANC membership cards, and I thought this was quite a contradiction: he is sitting there in uniform and he buys two ANC membership cards! I said: 'Why did you do that?' He says: 'I'm a member of this community. I just work there as a policeman.'

What sort of an education did you get at that time?

I went to school just like any other person in New Brighton, at the Newell High School in New Brighton, Port Elizabeth. I completed my high school education about the time when my eldest brother was arrested.

What was the reason for his arrest?

He was a member of the ANC youth movement at school, and he got five years. My father brought up his children as law-abiding, straight people. He spent his life-time savings in my brother's defence. We didn't even know where my brother was going to be tried. Those were the days when the authorities were moving the trials. He was actually tried five hundred and sixteen miles from our town in a small town outside East London, called Cambridge.

So my father went there on the morning of the trial, and just caught the tail end of it as he walked in. And he came back and said: 'I am sorry. I was going to go to the university and get a law degree, but now I don't have the money.'

After school I looked for work. And after six months of looking for work, applying saying, 'I have a matric, I've got a high school education, I want a job,' my father said: 'There are a lot of firms around here that need people to work. You are looking for a particular job. You're not looking for *work*.'

So I went to Ford Motor Company, and I got a job as a janitor. Coming straight from Bantu Education I'd never come across the word janitor. I knew what a cleaner was, I knew what a servant was, so I didn't understand, actually, what I was supposed to do. Then the man said to me that there would be clerical positions opening a little later, but they would like to keep me because I had a high school education. Could I just do for a short period as janitor? I said yes. And I cleaned toilets for two months, and then, because I could speak Afrikaans fluently, and could translate when he addressed the workers in Afrikaans, I was brought into the assembly line by a very famous (in my life) general foreman, *Mr Baas Bradley* – he wanted them both! And he is a character in *Sizwe Bansi Is Dead*.

So there I was working in the Ford engine plant assembly, and I could assemble an engine with my eyes closed, from beginning to end.

It was then that I discovered that there was this group of black actors who were doing plays – not the usual song and dance things, and they were working with a white person called Athol Fugard. This was in 1965. I went to see them and they were doing a very strange play called *Antigone*, by a man whose name I couldn't pronounce properly, called Sophocles – a Greek. And I knew that these brothers and sisters sitting there with this white honkey were duped. This white man is here to suck their brains out! He's one of those that say 'I know black people'. And in the meantime he's writing volumes and becomes an authority on them. I was very, very suspicious. And I was surprised at how the elderly guys in the group were so trusting of him. They had been working with him since 1961, you see.

I kind of stepped back, and the strange thing was that Athol was aware of that: I never drank a glass of water in his house, I never drank wine, I never ate in his house. I was always analysing everything he said. I was so suspicious. I was very angry – my brother being on Robben Island, my family in New Brighton being hounded by the security police.

And there you were as a young person – you got home, you were taught what was right and wrong. You go out into the street, *there* there are political commissars that are conscientising us about the struggle. We attend secret meetings in the evenings where we are taught to hate the enemy, detest the enemy, kill the enemy. We are singing songs about this being our country, keeping names like Nelson Mandela, Govan Mbeki, Walter Sisulu alive, our heroes – Oliver Tambo in exile, all those people.

Then you go home, and you become a nice young man, listen to your father. So those were the days, you know. I did hate, I did hate with a passion. And that was actually what kept me going. It was my hatred, and my love for my people, my love for freedom, but my hatred for white people and the 'enemy'.

And I knew something after one year of working with Athol. We did this play, of course, called *Antigone*, and I played Haemon, as I said, which led to *The Island*, later. I began to be attracted to what they were talking about, the way they discussed this Greek play – authority, loyalty to God, to men, to dignity, to the state. The language was quite similar to my meetings in the evenings with the political commissars, and I felt like I could do this. I began to like being there, and I began to understand one thing: this white man knew a little more than me about what I wanted to know more than anything else: the profession, the craft of the theatre. And I could only get it from him at that particular time. And sticking around the group I would learn more.

I began by asking to borrow a book, because there were no libraries, and he had books in his house. So he gave me Albert Camus' *The Revolution* and I read it, and I was so excited that he had this book, and I began to take another book, another book, another book . . . And in the later years he is responsible for having messed up my Revolution. Because suddenly in my mind I thought 'Not all white people are bad, not all white people are evil, not all white people are racist and not all white people are agreed and support this government of apartheid.'

And that made me think when I see a white man in the street, that he could be like Athol. So what do I do then? How do I kill? I might make a mistake that I might not like to live with the rest of my life. And slowly our relationship developed. We began then to write together and he began to develop my skills in writing and in understanding. I might come with a story and I was excited. And he would say, 'Where is the idea?' I said: 'Well, that's what I am thinking about,' and he would say, 'No, what do you *feel*?' And then – 'what do *you* think?'

We began to discover that many people, especially in the theatre, were writing from the memory of work they'd seen, or they were the radicals who wrote from the Government Gazette, who took just one law that was oppressing the people, and wrote a little story around it. I mean one compromised a lot during those years, which was the time of Protest Theatre. One compromised a lot – standard, quality. If the *message* was correct, if the message was talking about the people, and was informing, educating, exciting, conscientising, it was ready, it was right. But we in the Serpent Players with Athol, were always bound by the story, by the quality, the standard, and if there are politics, those will take care of themselves.

And that's my background. And finally, in the late '70s, I began to tour and travel abroad, and in the '80s I came back to be part of the Market Theatre. Now I am the Executive Director of the Market Theatre. I am still acting, I am still writing.

Were there any other persons, besides Fugard, that influenced you deeply in your formative years?

Yes, my father, really. He was such an important man in the community, and he also was a traditionalist. He believed that when he died, he would go to the ancestors. He had no problems with Jesus Christ and God and Heaven. He had *no* problems with those things. He knew exactly where he was going. And even when he died he left a message how the whole ritual was to be performed so he could become an ancestor. And he was an authority; in fact I used to say to him 'You've not entered the twentieth century.' He believed in the tradition of being an African, and an African for him was a person who embraced all other people, and all other cultures. But you have to be yourself. And the law was through him rendered to the ancestors and rendered to God. But it had to go through him. And that's what I am trying as well to instil in my children: I am the man, and they, through me, will communicate with the ancestors, who are my father, my great-grandfathers. And they go to church. My younger brother is an archdeacon in the Anglican Church. And this is wonderful. But when the time comes and we want to perform certain customary rituals, he's present.

We couldn't have any kinds of heroes in the art world, at that time. The South African community was a closed community. We didn't even know there were black actors in other worlds. The movies we saw were carefully selected. Black people were servants in them. There was no television in our age. At school the heroes and giants were from Jan van Riebeeck to Simon van der Stel, Governor of the Cape, to Napoleon, to Stalin, to Lord Nelson, to Abraham Lincoln – very briefly how he freed the slaves, while the emancipation in 1834 was misinterpreted here, as 'We don't have slaves, but we will maintain our relationship with our servants, as a master and servant relationship.'

That was my education, and yet in the struggle we had heroes, but we didn't know who they were. People talked about Nelson Mandela, about Govan Mbeki, about Walter Sisulu, Raymond Mhlaba . . . We knew the old men who lived in our area. I remember when I was very young, our job was to watch for the police, because the meetings used to be held in an open place called Embizue, where there was an incredible excitement some day in the late '50s. There was this man coming from Jo'burg who was going to address the crowd, the people in the Eastern Cape. We had heard it was going to be Mandela, but we boys were too far away to even catch a glimpse of his face.

So politically we had those as heroes, as heroes from some myth that kept us going. But artistically, really, it was just working, and without modelling yourself on any other person. It was when we began to go to England in 1973 that we heard more of people like Laurence Olivier, John Gielgud, Richard Burton. Movie stars were what flooded South Africa's colonised communities. The big movie stars. We knew about those and the gangster movies, *Street With No Name*, a little bit of *Ben Hur*, *El Cid* with Charlton Heston. They didn't mean a thing to us. It was just going there for an afternoon. And it was very expensive to go there anyway.

So that's how we were brought up, like a community that was bound by their love for freedom as their part of that struggle, and by their love for each community and an understanding of the family structures within that community. Each parent around our block was my parent. I don't smoke, but you couldn't even be standing next to one who smoked if the uncle who saw you happened to be related to your father or close to your father's home. You would be in trouble.

And it was school. There were a lot of troubles at school with Bantu Education. But our parents said it was better than nothing. So there was struggle on that front as well.

And when you got into theatre, were you involved with other 'movers' of the time, or was it just Athol Fugard? What about people like Barney Simon, Rob McLaren, Don Maclennan?

When I got into theatre in 1969, we met this young man from Johannesburg, Mannie Manim, who was still with PACT, in the 'enemy camp'. Actually we refused to meet him as he was part of the 'enemy'. But Athol said, 'No, no! He's a nice guy, let's talk to him.'

That's when Mannie began to talk about his dream about this place called the Market. But he was talking about a place where people of various colours could meet and work. We were working already at that time. The same year I met Barney Simon, and he also came to Port Elizabeth. We talked, and I began to like those two, and I understood what they were doing.

Later, in the 1970s, I think it was '71 or '72 that I met Rob McLaren with *S'ketsh Magazine*. We also met in New York, and he came to interview us about our work for *S'ketch Magazine*. And I understood the work he was doing besides the Junction Avenue, and began to understand that there were people who were doing meaningful theatre, and who were not necessarily black. They were also concerned about the cultural struggle within the country, and were also playing an important role in the attempt to normalise the situation under very difficult conditions. Those were people like Rob McLaren and Rob Amato, who I met when I took Albert Camus' *The Just* to Windows Theatre in East London. We worked together with Rob (Amato), and we encouraged them to form a similar group, and they formed, with Leslie Xinwa, the Imitha Players, which means The Sunrise. And we kept visiting each other to help him set up that group.

I met Don Maclennan, who is now Professor at Rhodes University, and worked with him to set up the Ikhwezi Players. That's another group of people in Grahamstown working with him.

Then I met Brian Astbury with Yvonne Bryceland, who were running a little theatre called Space, in Cape Town. And that's where we took *Sizwe Bansi Is Dead* for the first time, and *The Island*, of course. So the circle of these strangers around me began to increase. And I began to know more white people who were not 'the enemy'.

At the same time in the '70s I met Frederick van Zyl Slabbert, the politician, who was then a lecturer at UCT. He saw *Sizwe Bansi Is Dead*, and invited Winston (Ntshona) and myself and Athol for tea. He said he had been considering a job offer from a university in Canada, but after seeing the play, and the courage of the people in that theatre, he was thinking no, he wasn't going to go. He was needed here. It was wonderful for us to hear that.

Alan Paton I met in Natal. After a performance of *Sizwe Bansi* he stood up, and came to shake our hands while we were standing on the stage, and he made a speech, saying that 'If there is any hope in this country, this is the beginning of that dawn.'

We began to work with the (Institute of) Race Relations all over Natal, performing in church halls and in open spaces. And then we went to Transkei and were arrested, and spent six weeks in solitary confinement. We were released because of massive demonstrations in London and New York. Even Kissinger was asked by Gerald Ford, the then president, to write a letter to the President here, to intervene on our behalf. We were then released. The international community was in an uproar about our arrest.

And after that we were able to flout, to defy and challenge the state, because we knew we had gained some measure of immunity because of that. So we became a nuisance to the authorities. And they knew there was not much they could do about it. They confiscated my passport. I couldn't travel, and Helen Suzman, that great lady, played a very important role in making it possible for me to travel. And finally I began to travel with a document by the South African government through interventions by foreign embassies. It defined my nationality as 'undetermined'. I still have the document.

Were you at all involved in the Black Consciousness drive in theatre?

Black Consciousness was launched by Steve Biko, Strini Moodley, Nangwin Nkulu, Barney Pichana. We performed *Sizwe Bansi Is Dead* at the launch on BBC. I was basically ANC. I came from an ANC background, and I believed in equality in the human race. Somehow my upbringing was very strange, because when I was a young man my father was in a senior position, as senior as a black person could go. There were these young policemen that used to come to my father, some of them white. There was always liquor in my dad's cabinet and there were these guys with high respect for my father. And my father was like a little dictator because he had a bottle of brandy and they didn't. So I never had that kind of reverence and fear for white people. And my father always said 'They are nice people. There are others who are pigs, but these are nice people.' That's how I grew up. So I could never be attracted to Black Consciousness. Biko was a friend, and we shared lots of experiences with all the people in the movements. We used to tease each other.

But the Black Consciousness Movement in theatre made a very great impact, because that was the time when we used the theatre to conscientise our people to give them back their sense of self respect, to give them their voices again, to make them stand up – to break the fear of whites, which was the most crippling element within this kind of struggle. And the religious stronghold: Thou shalt not kill, or: Thou shalt respect thy masters; It is God's will; It is in God's hands; God will find a way; Don't do anything. It was almost like that. So Black Consciousness had to break through that kind of wall that made our people impotent. And through the theatre we managed to do that. But me, I was always ANC.

I understand that Credo Mutwa has reintroduced traditional mythical themes into the theatre. Does that interest you as a theatre director now?

If you look at theatre according to a western definition, if you look at its origin right up to the Greeks, on Mount Olympus and all the other things that have happened in the early centuries, this is what was also happening in the African communities in the age of the great ceremonies of the harvest, of the rain; the great days when people went to Kamatha, the great Lord of the Ancestors, where we went and prayed on the mountain and came back with the rain. We're looking at the story-telling aspect, which is part of the handing down of our history orally.

We are looking at the *imbongi*, the praise singer, who was not a court jester, but a great performer, who would praise the king, but would also speak what people felt about him, whether the king was good, and he would not lose his head.

We're also looking at all the circumcision ceremonies, the initiation ceremonies, we're looking in the early times, the seventeenth to the eighteenth centuries where there began to be some formal structure of celebration, where young men from one village would orchestrate a performance-like dance ritual in competition with the boys from another village, and the boys who won that day, by the choice of the elders, would get the neck of the bull. That was the prize, because the older men don't eat the neck, that's boys' meat.

Then there would be stick fight, mock stick fight – a little bit of a bruise here and there, but that would be that. And then, in other great ceremonies like inaugurating a young chief, or a young king, or a great matriarch, there would be performances, like dances by girls, up until when older people would take over in the evening, and the dance would go on till the morning. And then the witchdoctors' ceremonies. All that is the basis of the African theatre.

If we go to the villages, beginning slowly in the eighteenth and nineteenth centuries, and the beginning of the twentieth, we had village entertainments. There was the little *xinole* there, which was the beginning of our violin. It's one bend of the reed with one string, and then you sing. And there is the mouth organ and the thumb piano. All those things were happening in the villages.

At the beginning of the twentieth century we saw the arrival all over the land of the white man with his dances and the ballroom dances and the preservation of the western culture in South Africa. Then in 1934 Guibon Sinxo wrote the first novel that was adapted into a play, *Unomsa*, which was about the men who did not come back from the First World War, where they had fought for the white man.

What Credo is doing is understandable. It has a history, it has a place within the African culture. It was those witchdoctors performing rituals. For instance, my father was also a witchdoctor. And when he died, none of his children at that stage had shown any indication that they would take over. That happens from time to time. We had a problem about his beads, drums and skins and everything else, all the paraphernalia (the Xhosas don't, incidentally, throw bones). What were we to do with all that? My mother consulted one of the leading witchdoctors in the Eastern Cape, and he said that what we had to do was to bury, to lay to rest, all the things that he used as a witchdoctor.

And then there was this great burial ceremony. The whole thing was done at night. And if any of the other seventeen invited witchdoctors were able to point to where all this equipment was buried, then the ancestors would not have accepted it. But if they couldn't, it meant the ancestors had accepted it. It meant the ancestors had taken it away. And even if you were to dig the hole, which we didn't, of course, they claimed you wouldn't find those beads there. Thank God we didn't dig, so the ceremony was accepted. None of the children at this stage has picked my father's diviner heritage, not mine, nor my brothers' nor my sisters' children. But the time may come, maybe in my generation or my descendants', when one of them would want to be a witchdoctor. Then an ox would have to be slaughtered to reconnect the link between that new person and my diviner father.

You mentioned that your son had a heart condition?

Yes, my son, who is one year old today, was born with a hole in the heart, right on the top ventricle, and it was mixing the blood. And at three months he had to have major open-heart surgery. And the doctors were quite surprised how he had stayed alive, because they had detected a second large hole at the bottom end of the heart as well. I wasn't surprised. I knew it was my father, I knew it was my ancestors. I knew they wanted him to live, to continue the generations of the Kani family. I also know that it was Jesus Christ and God who had blessed him and blessed my family. So with me they are compatible, my African tradition and belief and this Christian religion. As my father used to say, 'You've got to believe in both, boy, lest one of them should be true. You will die, and if there is a road turning toward heaven, if you did believe, then you'd be safe.' But I know my father went the other way, to the ancestors.

Fifty-fifty?

Yes, that's what my father said. 'We've got to go fifty-fifty, boy, in case this old religion thing is true.'

Some theatrical gurus claim that South African theatre today is in a kind of limbo. You have called it a 'breather', I believe. Would you like to comment on that?

The whole country is in a transitional stage. When Nelson Mandela was released in 1990 it was such an incredible moment for South Africa. When he made his first speech in Cape Town we expected him to say one thing: 'You know where the arms caches are. I am the High Commander of the Umkhonto we Sizwe (the military wing of the ANC). Let's go!' But when he revealed that he had been negotiating, we knew there was another way we could achieve our freedom. We gave him time. But then we had to quickly think, where do we go from here?

And during that time, the theatre and the writing that emerged were addressing the violence in our communities, were talking about the issues of reconciliation and of reconstruction.

Elections came and we won, and we have a black President. We have a government of national unity. We have a situation that is redefining itself. Almost every day we are grappling with a new order in South Africa. Things are not stable yet, the landscape is shifting all the time. So there's a moment now when the writing is beginning to emerge, we are beginning to understand what the New South Africa is. The position we held before was that of being part of a struggle against a government, against a white oppressive nation. These positions were held also through ignorance and misinformation by white communities of what would happen should black people be in power, should black people be in government, should this be a black-run country. The perceptions we had, the aspirations we had, were that should we be free, I was going to take over Helen Suzman's house. I was going to live there, because I knew we were going to take over the white areas. I am, of course, talking of my young brothers who were thinking like that.

Now things are settling down. We are a year old with democracy. We are beginning to understand what it actually means. It means we have to work together to make our democracy work, to make South Africa work. We have a hell of a responsibility. As artists there is now even a greater challenge than before of educating and informing our people, of proving to the people that we are not that different, that we are one nation although we could be culturally slightly different here and there.

So that writing is beginning to emerge. But in the interim, what we are doing is we are also meeting the other need, the other demand from our audiences through the falling of South Africa's cultural boycott, South Africa's isolation: the ushering of South Africa into the international community. We are importing new plays – not new really, but plays that the authorities didn't allow to come to South Africa before because of apartheid. We are also putting classics on, we are also going back down Memory Lane to touch and do historical moments in our lives. We are also attempting to rewrite the history of our people so that each culture, each grouping finds and feels that they too have a place in this new democracy with respect and dignity.

We are not yet ready to do what politicians and some critics and the media expect us to do: to write *about* the new South Africa. We are not journalists. We're not going to write about what President Mandela said in Parliament yesterday, what Dr Buthelezi said, what F.W. de Klerk is saying, or what new law has been passed in Parliament. We're still taking this whole thing in. It has to be digested. It has to come as personal stories. Not as a challenge to anybody.

Also our resistance mode has been put into neutral, because it does not mean a government, that now has a black majority, has to be the government the artists and the culture must support. We will not be tied to the apron strings of any political party. We've got to remain the conscience of our community. We'll entertain them, we will be part of the culture that one likes to exhibit. We have to put the African culture in its proper place in museums, in galleries, in libraries, in education classrooms, in the work place and in homes, both black and white. We are breaking down the walls and the remnants of apartheid that are still entrenched in our communities. Attitudes that are still entrenched in our people are in the process of being broken down. That's our responsibility, and I find that South African theatre is at a most exciting time. There's work to be done, and I pray we don't get the West End and Broadway type of theatre where we are just doing it as an industry. There is still a drive for us that is part of the reconstruction and development of our lives and our communities and our beautiful country.

Do you still see theatre going out to the dispossessed and the disadvantaged in order to educate?

Our theatre doesn't go there. It comes from there.

Yes, but can all those people participate if it is not brought out? Do they have access to the town venues?

I say again: our theatre does not go there. It comes from there. When we go into the communities where we live, we are surprised when we see these little community projects happening – doing some song and dance because they need to put a fence around their little garden patch where they have the garden scheme for the village. People who are addressing the violence in their own communities and they are saying in their plays: 'Inkatha and ANC – talk!'

People in certain communities who are dealing with the drug problem that's emerging, are writing little stories about it. We go there, lend a hand, apply skills, assist, upgrade, bring them here. We also take our plays there, and to take them to the community, I send, through the Market Theatre laboratory, about twenty-five field workers who go as far as Maputo, Botswana, Zimbabwe and Namibia, where they are called to go and assist – all over South Africa and beyond, where people have their projects. It is part of the African heritage, part of the African culture to sing your troubles, to sing your sadness, to dance your anger and stamp Mother Earth so strongly as if to ask 'Why are you just a witness?'

So, it is not a matter of us taking theatre to the community. It's happening everywhere. We respond. We'll just go there because something is happening. I got a piece of paper the other day that said 'You must come, we're doing something.'

There was a letter from a person in a village outside Alice in the Eastern Cape. He says could I, if ever I come through the Eastern Cape, come and see their group, and maybe talk to them, maybe help them? And now I'm already thinking I know someone who's operating in King Williamstown – East London. I'm going to contact him and ask him to visit this group. And they're probably doing some traditional dances and maybe trying to raise funds to buy drums and then become majorettes. Or maybe they're trying to find a space where they can work. That's how it happens.

Could we go back again briefly to The Island *and the performance which I attended the other night. Has it been resuscitated and brought back now as a breath of the struggle era, or what specific agendas brought it back?*

The reason why we brought it back was that last year was its twenty-first anniversary. But both Winston and I were unavailable to do it. And at one stage I bumped into the old man Walter Sisulu, and he asked me 'When are you doing that play *The Island*? I've heard so much about it. Do you have it on video?'

I said, 'No,' and he said, 'Well, I'd love you to do it some time.' And then, of course, we also thought, well, this guy is old – we should do this now. And then, together with Winston and Athol, we decided to pay tribute to all those men and women, black and white, who gave of their time, some even their lives, for what we're enjoying. So we're now bringing *The Island* as a celebration of the indestructibility of the human spirit. We won! We survived! That's what we brought *The Island* back for.

Also it is a great classic. It's been done all over the world. So like I did *Hedda Gabler*, like I did *Othello*, like I did Brecht, so why not revisit a classic? And many young people who saw me in *My Children, My Africa*, who saw me in *The Native*, or in *Driving Miss Daisy*, always say 'My father says I ain't seen nothing if I never saw you in *The Island*.' And, of course, *The Island* is part of the university literature curriculum. And I've been going to the universities lecturing about how these plays evolved, how we put them together, how we worked in those days.

Therefore it was quite timely to do it again. In 1997, on its twenty-fifth anniversary, we've planned to do *Sizwe Bansi Is Dead*, which has exploded again onto the stages in South Africa and all over the world. It is, as you know, about the passbook, the nightmare about the South African race laws.

So we're talking about that. We're also talking of doing other work, writing plays about the great stories of the African kingdoms, that were never written during those days. We're also thinking of doing those plays which were simply love stories, family good stories that could not be performed before, because the comrades and the political commissars would have termed them 'irrelevant' at the time. So there's a lot of work to be done.

Was I right in thinking I detected a slight jibe at the Fatcats in Kreon's speech?

(laughing) This is how it was written then by Sophocles.

Yes, but I mean, didn't you feel there was a point there?

A young man came to me and said that was my best speech. And I was so happy, because the President was sitting there, some of the ministers were there, and I hoped they heard loud and clear that Kreon says they're too fat! Yes, it came via the press too. Some of the media picked it up. And someone even asked did we adapt it to today?

But this is the way it was written. It referred to the white fat people and government ministers. Now it means the Fat-All-of-You.

Language-wise, do you see English surviving as a primary stage tool, or will it be more the sort of township Creole taking over?

Already the work that is now emerging at grassroots level is so mixed in the language, that you will find that if it is performed in the village, it becomes like eighty per cent in that language, in that dialect, and a little bit of English here and there to show off that 'I can speak English, too'. But once you say to the people that the play is coming to mainstream, they begin to adjust it and put in more English, because now the audience gets wider. If you perform in Thoya Ndovu you predominantly perform in Venda or Shangaan. When you're coming towards Johannesburg you've got a sort of cosmopolitan situation. The more English you put, the more the work is accessible to a greater community. And, of course, 'the road to Mecca': if you want your work to come to mainstream and succeed in the professional or the commercial world, you will be writing in English. I do envisage a situation in the future where we'll have subtitles, or above-titles, or where there'll be interpreters with headphones in the theatre, because some work is going to emerge in its true language. People are beginning now, and we are encouraging young people to write in their own language, so as to begin to make the connecting thread between their mind and what it is that is gripping their soul. But if they are handicapped by Bantu Education, if they're handicapped by constantly trying to translate and interpret their own thoughts into a language they have no strong command of, it handicaps the work development itself. You see this work in English that is stumbling and not anchored anywhere. And I often feel that there's an idea in there that's struggling to come out. And when I talk to that person in his or her own language, I suddenly realise what happened: it was in the translation that he or she lost. So we do encourage that.

Two weeks ago we had a community arts festival at the lab, to which thirty-eight groups came. And some performed in Sotho, Zulu, Thonga and the audience loved it! And some of them, that didn't understand, looked at the others and laughed when they laughed.

I saw the Suzuki company perform *Macbeth* in Japanese. And that guy who was talking too much must be Macbeth, and that other one that looked solitary and cold with strange lighting, must be Lady Macbeth. But I wasn't sure whether that was a man or a woman. But I understand that in Japan they are now casting women in those roles. It is no longer as in the olden days when men played all roles.

I had an interview with Mazisi Kunene some months ago, and when I asked him if he envisaged any particular trends in South African post-apartheid literature, he said that what is always important is a good story. If the story is good, good literature will in all probability be the result. I suppose it is the same thing with theatre?

It is indeed the same thing. We're now saying that protest literature, protest theatre, the literature of the struggle, the language of the resistance, are slowly going to not have a place in the new South Africa. It doesn't mean that there will not be investigative, exploratory, questioning work that is thought-provoking. But what is going to make that work survive is its having a good story, if the people will come to the theatre to see it. It's already proved. Theatres are empty in Johannesburg now. But if you put on a good one, they come. Already! And even people have tried heavy political ones: it's not working any more. People have tried entertaining high, like they have with *Umabatha*, the Zulu *Macbeth*. And it's running to empty houses. And you put on some song and dance at Midrand with Richard Loring, they come! Peter Toerien puts on a West End farce and a certain audience that wants to breathe the thing would say, Ah, thank God, we can see theatre from London! And they go.

We put on *The Island*, and they're coming because it's part of their history; it's nostalgic and it's part of a debate of what must happen to Robben Island. And the people are coming. As one lady said to me last night, 'D'you know why I came? I've seen these old men now, and seeing *The Island* makes me understand what they went through. They're heroes of mine now, these cabinet ministers.'

We did *Titus Andronicus* with Anthony Shere starring. They didn't come. *They didn't come!*

So that's the state in which theatre is today. We as theatre practitioners are making note of what's happening. It's almost like a survey of your market. What is it they want? But I believe we must not just yield to what they want. We must give them what they want, but there has to be some form of education and information that will begin to shape South Africa. So that we could have an identity that is strong and South African, so that we are able to exhibit it all over the world. It would be sad for us to do Shakespeare and write like Shakespeare and do African stories on the model of Shakespeare and take those abroad. People abroad are hungry for what the culture of this country is about.

We need stories from the Free State where we know what the Afrikaner is about, we need stories from the Zulus, from the Thongas, from the Xhosas, from the Jewish community of South Africa, from the Italian community of South Africa. We need those South African stories now.

Could you envisage Gibson Kente come back with a twist?

Gibson is a legend in his own way and in his own time. He's always taken one route and Gibson is an entertainer. And Gibson is a very religiously based person, and a song-and-dance man. He'll always be our Broadway version of South Africa. He'll always come with this kind of light entertainment, maybe one question here and there, but basically Gibson is Broadway. It's vaudeville, it's 'Come and have a good time, pretty ladies, and enjoy yourselves!' That's Gibson, and he has a place in our culture.

Would that be a mode that could still remain as a sideline throughout the further development, do you think, or is he passé?

No, I think he's in a sense passé. Now look at Mbongeni Ngema. He's a version of Gibson with a little bit of a political message thrown in. If you look at some writing of a young boy now, Aubsey Sekgabi's new play – it's another version of Gibson. He's there. It's just that at a certain stage he became irrelevant because the struggle demanded relevance. Everybody in the late eighties and the nineties exploited the struggle, everybody. People jumped on the bandwagon. People knew if you said in a play 'Release Mandela', it sold out and it's going overseas. And people were printing T-shirts in 1990, in January. I know a company that printed six thousand T-shirts. They were all written 'Release Mandela', and Mandela was released in February, and the T-shirts are stuck!

So there were many writers and entertainers who did that, who knew it was very opportune to hoist the flag of the struggle within entertainment, even in music, who wrote songs about 'We will be free one day' and sold ten thousand copies a day. And those people now are being phased out by the new South Africa. What's happening is that the non-artists aren't going through the turnstile gate.

Mannie Manim

You have been involved in Black Theatre in South Africa for a long time. Could we start by going back to those early days?

My past does not go back to the early days of Black Theatre in this country. Long before me there was the playwright called Herbert Dhlomo, who I am sure you will have come across. He probably was and remains South Africa's most prolific and successful black playwright of this century. I suppose my time with South African Black Theatre really goes back to the beginning of the Market Theatre, which means to about 1973, '74, '75.

Prior to that I ran the drama section of the Performing Arts Council of Transvaal for six years, which was not allowed to perform black shows, so it was a ridiculous situation. And I think that was what made me leave them and with Barney Simon to found the Market Theatre as an independent theatre for all South Africans. So prior to the late 1960s and the early 1970s it was mainly Gibson Kente and a man called Sam Mhangwane. I suppose you would call Mhangwane's work more a kind of moral rearmament. His plays all had social messages, and he was more the serious side of township theatre.

And Kente, although he did have social messages, they were encased in an entertaining capsule, if you like. Both of them ran productions throughout the country, and for a great length of time.

The other writer of colour that was prevalent in those times, was Adam Small. He was a writer from the so-called coloured community in Cape Town. He wrote major epic Afrikaans Gamma-taal dramas, and is still to this day one of the major forces in the shaping of drama of this country.

In Afrikaans?

In Afrikaans. He wrote one play in English, called *The Orange Earth*, which, I think, had one of its first performances in the Market Theatre. An excellent small play about the Karoo – describes the colour of the earth.

In the Market Theatre I think basically what we were doing was allowing a conduit for a great deal of work that was kind of bubbling away under the surface in and around Johannesburg. We gave it a kind of legitimate venue to perform in, and we allowed all people to write, direct and perform the plays in the Market. And that's really what the Market was built for at the time, for it was kind of banned activity in this country, as the races weren't allowed to mix. And we just decided to do this in that venue, and to try and give that chance to all those that didn't otherwise have one.

The major subjects of the plays through the seventies and the eighties were, of course, political, and a little bit social. But mainly it was to do with the reaction to the headlines of the day and the political situation of the day, and the events that were going on around us.

Every second thing was banned in those days. I'm actually just reading *A Long Walk to Freedom*, the Nelson Mandela autobiography, and it is interesting to have that big bracket of historic time and to see how, slowly but surely, all our freedoms were eroded during that time, and how we lived in a world of little information. The radio, the newspapers and television were all totally controlled. And so in a very small way, through the venues in the Market Theatre complex, we could participate in exchanging truths. On the stage the actors could address the audience, and very often did – a number of our plays were described as pedantic, and I think they were, and didactic, and I think they were that as well. But they were imparting information that couldn't in any other way be imparted.

And they were also done in a highly dramatic form, and all the dramatic tools that South African and African drama certainly uses – music and song and dance, as well as excellent energetic acting, of course. So I think that probably those two decades of the Market managed in that time to encapsulate and give voice to a style and a series and a sequence of dramatic presentations that helped also to move our theatre on to a kind of international dramatic platform.

We were invited to many different countries in the world, and many different festivals, because our theatre spoke this unspoken stuff, this news behind the bare headlines, you know, that kind of thing. It also afforded us a small bit of international protection, I'd like to think. We used to have friends in the four corners of the globe. And many people said, 'But why were you not banned? Why weren't you closed down?'

I can't explain this. I think to a certain extent we were a very small situation, and the reigning government could say, 'But look how liberal we are. We allow this theatre to function in this way.'

But certainly our growing international success, and the growing international interest in the work of the Market Theatre was definitely, I think, a protective factor to our situation.

Barney Simon was involved in all this, wasn't he? I was going to have an interview with him just as he was taken ill last June, and taken to hospital, where, sadly, he died. Would you like to put him in this picture as well, before we move on?

Yes. Barney Simon was the co-founder of the Market Theatre with me. We met during my time at PACT. We met through Athol Fugard who introduced us to each other, and it was our discussions that led to the formation of The Company, the acting company which then launched the Market Theatre.

Barney was a man who was deeply rooted in the alternative, or at that time black South African theatre in the '60s and so on. He had left the country – for his own reasons, but I think he was frustrated with what was going on here.

He had returned to South Africa. He was an editor of literary magazines and that kind of thing, and he was a writer in his own right. He was a poet as well, but mainly a prose writer.

Barney had a number of politically active friends. He was very, very close to the Slovo family for instance, and would always visit them when I was with him in London. Once Joe Slovo returned to South Africa he was a regular house guest with Barney.

And therefore he was connected with a lot of free-thinking black writers, journalists, poets and so on. When he returned to South Africa – I think in the late '60s – he was advised that really this was in the age of Black Consciousness, and that if he wanted to do anything, he should conscientise white people. And in fact he launched into what he liked to term a White Consciousness Theatre. In other words to re-educate white people about what was going on around them, because they had also grown numb to all that, with our lack of real news and the lack of real knowledge of facts of what was going on around us.

Barney directed plays. He directed Fugard's early works, such as *The Blood Knot*, and he directed plays at Dorkay House, which was the African Music and Drama Association, and later Phoenix Players, headquarters, and also a kind of a melting pot for a lot of jazz and theatre people. Athol Fugard worked there at that time quite a lot.

My first contact with Barney and his work was going to see productions of plays like *The Death of Bessie Smith*, I think it was. And he worked in very, very poor conditions in the so-called rehearsal room on the second floor of Dorkay House at the top end of Eloff Street, mainly with black performers. He also did a musical at that time, which had its première at the Wits University Great Hall. It was called *Phiri*, and it was based, I think, on Moliére, and Fats Dibeko played the lead; Sophie Mcina and many other people were in it. It was a big, big musical, and it ran for a short season in the townships, and drew a great deal of interest at the time. He wrote the music with someone called . . . I think his name was Cyril Magubane. And in general I think Barney was just trying to function wherever he could. And then Athol came and did *People Are Living There* and *Boesman and Lena*, which were his own productions with PACT, and we spent some time together there. He then introduced me to this other man that he knew here and who he had worked a good deal with, who was Barney Simon.

Barney and I started talking. Barney did *The Crucible* for PACT, the Arthur Miller play, with me producing, and I built an experimental theatre at the time called The Arena in Doornfontein, which was a forerunner of the Market. It was a found space theatre. It was a big old mining magnate's house in eastern Johannesburg, near the present Ellis Park rugby stadium. And there Barney was allowed to experiment more. He did an early production of *The Maids* by Jean Genet, he did *Six Characters in Search of an Author*, he did *Woyzeck*. In his play *Six Characters in Search of an Author*, instead of the players making a play by Pirandello, a play within the play, he started them writing a new piece, a Barney Simon piece, if you like, doing that with the actors, using the actors/writers as writers.

And that, in fact, was the launching of The Company, the actors who gave themselves to that kind of work – eventually we performed the play that they were making within *Six Characters* as a late-night production, so you could stay and watch the play you saw being made inside *Six Characters*, which we called *People*. And *People* was very specifically White Consciousness theatre. It was stream of consciousness stuff by a group of young white South Africans. And it related to their everyday lives. They were mainly monologues and some duologues, and with that we had a sort of a smell of the kind of theatre that could be created in this country, and that we knew would appeal to young people, like ourselves at that time.

And it was with that knowledge and with that excitement, that we then decided to break away from the existing state-run theatre of this region, PACT, and start our own little thing called The Company.

We didn't have any money – we had my pension from PACT, and we had the talent of the actors and Barney's directing and writing talent and whatever managing acumen I had. We very quickly realised – this was 1974 – that we needed a place. And at that time we were performing in various venues around the city; most of them were in hotels or wherever we could find converted restaurants. Most of these places had liquor licences, most of them did not allow black people into them, so we would still have to take our plays into the township areas for black people to see these plays. And there was still an enormous amount of compromise involved.

And at that time we found the Market, and tendered to save the old building, and then to win the building from the Council. We won the lease in 1975; started the conversion. And that is a whole other story that's mainly in that book called *Best of Company*.

And in June of 1976, on June 26th, we opened the Market Theatre. It was a very interesting time, as it was also the beginning of the youth resistance, and I think in a way that fed into the work of the Market Theatre.

Our first performance in the Upstairs Theatre was Chekov's *Seagull*, and the first performance in the main theatre was *Marat Sade*, both directed by Barney Simon.

We wanted to kind of nail our colours to the mast. We wanted to have a good classical repertoire, while we also wanted to do the best modern plays: Arthur Miller, Tennessee Williams, those kind of plays. And we wanted to do new South African theatre.

So the second play in the upstairs theatre was *The Blood Knot*. Benjee Frances directed and performed in that. And our third play was *Waiting for Godot*, in fact a black *Waiting for Godot*, doing the original Beckett with black actors.

Our second production in the Main Theatre was Fatima Dike's *Sacrifice of Kreli*, and the next play was Trevor Griffith's English play called

The Comedians, so we felt that we were showing that this was the range of work we could do.

As time passed we were drawn into doing more and more South African work, as more and more writers, directors and actors began to understand that we were open to performing this sort of work and to performing the work of previously untried writers, and open to new black people on the scene, that had not had the opportunity in the situation as it was. The rest of our theatre, as you probably still see today, is a bit of a pale imitation of what goes on in London and America, really. So I think that if the Market did anything, it helped to popularise and to make known a number of actors, writers, composers, musicians and dancers who might not otherwise in that era have had the chance.

To what extent is Black Theatre still under the sway of western influence through the conscientisation of the whites which you undertook?

Yes, I think that's a very real thing that has happened, and also through our education system being what it was over the last twenty, thirty years if not more. And we are in the middle of the process of reassessing that right now, as I am sure you know. I think there have been small attempts by people such as Rob McLaren, Matsemela Manaka, to a lesser extent Maishe Maponya, possibly to try to move away from that and re-establish an African tradition to our drama, but it may be that history has had its way with us. I think every country's culture becomes all the other cultures that have threaded through that country, and I do believe that, yes, there will definitely be a reclamation of the *African* character of this country, which was so badly mauled during the last three hundred years, and particularly the last fifty years.

With that it looks as if the new regime is not willing – and I think that is a good thing – to discard what is good in the European influences of the past.

Now, what about the influence of Gibson Kente in all this?

Gibson Kente – well, because he was Mr Show-Bizz of the biggest African township in this country, Soweto – because he was Mr Show-Bizz in terms of being the man who was most successful commercially at touring his work throughout the country, he became very influential. He was the man who ran productions in tandem, and sometimes two or three productions at the same time. He was running productions for three or four years – the longest runs in South African theatre history – and he was the initiator of the bus and truck tour of going from barnstorming to barnstorming, from township to township: – 'Slick plays by Gibson Kente' – absolutely extraordinary!

He also was a kind of a training-ground, and he became the *Gibson Kente style of performance*. He is still very much present in the work of Mbongeni Ngema and Percy Mtwa, with names like John Ledwaba and many, many others who had their early acting experience in Gibson Kente's theatre, and, of course, who have had their first taste of theatre in the audiences by seeing a Gibson Kente musical. He was the most popular theatre-man of his time.

It does seem that in the last ten years Kente himself started to become an unpopular figure with the youths of Soweto and others, when he started to do plays which, to them, were toeing the state line, and which were not 'resistance theatre'. Kente was still wanting to do theatre of the masses, 'popular theatre'.

It does look like there may be a re-emergence now, and there is also a sense by the historians, which is possibly what you are alluding to now, that Kente has to be thanked for training a whole generation of theatre practitioners. For better or for worse, he was the major source of employment for people in the acting, singing, dancing, music profession on the legitimate theatre stage in this country. So there is a tremendous debt of gratitude that's owed to this man, while understanding that over the last ten or fifteen years he has drifted from the major limelight because of his choice of material. And he wouldn't be the first artist that went his own way, as it were. He wasn't waiting to take on what was 'politically correct' at the time. Which I think is to his credit in the end – that he was going where his muse took him, which wasn't always a popular route.

In recent time he has started to work in television. I haven't seen his latest series . . . I think he is on the screen now, or about to come on. And I would like to see that, in order to understand what he is thinking about and what he is writing about now.

I have also got the impression that there is a different side to this, as seen from the view-point of some of the young practitioners on the profession, viz. that with his slick popular style he is a hurdle in their way – that he is hampering their development. The public has become so used to his entertainment tradition, that they refuse to sit down and listen to straight, serious talk. Would you like to comment on that?

(Laughing) Yes – look, that has always been levelled against him. I can remember articles in Rob McLaren's *S'ketsh* magazine from twenty, maybe twenty-five years ago, where this was being addressed and Kente was being castigated and taken to task for doing this 'popular theatre'. You know 'With his talent and ability and influence he should be doing more serious things . . .'

We had a similar criticism levelled at some of the pieces we did at the Market, where the entertainment factor was seen as too high compared to the content factor. And for us it had to be seen again, and I think it was the same for Kente, against the fact that we had no subsidy, no sponsorship: we were surviving on the box office. We were trying to pay reasonable, decent money, earning salaries, and we were trying to run a professional organisation. And therefore there had to be the popular element, because you couldn't beat the public over the head and say, 'You must buy another ticket and come back next week to be beaten over the head again.'

There had to be that element of entertainment, of – I used sometimes to call it 'Entertainment Plus' – which is entertainment plus content. No entertainment just for entertainment's sake. So that was the other side of the coin. And I think I understand what Kente's problem was. And I also understand that Kente had developed a style of which he is very proud. And why shouldn't he be? It was his own *forte.* No one else could do it quite like him.

Do you at all envisage a fusion of what used to be the Black Consciousness emphasis on content, of conscientisation or empowerment, and Kente's entertainment style? It seems to me that some of the young black writers/producers tend to be looking for a kind of synthesis there. How do you look at this?

Well, some of the younger writers, who are trying to strike out new directions still – I don't know whether it is a Kente-ism or it is the fact that the last thirty to forty years of resistance politics are gone, together with singing of protest songs, the development of toyi-toyi as a dance of resistance, the rise of praise poets like Mzwakhe Mbuli, who have shown that through classical African forms – song, dance, praise poetry –

you can encapsulate the deepest, deepest and strongest political statement. And so the young writers now, wanting to emulate the idols and the heroes of the struggle – it is a natural thing still to try and incorporate that instead of going just for the word only – and work in that sort of more western oriented dramatic form.

But how are we going to re-claim a purely African tradition of drama? I think maybe in fifty to a hundred years we might see some kind of re-establishment of that, because of the energy of people like Matobe Mutloatse now, and others.

How about the ideas of Credo Mutwa?

Yes – yes, well, I attended that production. It was interesting, in that it was different. I found it meandered . . .

You are talking of u'Nosilimela*?*

Yes. I am not sure yet, you see – there is the influence on public taste by the tape recorders, the television, the radio, the film and the computers now – I am not sure that a playwright today can write in the same way, writing with the breadth of subject and the breadth of intention that for instance Shakespeare did, and have success. I am not sure that the young African playwright, if he steeps himself in that traditional African dramatic form, will be able to re-kindle the interest of a modern audience in that form. That's mainly what I am talking about. Or even his own interest. He might say, 'Everything is more zappy, more clear-cut, tighter – if it stretches that long, we lose the audience now' – all that sort of thing. So I think that in the immediate future the young men and women that are writing now are going to be going for forms that are maybe more western – in the immediate future, with the colouring of African music and dance input, which is so rich and so strong. And maybe out of that will evolve something that is more African, and maybe even more specifically South African.

Would you see Mbongeni Ngema as an exponent of that line? I understand that some people saw him as their new hope when he first came onto the stage.

Yes – this is very difficult, he is a very close and dear friend of mine, and therefore I talk as someone who cares about him very deeply. And as Athol Fugard says, you always respond to a question with what you want the answer to be. That's a way of influencing your answer. So I'm telling you that my answer will be influenced in that way. I was the original producer of *Woza Albert* and after he'd moved out of the township into the city, I produced *Asinamali!*, and these were great works of that time. Perhaps *Woza Albert* is going to survive because it was a story of the great classic tale of the Second Coming. *Asinamali!* was a theatre specifically of what I was talking about earlier of newspaper theatre, describing events in a specific township in Natal, and telling people of the stories that happened around that Asinamali campaign.

Then came *Sarafina*, which was a telling the story of the youth of the time, in a very commercial, Gibson Kenteish form, using the music of the time. Maybe more 'pop' and zappy than Gibson Kente's music is inclined to be, with more of the popular recorded rhythms and sounds of the time.

And since then, since the enormous success of *Sarafina*, with a small diversion into *Sheila's Day* alongside of Duma Ndlowu which I told you about, which is fourteen women, no band, no instruments, but using song and dance and story telling and poetry. *Sheila's Day* is currently running in America, heading to New York any minute, or has maybe got there already, and it's an important piece of theatre. Fourteen black women – I think it's seven South Africans and seven Americans. They parallel the freedom struggle in South Africa and the civil rights movement in America.

Apart from that he has done *Township Fever*, which was an attempt to retell the story of a great upheaval in the COSATU union situation, when union members killed scabs, and put that in a popular musical theme (laughing). Mbongeni was perhaps trying to bring the world of *Asinamali!* and the world of *Sarafina* together. In the end more people said he did not succeed than said he succeeded.

Then his next piece was called *Magic at 4 a.m.*, and we are now in the time after Nelson Mandela was released. It was in a way a tribute to Mohammed Ali, the great black world champion boxer. And it was to show how black South Africans drew strength from their idols throughout the world. And 4 a.m. was the time in the morning when you could listen to the great Mohammed Ali fighting – 'the Rumbles in the Jungle'. It was when the great fights in the world history were done because it was 10 p.m. American television time, and 4 a.m. in South

Africa. And it tells the story of a black mine boxer, the champion of his mine, and he calls himself Mohammed Ali and listens to his tapes. And in fact, as history would have it, the real Mohammed Ali was here for the world première, in the Johannesburg Civic Theatre. It happened in 1991 or '92.

And since then he has done something called *Mama*, which was really a re-telling of Committed Artists story, the story of writing *Sarafina*. So he was starting to re-tell his own story or to re-live his own legend, if you like. And now he is branching out. I believe maybe this is the first step into something new for Mbongeni. Did you see *Sarafina II* while you were in Durban?

No, I only saw the television version of Sarafina.

He attempted to take a very important social message about Aids, to the theatre in a 1990s version of Gibson Kente, with what he has learnt in all his international touring with these various big musical hits he has had. So now we have a very big lighting rig with moving lights, we have first-class sound equipment, we have a wonderful stage design, and all this he can wrap up and put into a truck: the cast go into a bus, and they can move and they can be ready to perform within two days in a new place. And his intention is in fifty-two weeks of this coming year to play South Africa from the north to the south. Fifty-two townships in fifty-two weeks. Mainly the townships but some cities as well. In Johannesburg he will play in the City Hall, because we now have an urban population of blacks as well as a township population.

So there he is attempting, not a new story – he is continuing the story of Sarafina. She has now become a social worker and she is working in rural areas, and she is taking the message of Aids: wear condoms; women have a right to say No. This is very radical theatre in the black rural and urban areas in South Africa! Caution must be used, safe sex must be practised, and all this is encapsulated in Ngema's music and dancing and Zip-Zap step modern style.

And this is all piping hot? It has not been out for the public to see yet?

No, it had its première two weeks ago.

All right. And how has it been received?

Well let us put it this way: It had its première because it had its first performance, and the Minister of Health came, and the European High Commissioner came, and many international World Health Organisation dignitaries – those kind of people. And I think it is being seen as an important response to the Aids problem. I think that's the way it has been perceived at the moment.

And how was it reviewed?

It's not been reviewed. He has avoided the press, because Mbongeni needs a long time to write his works. *Sarafina* took two years to write, *Township Fever* took eighteen months to write, *Magic at 4 a.m.* took nine months, *Mama* took six months.

Mbongeni needs a long time to prepare his work properly. *Sarafina*, I believe, is the last work that was prepared properly. And he is *trying* now, because he only had three months. He had a deadline to have the first performance by World Aids Day, on 1 December, in Durban. So he only had three months to get to there. It opened as a four-hour presentation (laughing), and maybe in that way the African culturalist would think it was moving in the right direction.

But it is by no means a complete theatrical statement yet. And in fact he did say that at the launch. And we are hoping that the press won't get to it for another two months or so, so that he can keep working, keep writing.

But let me say, after saying all these positive things I've been trying to say about Mbongeni: I am concerned that he is not giving himself the time to reflect and to find new subject matter. And he is not responding to the world around him. But he is responding to commissions. The Aids play was a commission, and the *Magic at 4 a.m.* was a commission by the Johannesburg Civic Theatre, and *Mama* was commissioned by the NAPAC Playhouse Company whose Durban music department he runs.

So since *Township Fever* he hasn't responded to his own impulses, rather he's responded to the commissions of the people who employ him to fly their flag. It was very important for the Civic Theatre to have a Ngema production; it was very important for the Playhouse Company to have his production. I really want him to reflect and give his thoughts in response to our New South Africa. That will, I believe, be the next important Ngema work. If he gives himself time.

So this, I suppose, is skirting the problem of popular versus commercial theatre?

Ja, very much so. Very much so. He is caught in a two-way stretch there. Very much so.

How does it compare or conflict with the Community Theatre idea? It seems technically to be an almost head-on collision. How do you see that?

What Ngema is doing now with the Aids thing of course, is taking him full circle. In a way he is back to community theatre. But he is doing community theatre with a Class A technology. So he is taking his wife, Leleti Khumalo; he's taking the band from *Sarafina*, that played on Broadway, the same characters. He's taking a number of the characters from his previous plays, and those original actors have become, thanks to the movie and various other things, have become role models for the youths.

The 'slick Ngema show', eh?

The slick Ngema show. And there is Leleti Khumalo standing on the stage saying, 'Woman, you now have the right to say No! when you do not want to make love.' I was there for the first two or three performances, and you could hear the men in the audience go B-O-O-O-O. So, maybe . . .

But the message is – put crudely to your face – AIDS KILLS YOU, and you have to be careful. Mbongeni doesn't necessarily get to the changing-the-lifestyle yet. He's speaking about prevention and protection rather than trying to change the whole lifestyle – of not having sex before you're married and so on. It can, really, potentially, save many lives.

Do you see any interesting themes coming up now as one enters the phase of the New South Africa?

Aha, the big question! Everybody's question. Ah – the New South Africa; the drama for the New South Africa. My theme is this, and this is the way I have answered this question maybe for the last two or three years – I've used the same answers so I know the line very well – I believe that the real artists at the moment are experiencing the New South Africa, with all the rest of us. We are experiencing this wonderful, exciting, terrible, terrifying, extraordinary event, maybe the most wonderful historic event in recent years alongside the Berlin Wall coming down and all that. We are experiencing that South Africa is now a free country for all people, that all people have the franchise and can vote, and that in three years' time we will have a majority government, I think. We now have this in-between national unity government. At the end of the five-year period we will have a government that is voted in by the majority of all the people of this country.

And our writers, our artists, our creators have to taste this as well. And what is going on now, I feel, is under-the-ground growth. They are experiencing this, they are feeling this, they are sensing this. And I don't believe the really deep responses can be seen yet.

I'd like to look at someone again that I am very, very close to, and that's Athol Fugard. I have produced all the original productions of his works in this country over the last twenty-five years. And in the last five years he has done three plays. The first one was called *Playland*, which was a play about reconciliation. It is a black man and a white man, late at night outside a play-fairground. They both have a terrible secret – they've both killed somebody. The black man has killed a white man, who was raping his wife. The white man killed a soldier on the border, a Swapo soldier. And at one o'clock in the morning the black man, who is a Bible-believing night-watchman, and the white man, who is a liquor-swilling paratrooper – whatever – find each other in a kind of exorcism of both their lives, and find a kind of peace with confessing their deep sin to each other, that they've never told anybody else.

The next thing Fugard did was he took five young South African girls, they were fifteen-, sixteen-year-old standard eight, standard nine school girls: two black girls, one Indian girl, one mixed-race coloured girl, and one white girl. And he acted as amanuensis to them, and they did a piece in the end, entitled *My Life*. And they told simple stories of their lives, in the New South Africa. The rehearsal period was up to July. And we performed in July 1994, after the 27 April election.

So this was another co-operative venture?

These were five girls of some sort of acting ability, only a little writing ability, who were turned into their own scribes, if you like. And we presented it in Johannesburg; we took it around to some schools and townships and so on, and then we presented it at the Grahamstown Festival. Fugard used the words of the girls. It was their words and their story. It was called *My Life*.

And it was a very interesting thing. Many people got very excited about it, and said, This is the theatre of the New South Africa! This is us telling our story! This is Uhuru.

I think, maybe yes, this *is* the story of the New South Africa. I don't know that that was a great work of art. I think that was the beginning, the first scribbling of new South Africans, saying what was going on to them during the pre-election time and after the election. And also talking about how all of this did or did not touch their lives.

The next piece, which just opened this year, is called *Valley Song*. It is the story of a grandfather and a granddaughter. Mixed race, coloured people of the Karoo, his beloved Karoo. And the daughter wanting to move away from the small town, wanting to go to the big city, and the grandfather wanting life to go on like it has always been. Here are the different images of the New South Africa – of the young girl of seventeen wanting to grab this new world that has been given to her through the recent election, and the grandfather not trusting this new world, saying 'Don't get anywhere near this kind of life!'

And it ends, of course, with the very big hopeful situation where he lets her go – he finds a way to let her go. And he continues as he was, but he understands that she has to move on.

So I think, I think that the new plays – I'm smelling that they're just starting to come. They're *just* starting, they haven't come yet.

Could we end by going back to the Market again?

Yes.

I want to ask you about the city venues, the big theatres – do they have a future? Does the Market have a future? Is it on the right sort of course?

All right. This is another very difficult question. I've just been asked to go back to the Market Theatre, in fact, and I am pondering that very question myself, 'Does it have a future – Is it on the right course?'

Mannie Manim

I think it has lost its way. I think that in the last three years there have been terrible forces pulling at the Market. I think the Market had a very clear course, virtually until the time I left it in 1991 (laughing). With the coming of the freedom of Mandela, the unbanning of all the political parties and so on, the Market initially started to celebrate this, but a lot of the power in the Market was with white business, from the Board, where we drew our funding. There was tremendous pressure on Barney really to start to sell out to western popular theatre, and to make the white northern suburbs feel comfortable and friendly in this Market, 'where they had been attacked for, oh, so long about their terrible ways of life'.

White business was demanding that the Market move from the Theatre of Protest, but not to the theatre of celebration, which Barney Simon was advocating. In my book they would have continued that line at the Market, and that would be using all the peoples of South Africa and still turning the stories of this country and celebrating our diversity, our liberation, our unification, all those things, which are totally worthy of celebrating. And in my book this tension was very bad for the Market, and it was very bad for Barney, as a creative person. It might even have assisted in his death in the end – this terrible pressure he was under. I know that in his heart of hearts he knew that the right way to go was what I have spoken about, the celebratory theatre. And he was asked almost to forget the first twenty years of the Market, and now suddenly to turn it into a pleasure palace. And everything is just wonderful in the garden – 'Oh, isn't it wonderful! We can have all the international stars come here and perform in our theatre, because we have got this international reputation. Now we can do popular theatre.'

But we are now at a very important time, and I suppose that part of what I've got to decide is whether I believe I can make any difference. They just have lost their way, and with Barney dying I think they've lost the way even more. I must decide whether I think I can help to influence them back on the path.

They've also had very poor management. I am a reasonable manager, and I think I could put them back on course. Whether it's right for me to go backwards in life – I am enjoying *my* freedom, I am enjoying the New South Africa, and I am working at the University with the young, new thinkers that are coming through. And thanks to the University's position I am also able to run my own little company, and through this company I produce much new work, but am free of any board structure, free of any of the tensions that poor Barney had. My only tension is, what shall the next play be? And I can decide. And if I've decided, we do it. And if I don't like it, we don't do it.

So it's a difficult moment for the Market, and I believe that its way to survival is through becoming truly the Theatre of the People, which they were trying to be before. And with the urban black population they have a chance to do that too.

Isn't that what John Kani is trying to do?

I think so. But he too is under these tensions. Maybe that's what he wants me to come back and help him with, because we have been comrades in arms. John Kani has been for me one of the most important influences in my theatrical life.

So you would pull in the same direction?

Oh, yes. Oh, yes. There is no doubt about that. It's a matter of not throwing the Market away, but taking the reputation that the Market has and build on that. Not to throw the baby out with the bathing water, but to use the new country and make the Market a celebratory People's Theatre, because it had this wonderful reputation for being the place where Mandela celebrated his first birthday after coming out of prison. It was in Kippies, where he was invited to a 'birthday' party.

We want it to be seen as the place where Hugh Masekela blew his trumpet the first time he came back to South Africa. That's what we want it to be: a place to celebrate the Victory.

Don Maclennan

Don Maclennan, you were involved in Black Theatre in the early 1970s. I wonder if you would be kind enough to tell me about the activity of that period, the way you experienced it?

Well, let me tell you really how it began. All my life I've been interested in drama. My sister and I made up plays and acted them when we were children, and I acted when I was at school and university. And when I got here, to Rhodes University, that was 1966, I had a play in my pocket, a satirical play called *The Third Degree*, and it so happened that in 1967 Athol Fugard's wife had a nervous breakdown, and came here to Fort England where she stayed for something like six months.

While she was in Fort England, Athol and his daughter lived with us in this house. I had met him before, and I was very stimulated by his company. And during the course of his visit here, we decided we should put on a couple of plays. He wanted to do *Krapp's Last Tape*. I gave him my play *The Third Degree*, and said, 'How about this?' He said, 'Yes, of course. Let's do it.' It was a one-act play. We were doing it for a theatre club. We had to have theatre clubs in those days, because you couldn't mix blacks and whites, you see. So it was a membership issue of tickets. And we decided to do it to raise money, probably for Grahamstown Area Distress Relief Association (GADRA).

It was very exciting watching him rehearse *Krapp's Last Tape*, and being directed in my play, because he said, 'You wrote the play, you bloody well act in it.' It was very, very exciting.

It led to a number of other plays I got involved in when he left, plays I got involved in with students at the university. I wrote several plays which we acted on various occasions. One was on Hiroshima Day in 1969, I think it was, which we performed in the physics lecture theatre. There was another one about two cities – large white boxes – which was about apartheid or them-and-us.

And in 1970 I wrote a full-length play called *A Winter Vacation*, and staged it here, in the Rhodes Theatre. It was a gloomy piece of work, a bit like a mixture of Chekhov and *A Long Day's Journey into Night*.

It worked very well for the Rhodes audience, they were impressed.

And then a couple of people from the township said, 'Why don't you bring it up to the township and let us see it?' So we took it up to the old Municipal Hall for a performance. The Municipal Hall was a run-down place. At the back there was a very narrow stage and the rooms on either side were full of dirty cardboard boxes and sweaty boxing gloves. There was very little space to do anything. It didn't matter. We said 'OK, we'll perform there.'

So we performed. It was meant to start at eight o'clock. At eight-thirty people were still coming in. European and Xhosa time are clearly very different entities. At eight-thirty I said, 'Shut the doors, we're starting.' And they were still banging on the door. Now this particular play begins with a forty-year-old woman reading aloud a Wordsworth sonnet. The old woman in the bedroom offstage is dying of cancer. She rings a handbell to get the young woman's attention. At that moment a black man in the audience shouted 'ice cream!!', and the whole quality of the performance deteriorated. We finished in the most violent Senecan mood imaginable. All the subtlety was gone!

What the audience liked was when the old woman came in and spoke to her son she was walking in with a stick and she raised her stick to hit him. The audience loved that part, you know. And when the son and the father met and drank whisky, whenever they knocked back a full glass of whisky, the audience cheered. It was absolutely marvellous. And when the production finished we were exhausted, absolutely buggered.

The chairman of the council said, 'Please, come and stand on the stage. I want to make a speech.' This was a man with a public front and a big strong voice. And he went on and on. I thought he was going to say, 'Here at last we have crossed a bridge. We have shaken hands across a divide!'

But he finished by saying, 'There are two very important things that we have learnt tonight. The first is that when you put on a play, you must talk very loud so that everybody can hear you, and second, you must never turn your back on the audience when you are performing! Cheers!'

I think we went home and drank ourselves silly. Anyway, that was my first real exposure. I then put on a couple of other plays, once doing at the festival here a comedy called *The Wake*; that must have been in 1971. That was in a sense about my own father's death, and it was about that wonderful wake that we had with all the family, and the comedy and the absurdity of it. It ran throughout the festival, in the Shaw Hall.

About that time two women came to see me from the township. And they said, 'We want you.'

And I thought, you know – me? What for? To put on plays. So we arranged a meeting, and there were about thirty or forty people there. So I said, 'Have you ever had any dramatic experience before?' And they said, 'Yes, we have just put on a musical called *I Regret*.'

'If you've just put it on, is there any way I could see it? Do you think you could revise it and put it on for me?'

And they said, '*Ja*, sure we'll do that.'

They had a piano and a saxophone and a trumpet for the music. It was a musical and it involved a *sangoma,* you know, and a gangster, a chap who goes bad and dies in stabbings, and a love affair, and in the end he regrets. Everything, you see. I was really quite impressed that they had managed to put it on. It had run for something like a month in the township. And they'd had some wonderful parties after it. So they said to me, 'OK, you direct us.' So I said, 'First of all I've got to see how well you can act, so I'm putting you through some acting exercises.' And I selected a handful, and I actually finished up with about six out of the whole lot, two women and four men.

We then mounted Soyinka's *The Trials of Brother Jero*, which is very funny. It's an attack on politicians and religion. I used the six actors and a couple more, and we performed it at St Philip's church hall, which is up in the township. The church hall is a building about the size of this entire house. It was divided into three sections, one big section and two smaller sections, which were used as classrooms. But it had something like an Elizabethan thrust stage, with wooden pillars going up like that, on the sides.

We performed there and I said, 'OK, now if you're serious, let's constitute an acting group.' They decided that the name they wanted was the Ikhwezi Players, which means, in Xhosa, the Morning Star. I think it is Venus. So I said, 'I am thinking about a play for you.' It was based on the book of Job, and I adapted the story to fit the local shoemaker, Job Mava, who has suffered a fate not dissimilar to Job's. You can get a copy of the play at NELM, it's printed.

You start seeing the shoemaker with his house and his shoemaker's shop burnt down. He's sitting in the ashes. And various people come along, and he tells his story to the audience of what happened. The government wanted him to move to Committees Drift, to be resettled, even though the land was given to the Fingos in perpetuity by Queen Victoria. The house has burnt down, his wife comes along to nag him, 'Why are you sitting outside? Let's get on with life, let's rebuild.'

He says, 'God has done this to me. I want to know why.' And then the minister of religion comes along. I forget his name now. I think it is something like the Reverend Mabandla. And he brought a thermos of coffee along for Job, you see, and says, 'Oh, come on, Job. Pull yourself together. Accidents happen.'

But Job says, 'God . . .' etc. And Mabandla says, 'I brought you some coffee,' and Job says, 'I don't want it.'

'OK,' says Mabandla, 'I'll drink it myself, then.'

And all these various people try to give him advice and to comfort him. In the end he falls asleep, and there is a man called Zizamele, which means 'Help Yourself' in Xhosa, who's a garbage collector. He lives on the rubbish dumps, looking for things, you know: bottles, keys, food, anything that's useful. And Zizamele turned out to be a brilliant comic actor. We didn't know that, but his timing was absolutely perfect. And Zizamele, the fool, the stupid one, has this relationship with Job, and he shows Job how foolish he is.

It was not a great play, but it was wonderful doing it. We performed and performed and performed. That was 1973, I think. And do you know, to this day, 1996, people who saw the play still come up to me and say, 'When are you going to do *Job Mava* again?' They remember it, you know. It spoke so well to the people there.

We did a number of other things. The play we finished with was an adaptation of Maxim Gorky's autobiography, *My Childhood*, which I think is the most interesting of all Gorky's works. I think he is very much overrated as a writer, but *My Childhood* is very rich. It hasn't got any social fury, it's just got the raw experience. There are about six or seven fairly important characters. But by this time I'd actually 'got rid of' all the women actors, partly because they were a bit unreliable. If you said 'We're starting at seven-thirty,' they would say, '*Ja*, Mm', and maybe come a bit later. But the other reason, of course, is that some of them had to walk through the township at night, and that was dangerous for them. In the end I finished up with four men.

I'll tell you a story about them. We had by this time set up properly a financial situation. I'd been given four lights by Rob (Amato), who was in those days very flush – theatre lights. I had been given a grant from the university – not much, a thousand rands, to get things going, and I decided we should not own a hall, we should not own anything, we should just do grassroots theatre. Also the agreement was, any money we made we would put into a savings account. And if anybody wanted to draw money, he had to have two signatures of committee members. There were only five committee members anyway, but you had to have two signatures. So the money began to accumulate, you see.

When it came to Gorky's *My Childhood*, we had four men, a big table, covered with an orange cloth, and a proper Russian icon, a samovar, pictures of the Czar and the Czaritsa hanging up on the wall, and the four men came in carrying candles, singing Xhosa songs. They had taken Russian tunes and put Xhosa words to them. We had these wonderful songs like *Rise, Red Sun*, *Along the Peterski*, the *Volga Boatmen* in Xhosa, and it was an absolutely perfect match.

In the acting area there were simply four chairs. Each actor took it in turns to be Gorky, talking about his childhood. When it came to grandfather and grandmother, who were the main characters, it was usually the same actor that played grandfather/grandmother.

We performed that in St Philip's church hall, we performed it in the Rhodes Theatre during the Festival, and early in 1975 we were invited by the University of Cape Town NUSAS Arts Festival, so we came down there to perform, and that was the last time the group met, in January or February 1975. I'd had enough. I'd been running them for about four years now. I had to provide scripts, I was the director, the financier, the transport manager, the provider of wine and food, the organiser of banner and tickets and everything. And I was holding down a full-time job at the university. And I'd had enough.

So we looked at the bank balance. And this is interesting. Of the four men who remained with us, grandfather was a teacher anyway – he went on teaching in Grahamstown, and he became finally headmaster at Pedi. We divided up the money and split it four ways. Zizamele went to Fort Hare University, and got a degree. Bob was teaching anyway but he took the money and he was working for a degree. I think he spent a couple of years at Fort Hare, and he is finishing a degree in history through UNISA. The chief actor, the most articulate one of all, came to Rhodes University and did a degree in sociology. Of course the money didn't pay for everything, but it was a tremendous start. Oh, and there was one other young bloke, Chris Baskiti, who went off to become a professional actor. I think he started off with Gibson Kente, who you may have met.

I am meeting him for an interview next week.

Interesting fellow. A really charming bloke. A bit of a tyrant, I believe, but he really gets things done.

So there they were off my hands. But we stayed good friends. We're always meeting each other, because Bob and Zizamele are still teaching in town. And we meet and chat and keep in touch with each other.

For the rest of that year I had been working again with students at Rhodes, trying to put together a play called *The Voyage of the Santiago*. I had been reading stories of Portuguese voyages of exploration, and there is an extraordinary story of the *Santiago* that left Lisbon about 1540 and sailed round the coast of South Africa heading for Goa in India. On board it had something like fifteen priests. It was an extraordinary story, because there was obviously some kind of authority difference between the Master of the ship, who is technically the owner of the ship, and the Captain of the ship, who should be in charge at sea. And because they had been delayed coming around the Cape of Storms, and had near mutinies from the poor Portuguese they were taking out to colonise Goa, they were delayed, and they had to decide whether to winter on Madagascar, or whether they should sail straight to Goa. The captain of the ship said, 'It is my advice to winter on Madagascar,' but the master, to put it very simply, was greedy. He did not want to lose money, and he said, 'I insist that we go to India.' So the captain said, 'You have just committed the whole lot of us to certain death,' or: 'You've turned this into a living hearse,' or some such expression.

So they sailed – that was in the afternoon, and that night they were sailing along and even though they had men on watch the ship ran straight into a thing called the Jews' Shoal, south of Madagascar. And the top half of the ship slithered over onto the coral, and the bottom part sank, and a hundred and fifty people drowned at once.

And scattered around on the top of the coral reef there was money everywhere, bales of silk, all kinds of things. And almost immediately those who had guns and swords, the aristocrats, commandeered what boats there were – there were only a couple of boats. Others began building rafts. But that wasn't enough to take everybody off. There were still thirty to fifty people left. And the tide was rising. It's quite an interesting play, the best I ever wrote, I think. It was performed at the Arena Theatre in Johannesburg, and was directed by Ken Leach, and it ran for three weeks – packed houses. That was early '75. It finishes the way it started – one priest is left holding the hands of the people who have survived. It was all done very simply. The sound was complex. There was sound all the time, but the acting was very dynamic. There was a set with a ladder, a box, and some lids you could lift up and drag out costumes. And the actors wore black leotards and could change costume very easily by donning a chasuble or a hat or something like that. It's the only play of mine that got me excited.

That was the last thing I did. It's not that I don't like drama. I think it's wonderful stuff. It's just that I have moved somewhere else. I was trying to write novels. And I had written nine novels. And twenty-five years ago I got so sick of them I took the lot outside, to a forty-four gallon drum, and burnt them. Burnt the lot. It was such a relief to me.

When the plays were over I also felt some sense of relief. But I've been writing poetry, you see, and my sixth volume was published last April, called *The Poetry Lesson*.

So that's where I am. That's what interests me. And I am retired from the university. I have been retired for a year now, but teach twice a week free of charge, just because I like teaching. It keeps me in touch with my colleagues. I have an office there, and I get tea. I feel that if I suddenly stopped working I wouldn't know what to do with myself. I've been teaching most of my life, you see. So you must keep doing what you like doing as long as you can. But in terms of creativity, it is now poetry.

Matsemela Manaka was saying that he didn't feel it was wrong for an Africanist to work with whites. But it was his experience that when blacks and whites work together, the leader or the leaders of the group are invariably white. What are your experiences in that respect from your work with Black Theatre?

I don't know that I can answer properly.

I had seen Athol Fugard work with the Serpent Players years before, probably early 1966, and I watched Athol directing, and I watched Rob and his Imitha Players, and Rob was saying, 'You should start a group.' And I said I can't just start a group like that. And it was only when those two black women came to my house and said 'We want you,' that I got into that work. I asked, 'Are you sure you want me to do this? Want *me*?' And they said 'Yes!'

And I had no sense of resentment whatsoever with this group of people. It could be that they were not as politicised as Matsemela Manaka, that's quite possible. But we got pissed together, we embraced each other, there was no exploitation. And I never sensed any resentment.

My impression from talking to Manaka and others, has been that it was not so much at that time as later, when some of these actors and collaborators felt gratitude was due to them, but not given, by some of the white producers/directors they worked with. I think that's more where the resentment came into it.

I suppose you could explain that in a number of different ways. I know, for instance, from talking to Athol, that he picked up that John Kani and Winston Ntshona were saying, 'Athol has surfed to fame on the backs of John and Winston.' I just don't think that is true. I think Athol was going there anyway.

He happened to have, in John, a superb actor. He is a hell of a nice bloke and a wonderful actor. I haven't heard John say things like that since he became director at the Market Theatre. So it could be explained as a resentment that the guy one worked with has gone on much further. But it also sounded like the right thing to say that you were exploited by whites. And I just don't think it's true. I think Athol is a person of such integrity that he completely recognised the authenticity of the people he was working with. What makes him a good director, of course, is that he listens carefully. He knows what he needs, he knows what he wants, not rigidly but creatively – he has a vision. It is one thing to look at a Fugard written text. It's another to watch him directing. The real magic of Fugard's theatre is not so much in the play as finished product, as in the rehearsing, in the psycho-therapy, if you like, of the actual contact between Athol and the actors, and that is very extraordinary. As a catalyst he is incredible.

The art is a very complex one. Of course it is also shaped by a Black Consciousness view and probably a PAC view, that anything to do with whites is a colonial imposition and hence must be distrusted. There were lots of attempts to discredit, say, Athol's plays, on the grounds that he was writing about black people and he wasn't himself black. What could he say? How could he find the balls as a white man to talk about black and Black Africans and Black experience? There is some truth in that, of course there is. But you must think of other playwrights, like Shakespeare. Shakespeare, who wasn't a soldier, how could he talk about soldiers? He wasn't a king, how could he talk about kings? He wasn't a woman, how could he talk about women? Someone with imagination can project himself into a situation and talk about it. So it becomes very complicated, you know, if you are fighting a political battle. You'd use any weapon at your disposal.

Have you been involved at all in this dichotomy between race and class as you see it in some of the white people behind Black Theatre as well? Which was the basic thing that created apartheid, was it class or is it race?

You'll have to explain this, I am not sure I understand what you mean.

I suppose the simplest and most 'popular' way of explaining what apartheid is to people who don't know the problem too well, is to call it a racist thing. Others, like for instance Rob McLaren (Mshengu Kavanagh), will say, 'No, it's a class thing, it's rooted in capitalism. It is capitalist exploitation of the working class that is at the core of apartheid.'

I would disagree with McLaren. Actually, it's both. I think money and power give you opportunities, keep you safe, keep you where you are. But from having spent a lot of time in the country with Afrikaners and farmers, I know that fundamentally it is also a racist problem. I am talking about the old days during the war; we used to go up every winter to spend a month at an Afrikaans farm to improve our Afrikaans. And there wasn't a farmer we met there who didn't think that black people were the same as baboons. It was that racist. And there was no talk about class. What class boiled down to was the ownership of the land. Even those black people who did own their land in places like Lesotho or the location were still regarded by Afrikaners as baboons. Perhaps there's a third category. A guy we stayed with, called Gideon Pienaar, would say to us, 'Of all the animals the kaffir is the dumbest.' And that is not class . . .

No, that's plain racism. Against your own personal experience in this country how do you look upon Bishop Tutu's Rainbow Nation? Are there any chances of this concept amalgamating into any sort of nationhood?

I like Tutu. I used to know him slightly here in Grahamstown. He's a great guy. Mandela I've never met, but I have enormous respect for him. If I were to use the phrase A Man of Spirit, I would like to use it about him. I am not quite sure what I mean by it, but there is such integrity there. I'm deeply impressed by him. I like the idea of the Rainbow Nation. I've always hoped for one, always. But I have always believed in change, that real change only comes by living next door to someone – that you can't *impose* real change. I'm prepared to wait and see. I am very happy that we've had an election, rather than a blood bath. I think that's amazing in itself, it is.

But what worries me, of course, is the inexperience of people in government, the huge amount, still, of fraud and corruption that is going on. And the worry that I have is that the ANC has made election promises it might not be able to fulfil. First of all to pay the bill of the new parliamentarians, and at the same time to provide houses and sewerage and water and education and policing for the rest: there simply isn't enough. If the ANC can't live up to its promises, what I am afraid of, is that another force like the PAC will become troublesome in opposition, although it wasn't particularly well represented in the last election. The chances of civil war between black and white have disappeared. They haven't disappeared between black and black. Those are the only worries I have: promising the right things, but *unrealistically* – that and the situation in Natal – if those matters could be sorted out, I'd be happy.

To round off this interview somehow, let's go back to where we started. One thing I have picked up from some of the interviews is the idea of theatre acting as a kind of educational institution. Could you envisage the development of that sort of theatre? A sort of marriage of the Gibson Kente and the conscientising 'committed theatre'?

Oh, *ja*, I can imagine it – I just hope that I don't have to have anything to do with it (laughing). I think it could be the most dreary stuff in the world.

Can you see anybody serving as a vehicle for that now?

I think all theatre willy nilly reflects social, political, spiritual realities. I don't think the best theatre is about social, political or spiritual realities. I think theatre is a special kind of human magic, that is able to transform the present and take you a bit out of the present, to something else. Theatre which is reformist in intent or educational in intent I would say is uninteresting to me. I am much more interested in what you can pull out of the human psyche. I am much more interested in what Jung would call *Integration* – how well people know themselves. It's easy to talk about society, politics, poverty, police brutality, etc. It is not easy to fish out from inside someone the chemistry of personality, the chemistry of compassion, grandeur, understanding, love. That is theatre.